STEEL BEACH

---•---

MY LIFE AS A NAVAL AIRCREWMAN

1972–1976

To Les Potter

By

Jeff Lee Manthos

[signature]

INKWATER PRESS

PORTLAND • OREGON

Dedicated to the men and women who have made the ultimate sacrifice while wearing Navy aircrew wings.

Acknowledgements

This book would not have been possible without the love, support, editing skill and encouragement of Karen Gordon. My life would not be possible without her, either.

A special thanks to Master Chief John Dungan, U.S.N. (ret.) for his invaluable technical assistance with this book.

I'd also like to thank the following for their feedback, support, advice, constructive suggestions and trust that I could do it: Nancy Conescu, David Willson, Wayne Mutza, Barbara Van-Nix, Dan Manthos, Kim Cook, Kim Wilson, Marilyn Johnston, Jim Howe, my friends and veterans writing groups colleagues. Anyone left out deserving mention is due to my own error.

TABLE OF CONTENTS

PART FIVE: 1976

We are older men now, those I write about that have survived naval aviation and time. Our memories are imperfect visions, rendering them unique in their vividness and beauty. Our memories are our truth.

This is my truth. This is how I remember it...

PART ONE
1972

1: "ONE IS THE LONELIEST NUMBER..."

February second. Marsha slid the front section of the Fort Collins Coloradoan across our tiny kitchen table as we lazily enjoyed some breakfast. "Did you see this? It says 'draft lottery completed.' Do you want to look or should I?"

I set my coffee cup down and reached for the paper. "I'll do it. What the hell, how bad could it be?" I thumbed to the page with the list. My birthday, March 6, had been picked number 1 in the draft call-up. "I'm fucked, babe."

It was too cold to escape on my Triumph motorcycle up Poudre Canyon so I just stared out the little window at the snow. Marsha started telling me about her brother-in-law who had just returned from Vietnam. His hands shook so badly he could only fill a glass half full so he wouldn't spill anything. Her voice receded into a dark distance as my mind grappled with the inevitable.

She and I had been living together in a small one bedroom apartment in an old house on Matthews Street, setting up housekeeping and spending most of our time working minimum wage to make the rent. She was a bartender, that's where I met her, in a bar, as an underage eighteen year old without even a fake ID, just bluster. It had worked, we started dating and found ourselves playing house. I worked construction jobs and tried the summer session at Colorado

State, but I couldn't focus, I kept seeing the draft headline in my mind's eye and the war in the paper.

With the draft number thoroughly soaked into my marrow I quit work, quit college, quit everything but drinking where Marsha worked, worrying about what I was going to do. I decided to join the Navy. It seemed a solution I could live with. Marsha had a shitfit.

I enlisted on September 15 and after the swearing in and a cursory physical I was off to Recruit Training Command, San Diego.

Two months of indoctrination, marching, folding clothes and watching *Victory at Sea* movies passed with the slow hum of a giant man-processing machine. I had been poured into a funnel at the receiving station in Denver and bootcamp concentrated us into a steady stream of blue clad recruits destined for ships that sailed the world's oceans.

Mail call was the high point. Marsha had been writing every other day, her letters feeling soft and warm, like she had slept on them the night before. I had some pictures of all four foot eleven of her and would lay them out on my rack when I read her words. I missed her. And I worried; she was cute, effervescent, had a dreamboat build and worked in a bar. I was twelve hundred miles away and wouldn't be home for months.

The pinnacle of my bootcamp accomplishments was being made the sock folding petty officer. I had them rolled tight, looking like a fuzzy black hand grenade. I was to pass on that technique to the guys who were more challenged by the task.

I had a stirring moment as I gazed at a giant helicopter one day as it hovered—defiant of gravity—right in front of my eyes as we sat on splintery bleachers for an outdoor lecture. I had enlisted for three years and with that I was guaranteed my choice of coast—which took me to San Diego—and the aviation branch of the Navy. "Aviation" meant I could be cleaning toilets on an aircraft carrier instead of on a destroyer. But watching that big helicopter was a wondrous thing, I thought man, wouldn't it be amazing to be on one of those machines. But I had no "rate," or job, to train for with a technical school, just a two week flight deck indoctrination class after bootcamp was all I was going to get before being shipped out to the USS *Hancock*, CVA-19. It was a holdover from WWII and rumored to be mostly rust and ghosts. And she would be my home for two years and ten months. But no glamour awaited me there, just exhausting work on four acres of flat American steel dodging propellers and jet intakes. I would ship out of bootcamp as a 0000, a "quad zip," with no numerical designation marking my specialty. I didn't have one. I was a quadruple nothing.

Once we had proven that we could march, do the 16 Count Manual of Arms and spitshine shoes, we were graduated in grand naval tradition and set loose upon the world. I was shipped out to the Naval Air Technical Training Center, Millington, Tennessee, near Memphis. There I would begin the flight deck orientation class full of tales of the terrifying accidents and endless hazards that made a carrier flight deck the most dangerous workplace in the world.

2: THE TIDE CHANGES

Marsha wrote a lot during bootcamp but her letters thinned out. I told myself I just needed to get home on leave, that would take care of things. I missed her terribly and the harsh winter added to my melancholy, but I had a few weeks before I could go home. First I needed to get through the flight deck accident films and lectures on the dangers of fire, liquid oxygen, fuel spills and steel arresting cables slithering across the deck like iron pythons, ready to coil around a young man's body and squeeze the life out of him in seconds.

Just as I was getting used to the idea of going to the *Hancock*, or "handjob" as I had christened it, my future changed in an instant. I was only a few days into the school when a tall, athletic looking young officer stood at the classroom doorway.

"Is there an Airman Recruit Manthos in here?"

"Yessir, right here," I said as I raised my hand. Just like in high school.

"Manthos, would you come with me?"

My heart skipped a beat. What kind of trouble was I in? I was thinking as fast as I could; did I miss a watch? Everyone stood watches, four hours of stomping your feet to keep from freezing in the middle of Memphis winter pacing endlessly, keeping watch for fires, spies, whatever. I followed the Lt.j.g., I was finally recognizing rank, into an adjacent office. He sat me down and plopped my thin service jacket on the table. I gulped.

"Manthos, I've been going over your records. Your GCT, ARI and Mech scores are pretty good. I have an offer for you. Have you ever dreamed of flying?"

Flying? With Lt. Col. Manthos, a career Air Force pilot with combat tours flying high powered fighters in two wars as a dad? The idea of flying had been drummed into my head from the age of five. "Sure, I've thought about it. But how can I fly? Sir?"

He grinned. The hook had been set. "I'm offering you a rate where you can fly in one of four types of aircraft. We have an A class school right here that trains men to fly and operate electronics gear. To detect Soviet submarines. They have 400 subs and we need to be able to stop them. The rate is AW, Aviation Antisubmarine Warfare Operator."

Shit, maybe I'd get a designation besides 0000. "What do I need to do?" After looking at films of jets crashing into carrier decks all day I was interested in what he had to say.

"Well, it's a long A school and that's just the ground phase. But you'll eventually earn Aircrew wings, sort of like my Aviator wings, but for enlisted. It makes you awful proud to wear them, believe me. I see you had some college." He had no idea what my grades were: a C average my first semester, and two Fs just that summer.

"So you should be able to handle the school no sweat. All you need to do is extend your enlistment. One year, that's all." I knew I had to sign for at least four to get a decent school and a better assignment.

"And you'll be in training almost a year anyway. By the time you finish A school, FRAMP, SERE, D-WEST, and some others, you'll have three years to be in the fleet, same as now, just with a better job. Flying. And you'll collect flight pay; that's fifty extra bucks a month."

D-WEST, SERE, I had no idea what that meant, but it was sounding better than dragging heavy fuel hoses or canvas bags full of chains around a flight deck twelve hours a day. And the extra $50 would come in handy; that's what my motorcycle payments were. I didn't realize it was hazardous duty pay—he didn't say anything about that.

"By the way, how good of a swimmer are you? You need to pass the first class swimmer's test to be an aircrewman."

I was a terrible swimmer, didn't like to be in water over my head. I had barely passed as a third class swimmer at bootcamp.

"I do OK." I lied.

It was a done deal. I signed up for another year, said goodbye to my buddies headed for the fleet's flight decks, packed my sea bag and checked in to Company 4-C, 4th Battalion, room 403. A real room—damn what a luxury.

I couldn't wait to tell Marsha. If she would just answer my calls.

———◆———

WHEN I REPORTED TO the sterile, buff colored brick building that housed the AW A school I was sent directly to the master chief. A master chief is an E-9, the highest rank an enlisted man can attain. It was rumored he knew God personally.

"So tell me," he said pointedly, "could you torpedo and kill 250 men you don't know well enough to hate?"

"Sure." I wasn't sure. I *was* sure I didn't want to go back to flight deck school. The master chief gnawed on a cigar stub, looking me over closely.

"And?" His look told me he sensed I had something to add.

"Well Master Chief, I can't swim very well." Hell, I couldn't swim at all.

"We'll teach you, and you *will* pass the 1st class swim test. Now turn to, you have classes to attend."

I started AW A school that day. Twelve weeks of intensive ground training stood between me and a fleet replacement squadron. That, and passing the 1st class swimmer's test. I finally reached Marsha on the barracks pay phone and told her the good news.

"Well, OK, if that's what you want."

"But it will be good for us, can't you see that?"

"When are you coming home?"

"In a week or so, if I get my leave chit approved."

"Your what?"

"My chit, it's like a hall pass, sort of. Never mind, anyway, I'll be home soon. Will you pick me up at Stapleton? I'll make sure I'm on a flight that arrives in the day so you don't have to take off work. Is your Impala still running OK? I'm sorry I'm not there to help keep it tuned up."

"That's OK, I have help, uh, from time to time. Just make sure you let me know when you're coming back, OK?"

It was December 11. President Nixon would order Operation Linebacker II, the bombing of North Vietnam, within seven days.

My class was full, thirty men starting out in a new rate developed in 1968 in response to the Cold War. Attrition took its toll immediately. Chairs emptied daily. And that was the easy phase.

AW training included a lot of electronics. AWs operated "black boxes," exotic gear with secret code names, and we had to understand the basics of how they worked. We studied how to fix simple problems with the equipment, but the instructor said a steel toed flightboot usually got it working, if you knew where to kick.

We had four possible aircraft assignments as an AW "striker." The king of the hill was the P-3 Orion, a four-engined turbo prop beauty. It was designed for long range maritime patrol, replacing the aging P-2V Neptune. Everyone wanted P-3s, and a good reason was they never landed on an aircraft carrier. That meant, even after twelve or more hours airborne, you came back to terra firma, a real bed and maybe even an EM club. The terra firma could be the Backside of Beyond, but it would be solid ground. You stood a good chance it could also be Adak, Alaska, a tiny Aleutian island hundreds of miles from nowhere.

The other three were shipboard. The S-2F Tracker was a twin radial-piston engined relic and the worst horror stories were about S-2s succumbing to gravity in a variety of ways. And they were catapulted off the flight deck and arrested by a wire, adding to the potential mishaps. But it was naval aviation and that was what it was all about; if you didn't care for it, the Navy could find some place safer for you, like the scullery.

Helicopters rounded out the slots. The H-2 Seasprite was an odd looking machine deploying on ships like destroyers or frigates. The other option was the SH-3 Sea King. Sikorsky's triumph of maritime aviation design, the SH-3 was fully night and all weather capable. It carried sophisticated computers and of all things sonar. Didn't sonar belong on ships? What the hell was it doing in a helicopter? How did that work? But it looked a lot like that big helicopter I saw back in bootcamp—that machine impressed the hell out of me.

One problem with getting helicopter duty. You not only had to be a 1st class swimmer like all aircrewmen, you also had to be a SAR rescue swimmer. That meant you had to save other people by jumping out of the helicopter into the water, any water, and perform life saving techniques. No way would the Navy send me to helicopters, not after they saw me trying to swim.

We studied hundreds of slides, needing to know by sight every class of ship and submarine the Soviets had. Their navy looked impressive; cruisers bristled with guns of every caliber, subs held tubes of missiles and torpedoes, their hulls looking sleek and seaworthy. And we learned why pictures were classified. It was less what the picture was of, than who might have taken it. I hadn't thought of that; that there were spies, for us, in places like Russian shipyards, so if the image was made public it might compromise the source. There was always room in the Soviet gulag.

Hours were spent in class studying sound in water and the variety of ways it could be "heard." One was sonar: SOund NAvigation and Ranging. Actual sonar tapes played on and on as we strained to hear sounds through headphones. Snapping shrimp were a favorite, as were dolphin squeaks and groans. The sound of a torpedo tube opening was a different matter.

Another method of listening was through sonobuoys—long tubes tossed into the ocean which would relay sound to electronics equipment to be analyzed. The sound would be mapped out on a time/frequency grid; repetitious sources like engines, propellers or motors, would show up as lines. Knowing what the lines represented meant knowing what was out there, could be a rusty Liberian freighter, could be a Yankee-class Soviet sub patrolling the US coast. Should the Cold War escalate, knowing the difference could mean preventing the destruction of every major city in the US. That was the mission of the AW—stopping Soviet submarines, all 400 of them, should world affairs spiral out of control.

It was getting serious.

As weeks dragged on in the ever-shortening days, I felt an increasing heaviness. Several things loomed on the horizon. The 1st class swim test was approaching. And I was due for Christmas leave. Could I tell Marsha I passed the test? Would she be there to hear?

THE OLYMPIC SIZED POOL was indoors, the pervasive chlorine almost forming a gas cloud above it. The day's swim test candidates gathered at one end, standing around in tan bootcamp issue swim trunks waiting for it to get started. Joking gave way to the present when the facilitator showed up. The sailor was lean, his blue T-shirt sporting the SEAL emblem. His clipboard held the day's roster.

"OK you hamburgers, quit your skylarking and listen up. I am Petty Officer 2nd Class Harper. My job today is to give you the 1st class swim test. If you don't pass, you don't fly. It's that simple. We have the whole pool this morning but that doesn't mean you get it all to yourself. I don't expect you to be Mark Spitz; if you had just won seven gold medals you wouldn't be here, that's a fact. I do expect 100 percent from each of you. There are several categories including distance, burning oil, underwater distance, treading water, and buddy tow for starters. We'll start with distance, three laps of the pool using three different strokes. All right, begin."

Twenty sailors plunged in and made for the other end. Within seconds Harper boomed, "Who is the fucking wounded water buffalo thrashing around for dear life in *my* pool? Hey, you, what's your name?" He had his clipboard at the ready. He was staring right at me.

"Manthos," I chimed as I swallowed a mouthful of chlorine laced water.

"Hmmm, Manthos, OK." He ran his finger down the column of names on his clipboard and made a check. "You're giving 'dog paddle' a whole new meaning. My grandmother can swim better than that and she's in a wheelchair. You have the burning oil swim next, hope you don't drown before you tackle that one."

I managed to do my laps in an ugly but barely acceptable way, and pounded water into droplets in the burning oil phase. My final undoing was the underwater swim. Harper had cut me slack all morning but there was no way I could fake swimming under water. Harper called me over.

"Manthos, you get one more chance at this; I don't want your aviation career to be deep-sixed over a few feet of water. Take a few minutes to catch your breath, shit, you look hyperventilated, and then go over to that guy there and try it again." He pointed to the other end of the pool.

I sat on the cold wet concrete pool apron and let my breathing slow down. Then I walked to the opposite end and stood for a few minutes looking for the other instructor. He had disappeared into thin air, or water, perhaps, but he wasn't there. I waited five minutes and still no swim instructor. When I returned Harper was busy with another group so I waited a bit more. He finally noticed me and asked, "Did you do OK?"

I hesitated, then nodded in the affirmative. Another lie.

"OK, you passed. Barely, but you did it. *Somebody* has to be last."

I had lied again, but I was in. Hotdamn, no more swimming, that was it.

I bypassed the pool from then on and instead started working out with the base wrestling team, a sport I had enjoyed through school. I felt out of shape and wanted to cut a few pounds and wrestling was an excellent way to do that. It was looking like I might make the team. And I was able to stay in AW A school.

Finally, I could go home on leave with something positive to tell Marsha. She was going to pick me up in Denver and take me back to our little apartment in Fort Collins. It felt like years since I held Marsha close, hearing her laugh, feeling her warmth. Everything would be OK, once I got back.

As I flew into Stapleton, snow was falling on northern Colorado. Bombs were raining on North Vietnam. Operation Linebacker II had been unleashed.

———◆———

MY EYES SEARCHED THE waiting crowd as I disembarked the plane. I didn't see Marsha but she was so short she could have been hidden in the throng of holiday travelers. After the crowd dissipated she still wasn't there. As families reunited with hugs and smiles I walked the long concourse to baggage claim, maybe that's where she was waiting. I collected my bag and not seeing her there either, waited by the front doors, looking for her blue Impala two-door to pull up. Men in all kinds of uniforms streamed by, some looking fresh from bootcamp, some fresh from war.

After waiting an hour I called home. "Marsha? Where the hell are you? Weren't you going to come get me?"

"I'm so sorry, I worked late and overslept. I'll be right down."

"Right down? You're over an hour away! Guess I'll watch TV or something; I'll be by the Western Airlines counter."

After grabbing a hot dog and a Pepsi I stood watching the news. B-52s continued to pound Hanoi and Haiphong. 15 of the big bombers were being shot out of the sky. The Watergate scandal was getting bigger. I wondered how far up that went. Nixon had been reelected so whatever happened it was his administration dealing with it. I hadn't voted even though it was the first time eighteen to twenty year olds could vote in a presidential election. I didn't realize it, but perhaps if anything was being "won" in Vietnam it was that voting right.

I felt a small fist gently punch my arm. Marsha. Damn it was good to see her.

"I didn't recognize you, your hair is so short! And look at your clothes, it's a, a uniform! And no mustache, I've never seen you without one. If you hadn't written your name on your bag I would have walked right past you."

"But it's me, it's really me, and I'm back. I'm back to get you."

"We have so much to talk about, Jeff, so much. Tell me everything."

And so I did, on the drive back. I was beat, she drove, and when we got to our little apartment I felt wonderful. I couldn't wait to get out of my woolly dress blues and into civvies again, so I rifled through drawers looking for some comfortable old Levis. The clothes I wore to bootcamp never made it home so I didn't have my Dingo boots, but there were some Converse Allstars which did the trick. And there were some clothes in the drawers I didn't recognize.

Sex was on my mind and she knew it. It didn't take long before I was out of my comfortable civvies and we were in bed making love. It was everything I was not hoping for. She felt cold, distant, detached. Dammit, it just wasn't like it used to be with her. Something was wrong. The next morning we talked.

"You were cold last night, like you didn't want to be there."

"I know, I know. Things have changed since you've been gone."

"Is it somebody else?"

"Yes. It's somebody else. You were gone, he's here, he's older, he has a good job, he's not going anywhere."

"Are those his goddamn clothes in my dresser?"

"Yes..."

"But I came to get you."

"I don't want to be 'got.'"

My heart sank. We were due at my parents' house in half an hour.

THE CHRISTMAS TREE STOOD in the corner, full of decorations I remembered from childhood. My favorites were long thin tubes that held ruby, amber and emerald colored oil which bubbled happily when plugged into the string of lights.

Mom was full of questions: where was I going, what was I learning, did I like the Navy? I didn't want to tell her I felt like I was tumbling down a deep well after Marsha's revelation. But even with Marsha propped up on my lap, Mom sensed something was different, besides her son with no hair. Dad said I walked like a sailor. That I folded my clothes almost made Mom faint; my pre-bootcamp method had been to cram everything into a drawer.

Mom filled me in on the evening's plans. I could tell she was happy, she called me "JeffLee." That was reserved for when things were going well between us. "JeffLee, the Matthews are coming for dinner and they'd love to see you."

After a few hours at home I needed to get Marsha to work and hurry back so I could see Matt and Millie Matthew, who were old family friends. It was a quiet drive to the Black Knight Inn where Marsha tended bar, where I met her, fell in love with her, drank hard liquor illegally. It had all started with a bluff. I went in to the place with a bunch of guys, several were Vietnam War vets, and all friends older than me. We were seated around a big table, the guys primed to joke with Marsha. She was wearing her usual tight, low cut top and laughing her special laugh at our bad jokes.

"OK guys, I know you're all old enough but I need to check IDs. Boss says so." She started to my right and worked her way around the table; everyone else had an ID, most were even legal. I was the last one she checked.

"Just bring me a damn drink, OK?" That's the best I could do, for an eighteen-year-old in a twenty-one hard liquor state.

"All right, smart-ass, what will it be?" It worked. I was good at bluffing.

I couldn't take my eyes off her that night and soon found excuses to go to the Black Knight Inn just to see her. We hit it off, well enough that I had to finally tell her I was only eighteen. She said she didn't care. I was as much a man as anyone else she knew, she reassured me.

After dropping Marsha off I went back home to see the Matthews. I really liked them, so much so that there were times I had wished they were my parents. Matt had flown P-51s with Dad in the 357th Fighter Group during WWII. Both had flown combat in Korea. Between Dad and Matt there was a hell of a lot of flying, combat and bravery. There I sat between them at dinner, an E-1, the lowest rank possible. Talk turned to bootcamp, fresh in my mind but distant memories for them. Mom couldn't help herself. "JeffLee, show us how you folded socks so well you were made the sock Petty Officer."

Jezuzchrist, I couldn't fucking believe it. I turned red. There I was, wedged between war heroes and all I had to show for myself was how well I folded a pair of goddamn socks. Moms, they could be proud at the worst moments.

Two weeks' leave went by in a blur. I tried to see as many old friends as I could, and my buddy Mark made sure I got to some parties. He introduced me to a girl at one bash who quickly took me to bed. She called me "lover" as we pressed flesh to flesh. My dog tags clinked together in a thrusting rhythm. I forgot her name. Maybe she forgot mine too. She needed the attention, I needed some tension release; it worked for both of us even though she wasn't Marsha and I wasn't really her lover. I got dressed, donned my peacoat and rejoined the party.

Marsha put up with the awkward arrangement while I was at the apartment, but when it came time to leave I knew I wouldn't be coming back to that place. I gave my stereo to Mark, left my collection of records at the apartment, packed what I had there and left.

Marsha and I had saved two mini-bottles of gin as a special little "something" between us. The last thing I did at the apartment was dump them in the sink and leave the empties on their side, drained of whatever it was they once held special.

Dad took me to the airport, bound for Memphis. On the plane ride back loneliness sat next to me like a big ugly dog that wouldn't go away.

PART TWO

1973

3: Submarines and Field Days

That winter in Memphis was miserable. It was damp, soggy, clear to the bone freeze-your-marrow-solid cold. Slipping and falling on snow and ice was routine. The thick wool peacoat added some cushion, and it was damn warm. With the wide collar up it afforded protection from the biting wind.

But there was a bright spot. January 15 marked four months in service and I was "awarded" automatic advancement to E-2. I was officially an airman apprentice. I was no longer a "boot" and no longer an E-1. A number of guys in school made E-4, Third Class Petty Officer, quickly. By buying it. With time. They had a "crow," they didn't do field days, clean latrines, pick up butts or empty shit-cans. They signed for an extra two years to get their automatic promotion. Six friggin' years total. We called those fast rank guys "rent-a-crows." Most didn't get the respect they were technically due since the rank wasn't earned, but a few were decent guys and didn't throw their purchased weight around. If I thought deeply enough about it I could see the logic in doing six and getting the advancement early. If you were dead set on doing twenty, might as well take all the advantages available if you're going to be a lifer. That's what we called career guys, "lifers." If I did twenty I'd be thirty-nine when

I could retire—seemed like old age and an eternity away. I just couldn't think that far down the road.

I made a couple of friends. Brady Turner had been in one of my sister bootcamp companies and was in my A school class. He was a stocky, dark haired and good natured half-Indian from some tired lumber town on the Washington coast, up where Orcas and Bigfoot ruled. It seemed like we always drew field day together, and watching him wrestle that buffer was almost as entertaining as my tango with the powerful machine. But we polished our swabbing technique and were able to lay a wax coating that would buff up nicely and pass any inspection. And he always had a bet to make.

"Hey Manthos, there's a big fight on today, gonna watch? My money is on Joe Frazier, that guy's indestructible. C'mon, bet me a pitcher of beer and a burger." Brady had an amazing appetite, especially for a guy his size. I saw him eat two burgers with fries and a whole pizza in one sitting at the bowling alley diner; no way was I going to bet dinner—that could be hard to define. But a burger and some beer, I could cover that if I lost.

"Ok, you're on. I'll take this guy Foreman. He looks pretty big, he might have a chance. And I'll take a pepperoni pizza, small will do, if I win."

Huddled around the small black and white TV in the barracks rec room on January 22, we watched Foreman TKO Frazier in two rounds. It wasn't pretty, but those fights never were. The free pizza tasted great.

Lyndon Johnson, the thirty-sixth president, died the same day. A day later the Paris Peace Accords were ratified, with a new ceasefire for Vietnam in place. It wasn't a victory. It wasn't a defeat. It wasn't anything but a way to close the door. U.S. ground troops were to be withdrawn. It didn't say anything about the 7th fleet.

Brady was married and soon brought his young wife down from Washington State. Watching him spend time with her made me long for Marsha, for the good old days that seemed so long ago, so short lived, so fragile. She was continuing to have a good time back in Fort Collins while I wrestled with electrical circuitry and aquatic acoustical properties.

Another friend I ran into was Mike Johnson. He had been on the flight from Denver to San Diego, was in my bootcamp company and now was in training for enlisted aircrew. "Hey Manthos, what the fuck are you doing here? I thought you were headed to the *Hancock*."

"Yeah, me too, but I got talked into going to AW A school. That was going to be your rate, wasn't it?"

"Almost. I switched to radio operator, but I'll get P-3s. No ships for me!"

"Yeah, asshole, no need to rub it in yet, I could get Orions too. Did you bring your guitar?"

"Yep. And my car, too, I'm a changed man! I might even let you borrow it sometime."

"A fuckin' car? You lucky bastard. You know it's only a half hour to get into Memphis. If you ever want any company you know where to find me. Hell, I'll chip in a few bucks for gas; your Volkswagen can't use that much."

A car; it was an amazing thing to have access to after boot and weeks of being stuck on base. On occasion Mike would drag me to an art house theater to see an Ingmar Bergman film, which usually left me dizzy and ready for the 3.2 percent EM club beer.

Mike was a real friend for letting me use his car when he was on duty. I loved going to Shelby Forest State Park; it was close to the base, woodsy, quiet, everything the base wasn't. Maybe I should have gone Army I loved the woods so much. Everything I had seen of the Navy was blue or gray, and most of the gray was steel. If it moved, salute it, if it didn't, paint it.

The country roads around Millington were begging for a high powered motorcycle to put tire to them and thunder miles and miles until the dark of night made it impossible to open the throttle all the way. I really missed my Triumph. Soon, soon, I would have it back. Meanwhile Mike's red VW bug had sufficient power to escape the gravitational pull of NATTC Millington's front gate.

THE BASE HAD A lot of Marines and I was about to wrestle one for the 165 pound spot on the team. I tried not to think of how hard Marine training was; I had faced tough opponents before, some I beat and some I didn't. I had nothing to lose. He didn't either.

The gym was old wooden WWII vintage: dark, moldy and musty. The mat looked like it had been keelhauled. Overhead fluorescent lights barely had enough candlepower to illuminate the huge cockroaches scurrying about in damp corners. Battleship gray steel lockers had been beaten with the fists of losers, flung open by victors, rusted by decades of Mississippi River moisture and neglected by sailors and Marines. Perfect. Wrestling was not glamorous; it was sweaty, smelly, hard bones, gristle, cauliflower ears, pulled muscles and bruises. As far as I was concerned other sports, especially basketball, had too many rules. We just had a few: no body slams, no choking or gouging of eyes, no full Nelsons. I had accidentally discovered a move while I was in high school called a "Turk." Maybe it was time to pull it out of my bag of tricks; I'd never seen anyone use it before. I was hoping the Marine warming up with fifty pushups hadn't either.

Nine minutes and one well executed Turk later I was on the team. All I had to do was imagine he was the guy sleeping with Marsha. I could see the disappointment in the Marine's eyes; he'd been beaten by a sailor, no easy thing to take. We shook hands after the match—no hard feelings, I just, finally, had a good day.

There was a tournament coming up in Norfolk in three weeks. I was still a ways off from being in top shape so I continued to work out wearing plastic sweats. They made me sweat profusely, obscenely, endlessly. But I shed pounds and started to feel good.

———— • ————

"OK, LISTEN UP. FOR those of you who have made it this far, it looks like you will graduate unless you fuck up in a big way, which has happened. But, barring hitting an officer, having major brain farts or going AWOL, here are your orders. Everyone is going to P-3s at

Moffet Field. You'll like the Bay area, you'll like P-3s, you'll rack up some serious flight time. But let's see, no orders for either Turner or—Manthos. I have no idea where they are; I'll check. In the meantime you two field day the classroom; I'll be back after I talk to the detailer."

PO1 Blank left the classroom in a buzz of excitement. P-3s, maybe even Barbers Point, Hawaii, for an active duty squadron. Everyone was delighted they didn't get S-2s, rumored to be flying oil slicks. Brady and I looked at each other quizzically.

"What the fuck's going on, Manthos?"

"Beats me, our orders must have been delayed or misplaced; I mean, everyone got P-3s, so we must too, it only makes sense."

"But nothing makes sense here. What if we get S-2s, man, those things scare me."

"Me too. Remember those flight deck accident films I told you about? Who wants to be in the thick of that. Oh well, we'll know soon enough."

As I waltzed the big buffer around the room with two fingers controlling its motion, I repressed that sense of dread I had in bootcamp when I got orders to the *Hancock*. What if I got helos? I couldn't swim worth a damn, then what.

Two days of agonizing over my next training phase were finally put to rest by Blank. "OK; Turner, Manthos, you report to HS-10, Naval Air Station Imperial Beach, California. You got helicopters. Call 'em 'helos.' Hooyaa."

Goddammit. Helicopters. I was headed back to the swimming pool. Aircrew Rescue Swim School was my fate after all. If I had only not lied two months before, not bluffed my way through the swim test, I wouldn't be facing something I feared I couldn't overcome. I went to see the master chief.

"Manthos, you again? What's the problem now?"

"Master Chief, it's the swimming. I can't really swim worth a shit, and I have to get through rescue swims."

"And what did I tell you back then? That they'll teach you everything you'll need to know. And listen close, I'm only going to say this once. You'll never know, unless you're tested, what is inside you, what you are capable of, what you may or may not be able to accomplish. They will give you the tools, young man, to do whatever you need to do, if you have the will to try. You don't strike me as being a quitter, and plenty of guys have quit this school already. Just try, Manthos, give it your best shot. See where that takes you. Now, take a hike."

As a cigar stub smoldered between his teeth his attention was immediately drawn to a pile of paperwork on his gray steel desk. Nothing else for me to do there, but I hesitated. A quick glance back up at me, with a raised eyebrow saying "you still here?" from the master chief, sent me on my bewildered way.

After I got my orders to helicopters I spent some time taking it all in. I had a possible way out. I was scheduled to wrestle with the base team in a tournament in Norfolk in a few weeks. If I went, my orders could be changed. To S-2s given my luck. I really didn't want the "Stoof" as seasoned crewmen called it. I went back to the master chief.

"Manthos, I hear you're a decent wrestler. You're here because if you go to Norfolk your orders will be changed. You're not sure what to do, right?"

He was a freakin' mind reader. I hoped not every master chief could do that. "Uh, right Master Chief. I'm just not sure, I mean, I liked San Diego, what I saw of it. I just don't know what might happen if I go wrestle and things change."

"My advice, and that's why you're here, is take these orders. I know going to the tournament would be fun, but these are good orders, I suggest you take 'em."

His pronouncement rated a fresh cigar. His suggestion almost sounded like an order, but he made me believe in his words.

I went over to the gym and told the coach I decided to stick with my orders and not risk something else. After I turned in my thin-soled wrestling shoes and smelly sweats I headed back to my barracks, feeling like I had just taken a certain path in Shelby Forest, leaving another unexplored and a perpetual mystery.

Two more weeks and A school was over. I managed to conquer electronics, sonar, and a host of odd sounding gear like MAD, Jezebel, Yardstick. I knew what a catapult was, what arresting gear did, how fast sound traveled in salt water, what a homing torpedo could do to a steel tube filled with 250 men 1,000 feet down. I knew the sound of a collapsing submarine hull.

I graduated fifteenth in a class of eighteen. A dozen guys had washed out and we weren't even in the air yet. I also got my first official looking certificate, not realizing the Navy gave them out for almost any accomplishment. It certified that "Jeff L. Manthos, Aviation Antisubmarine Warfare Operator Airman Apprentice, U.S. Navy" had satisfactorily completed training on March 14, 1973. Aviation Antisubmarine Warfare Operator Airman Apprentice, what a mouth full. And I finally had a striker designation.

I also got my first quarterly marks, grades in five categories that would follow me for the rest of my enlistment. I didn't pay much attention at first, but a lot rode on those marks, and decisions about my future would be made in part by them. Professional performance, military behavior, leadership and supervisory ability, military appearance and adaptability. Several didn't apply to the lower ranks, like leadership, since we weren't expected to "lead," just follow orders at that point. But the others did apply, and without trying I did OK.

Brady got his certificate too, and we would regroup in Imperial Beach, California, within days. I boarded another plane bound once again for San Diego, and a great big Navy swimming pool.

I had a chance to look over my service jacket on the plane. I had signed a contract of enlistment which was legally binding. The authority for my enlistment was "COMCRUITMANINST." That would have been at AFEES—the Armed Forces Entrance and Examining Station, in Denver. The contract said my physical profile was a "B." I had no idea who assigned me as a B, but I was, it said so right there. It made me wonder what an A profile was. So I had been a B in an A school. It also made me curious how many categories there were—was there an "F" profile? The contract also had my selective service number on it—05011530127. I couldn't decipher that number either, but in there somewhere was my draft lottery number of one, I was pretty sure of that. My new orders read that I was to report to Helantisubron-10 FRAMP, NAS IB. As an AWAA. The acronyms were starting to make sense. I was becoming a sailor.

4: SEA KINGS

I got checked in to Naval Air Station Imperial Beach—NAS IB—through the training squadron office. The base was small and had a friendly feel to it. The barracks were fairly new and I was put into a two-man room with another AW trainee a few months ahead of me. Life seemed promising, even without Marsha.

I reported to HS-10 Aircrew Training. The HS stood for "Helicopter Anti-submarine Squadron." Brady was already there and we were grouped with two other aircrew candidates, Mike Pater and Dan Diaz. Petty Officer 1st Class Bliven was to be our instructor. In dress blues, he sported a chest full of impressive medals. I asked the aircrew chief, Lawson, about him.

A big, barrel-chested man with a soft voice and keen eye, Chief Lawson filled me in. "Ol' Doc, see, we call him 'Doc' 'cause he was a corpsman with the Marines in Vietnam, did a full combat tour. Earned every one of them medals and there's prob'ly a few he didn't get. If you ask him I'm not sure what he'd say about which was more dangerous, flying in helos or walkin' patrol 'round Hue."

Jovial but strict, Bliven made his training synopsis clear from the start. He walked in to the small classroom and slammed down four thick, blue covered manuals onto the gray metal table. "This is day one of your aircrew training, and this is your NATOPS for the SH-3

Sea King. NATOPS—Naval Air Training and Operating Procedures Standardization. You each get your own. Tonight I want you to read the entire emergency procedures section; the pages are outlined in red hash marks. I will be asking questions on it tomorrow, so don't fuck off and spend your evening at the EM club.

"Listen closely. Everything you need to know about the Sea King helicopter is in here. NATOPS is written in blood; it is the culmination of thousands of flight hours, many of those ending in the loss of some pilot's or aircrewman's life. I don't want the next blood soaked page to be written about your mistakes. Flying is inherently dangerous and helos are no exception. You have six months of training before you are assigned to a fleet squadron. I haven't lost a student yet, and by 'lost' I mean killed, and you will not be my first. I never lost a Marine to wounds I treated and I'm not going to lose one of you now and ruin my record. Oh, and you can call me 'Doc.'"

Time to get very serious. And flight training for the Sea King helo was just part of the picture. There were additional schools to blend into the syllabus. Some were for aviators exclusively, others for sailors destined to be potential POWs. We fit that description.

The next morning Doc nailed us on NATOPS emergency procedures before we had even seen the gear. We didn't do so well but he made his point. Then we took a look at the opening pages.

"Remember what I said yesterday about NATOPS being written in blood? Turner, turn to page four and read what it says about warnings."

"It says, uh, 'Warning: an operating procedure, practice or condition, etc., which may result in injury or death if not carefully observed or followed.'"

"Remember: injury or death. Pay close attention to this warning, it will crop up all through the manual. Now, Manthos, why don't you read the next entry on wording. These words have very specific meanings, so don't go thinking you already know what they are. OK, Manthos, begin."

"Wording: The concept of word usage and intended meaning which has been adhered to in preparing this manual is as follows:

'Shall' has been used only when application of a procedure is mandatory. 'Should' has been used only when application of a procedure is recommended. 'May' and 'may not' have been used only when application of a procedure is optional. 'Will' has been used only to indicate futurity, never to indicate any degree of requirement for application of a procedure. 'Land immediately' is self-explanatory. 'Land as soon as possible' means land at the first site at which a safe landing can be made. 'Land as soon as practicable' means extended flight is not recommended, the landing site and duration of flight is at the discretion of the pilot in command. Hey Doc, what's 'futurity?' Oh, wait, never mind, I think I got it. It means like, in the future, right?"

"Brilliant Manthos, you must have figured out how to use a mop pretty fast, right?" Laughter rippled through the room as I turned a bit red. Sometimes I was just slow to catch on. But "land immediately" being self explanatory stuck with me as both a bit funny in its bare truth and yet very grave. It was all a lesson in semantics that impacted how I would read those words for the rest of my life.

Doc reclaimed control of the class after the fun at my expense. "Listen up you four, the months ahead will be plenty busy. Starting in one week is D-WEST, which includes the Dilbert Dunker; that will make or break some of you right there. D-WEST stands for Deep Water Environmental Survival Training, as in 'I'm floating in the middle of the South China Sea all by my lonesome and what the fuck do I do now?' You will get your flight gear in a few weeks so until then, start running so you're in shape for SAR swim school. I would suggest running around the base; it's about three miles and can be done over lunch."

SAR swims. I didn't know about that dunker thing but rescue swim school was going to be a bitch.

I was still without my Triumph motorcycle and slowly going nuts without any personal transportation. For someone raised in the wide open West I was feeling awfully restricted. At least my bike was still waiting for me, in my parents' garage. I planned on getting it shipped out to Imperial Beach as soon as I could. I told myself when

I turned twenty-one I was going to ride that bike back to Colorado and get drunk at the Black Knight Inn.

———◄●►———

IMPERIAL BEACH, "YOUR VACATION fun in the sun paradise" as the Chamber of Commerce suggested, is the most southwesterly town in America. Locals called it "Venereal Beach." The Tijuana bull ring stood on a hill to the south, just across the fence that formed the international border. To the west the beach hugged the Pacific just past the end of the runway.

Brady had a car and we would take off for short trips around the south bay area. Still too young to drink off base, we poked around side streets in places like Chula Vista and National City, towns that filled the gap between San Diego and the Mexican border. National City was a hard-edged town weaned on the 32nd Street Naval Base, the port for combat ships like destroyers and cruisers. Gray steel vessels lined up for a mile, and the heavy, thick fuel-oil exhaust permeated the National City air like a dark petrochemical cloud.

Inevitably we found a tattoo parlor. No self-respecting Navy town wouldn't have a dittybag full of them. This particular place belonged to Iwo Jima Eddie. It was quite by accident, just a turn down a side street and there he was. His storefront had an old photograph of Mr. Eddie, faded with a greenish tint. There in the photo he sat, tattooed from head to foot. The only places that weren't tattooed, that were visible anyway, were his hands, his face, and his feet. It was as if he wore a suit of ink: black, red, green, all swirled and shaped into a mosaic of images drawn from opium dreams and life at sea. Dragons, mermaids, skulls with glaring garnet eyes, and sea snakes coiled and contorted around his body.

It was twilight when we stumbled upon his shop. We stood in front of a weathered wooden door flanked by glass windows full of pictures of Eddie's subjects, poised like princes to his tattooed majesty.

Brady spoke first. "I dare ya'. Go in, I dare ya'!"

"Man, I don't know, I'm not even drunk. Aren't ya' supposed to be drunk first? At least that can be an excuse."

"C'mon, Manthos, just go in and look around, what can it hurt?"

"OK but dammit, you better be right behind me!" I pushed in the door on its rusty hinges and stood in the dim light of a single bulb, uncovered and dangling by braided electrical cord from the high, musty, tin covered ceiling. It took my eyes a few seconds to adjust to the dimness. The room was empty, nothing but wall space all the way back to a small counter. There, looking straight into my young soul, was Iwo Jima Eddie. His smile was a riddle as he beckoned me with open tattooed arms into his lair. I was drawn in by the sheer magnetism of his mysterious world.

"Welcome boys. You're in the Navy, I can tell. I can tell the Merchant Marines from the fishermen, the sailors from the jarheads, the crabbers from the tuna boat boys. I've been doing this longer than you've been alive."

I believed him. I think I would have believed him if he told me he sailed with John Paul Jones. The stories he had stowed away in his hold were bursting at the bulkhead. And he knew how to reel in a fresh catch. "Just take a look around fellas, I ain't goin' anywhere. I've probably been there already anyway. Been 'round the Horn, 'round the Cape, crossed the equator so many times Davy Jones pays his respects to me! Take a look around, I can do just about anything you want."

As I did a 360 degree turn my eyes were awash in tattoo patterns. There was nothing in his shop but tattoos, thousands of them, all tacked to the walls in random patterns: Marine bulldogs, three masted sailing ships, cobras, panthers, dragons, and daggers scrolled with the words "death before dishonor."

Brady started in. "Go ahead Manthos, get one!"

"Brady, I ain't got hardly any money! I'd have to go back to IB to get some more cash. Anyway, I'm not sure about this."

"Look, I'll loan you some money and you can pay me back. Go on, it won't hurt either."

"How the hell do you know that? You don't have a tattoo. And aren't you going to get one? How come *I'm* the one who is supposed to get it? Hell, my mom would faint dead if she saw a tattoo on me. And her advice before I joined made sense; she said if I ever get a tattoo, don't get a woman's name, no matter what. But I do kinda like that big dragon up there. Damn, it's a hundred dollars, but it's really cool."

"I ain't loaning you a hundred dollars; I'd never see it again even if I had it. How much you got on you? I've got a couple of tens."

"I got five bucks, enough for a couple of pitchers of beer at the EM club. So with your twenty that makes an even twenty five bucks. Hmmm, wonder what I could get for that."

Iwo Jima Eddie emerged from the shadows right on cue. "Son, I got a little dragon over here for twenty-five, she's real pretty and fits nice on the arm. Won't take but about an hour or so to get 'er done for ya'. And I'm open for a bit longer. I can do it right now, matter o' fact. C'mon back and have a seat."

The hook was set and the spell was cast. An hour and a half later I left Iwo Jima Eddie's web with a sore arm saturated with emerald greens and ruby reds outlined in coal black.

"Being mighty well known hereabouts as a fine deserving sailor of the Southern Seas, by virtue of having displayed an uncommon lot of valor, glory and hallelujah; for being intrepid, tepid, warm natured with cold steel nerve, shown by his willingness to sink, swim or walk water to join services with this great and glorious endeavor..." I was appointed Admiral. So sayeth Eddie's certificate. Right. All I knew for sure was the little $25 dragon was probably going to be there when I woke up.

Brady laughed all the way back to the barracks.

———◆———

DEEP WATER ENVIRONMENTAL SURVIVAL TRAINING at the Fleet Aviation Specialized Operational Training Group, Pacific Fleet. DWEST at FASOTRAGRUPAC. It was all in the name. "Faso" was slang for the training group, which held several other programs including

SERE and JEST. SERE was rumored to be nasty and brutish and not very short. But DWEST was up first and we were bussed to NAS Miramar, northeast of IB, for the start of the fun.

Our first introduction to aviation was experiencing vertigo: a dizzying, sickening, disorienting tumble into an abyss of confusion and contradiction. Your mind tells you one thing, cockpit instruments tell you another, and if you believed your brain, that marvelous organ that told you to eat, sleep, reproduce and survive, you would certainly die. Trust your aircraft's instruments, that was the only lesson for that phase; trust them no matter what your mind wanted to believe. Turning left might seem like a turn to the right, sideways might seem like up, and down might not feel like down. Aviators who didn't pay heed rarely had the chance to tell their squadronmates why. Their lockers were cleaned out and valuables sent to their families. Even the word "vertigo" sounded ominous.

Next we were herded into a large building where a huge swimming pool loomed before me. Jumping off a twenty-foot tower into the pool started things off; treading water in full flight gear followed. After tiring us out in the pool they lined us up at the deep end. Looking like a carnival ride from hell, a cockpit mockup sitting high on rails running into the water sat at the pool's edge. "This, gentlemen, is the Dilbert Dunker. For those of you who have not had the pleasure of riding my baby here, let me demonstrate." Our instructor yanked a lanyard and the cockpit sped along the rails quickly gaining momentum. With a whoosh and a bang it hit the water and flipped over into the deep end. And sank. Unlike a Disney ride, this machine didn't pull you out to safety accompanied by a giggle and blush of embarrassment at your primal fear. It just settled inverted under water. Your fear could pretty much do whatever it wanted while you were strapped in upside down, submerged.

As the line formed I could feel my heart pounding in my chest. I didn't like the water. I had done marginally OK in my 1st class swim test which I hadn't truly passed to even qualify to be there that day. But somehow I stayed in line and worked my way up, as if some invisible hand pushed me along.

In the deep end, deep down, was a diver in SCUBA gear—our safety net if something went wrong or we panicked. He wasn't there to hold my hand, just save my life if things went awry. Bubbles percolated to the surface from his tank as he sat weighted down with a lead belt.

"Now remember," the instructor boomed, "the cockpit will settle for a brief second before it sinks upside down. That's when you take a quick breath, not before—too soon, not after—too late."

My turn came and somehow I climbed the ladder, donned a soaked flight helmet and got strapped in. Before I could say hey wait a second I'd like to think about this I was gone. As sure as reveille is sounded at dawn, the steel tub of a cockpit struck the water with a splash and hung, for just a second, before it rotated on its hinge and flipped me over. I managed a gulp of air and hung on. The water was cold but it got my attention. Once the dunker stopped I found the release lever for the harness and freed myself. A glance at the diver on the bottom somehow made me feel like I had done well; he didn't move, just his flat glass facemask glinting back at me. Up was up—somehow I knew where that was—and I popped to the surface and cleared the deep end just as another flyer struck the water strapped into the cockpit on rails. Damn, it was actually fun. I would have done it again but we had yet another phase before the day was over.

Our big gray bus took us back to NAS North Island. Since most naval flyers had the luxury of parachutes, some even ejection seats, neither of which we helo guys had, we were to get the feel of being dragged by a 'chute in the open ocean. I had never swum in the ocean, never even got completely wet in the ocean, and now I was going to be dragged behind a speeding boat until I figured out how to release the harness and free myself.

The boat had a platform on the stern and two tall spires where the parachute rigging was attached. We were pushed off the platform into the water while the boat merrily sped across the sunlit sea. Some didn't *need* pushing, some did. I didn't know if it was a human hand or the same invisible one that propelled me toward the dunker hours before, but when my turn came I was launched into the Pacific with all the conviction of a guy who had avoided the draft by reluctantly joining the Navy and ended up in the ocean being dragged by a parachute harness behind a speeding boat before he really knew what had happened.

The water was colder than the pool and a lot rougher, but I luckily landed on my back as I bounced across the waves. The training kicked in as designed and I got free, floating in the water once clear of all the entanglements. A line of flyers, like so many fishing net floats, bobbed along for a hundred yards behind me.

The final phase was rescue by none other than a naval helicopter from NAS IB. It was a little green H-2 Seasprite from HSL-31. My turn came to be "rescued" by a SAR swimmer and he got me hooked up and hoisted into the helicopter. He had apparently made it through swim school. That dreaded phase still awaited me.

But I made it through DWEST, a short but important stage in aircrew training. And I got another certificate, dated March 28.

The next day the last American ground troops left South Vietnamese soil. The USS *Constellation*, and Task Force 77 of the 7th Fleet, were maintaining their positions in the South China Sea.

———●———

MY OFF-DUTY LIFE REVOLVED around getting my motorcycle under me. It was somewhere between Fort Collins and San Diego and I was somewhere between cabin fever and stir crazy. The base had the EM club with its cheap beer and grill, and the movie theater ran fairly new flicks, but I was still trapped. Save for a rare jaunt with Brady I spent all my time on the small base. But I finally started flying.

My new flight gear held the same odor as the clothes pulled from the bins at bootcamp, but it was special. It marked me as an aircrewman, a member of an elite group of enlisted aviators entrusted with million dollar aircraft and the mission of protecting the country from the Soviet submarine threat. The only people who were impressed were my parents and myself. IB was awash in flyers attired in exotic looking flight gear. I couldn't wait to wear my new leather G-1 flight jacket. As I slipped it on it felt cool, stiff, it squeaked that new leather squeak. The nylon lined sleeves welcomed my arms, up to a point. The cuffs had been sewn together. So much for the lowest bidder argument. It made me wonder what was wrong on the helicopters. At least I could don my new, right out of the box, distinctive naval aviator sunglasses. Or at least dangle them conspicuously from my pocket. And the gear was all temporary; as students we were not yet authorized to wear wings, and if we didn't make it we would lose the right to wear it all.

The SH-3 Sea King was a magnificent beast: a huge, imposing machine standing well over fifteen feet tall at the rotor head. From the tip of the main rotor to the tip of the tail rotor was seventy-two feet, 10.67 inches. There was a scant 3.5 inches clearance between the main and tail rotors and when turning, it seemed razor thin. I had visions of the rotors stretching and touching ever so slightly, just enough to shred themselves and me along with them. The main rotor blades folded back along the fuselage like the wings of a gigantic insect. Two pitot tubes protruding from above the cockpit pointing toward the front at 90 degree angles looked like antennae, adding to the bug-like image. The entire tail pylon—tail rotor, gear box and all—folded back upon the fuselage. This shortened the overall length to 47 feet 3 inches, a measurement every flight deck boss knew. It also made the helo look like a white over gray 20,000 pound anvil.

The Sea King had retractable front landing gear with a small stationary tail wheel—it was a true "tail dragger." The cockpit landing gear lever had a clear plastic tire on the handle with a red light inside, which illuminated when cycled up or down. Very "old aviation." And the helicopter I was training to fly in was the same kind that had hovered over the Marine field that day so long ago in boot-camp, when I looked in awe at that amazing machine. I had no idea I had been looking at my future.

My first few missions were basically "sit still and don't touch anything" types, mostly just dead weight while the student pilot learned how to fly the pattern and try autorotations. An "autorotation" was an event for which the first one experienced by a helicopter crew-member is unforgettable. It is a power loss simulation; that is, engine failure, and the machine drops out of the sky like a ten ton bowling ball. Airplanes—fixed wings—have a glider ability. A helicopter drops straight down. Controlling all the forces in effect takes a deft touch by the pilot, especially when accompanied by weightlessness caused by the rapid fall. Like a roller coaster diving down a steep incline, we would plummet towards the ground in a free fall until the last seconds before impact, when the pilot would bring on power to the blades and we would go around and do it again.

As my training progressed I began to operate the sensing systems aboard: the sonar was the main gear. We also had MAD—Magnetic Anomaly Detection—which could pinpoint an object made of steel in the water.

Doc also instructed me in the use of the rescue hoist, which required lots of dexterity. Your left hand had to operate the ICS—the Internal Communication System—the hoist, and the lever used to fly the helo laterally, keeping it over the spot where you needed to be. We would practice over smoke flares in a dance of wind, water and concentration.

One afternoon after a successful flight with Doc I asked him what ship he was on last.

"I've never deployed on a ship, ever."

"But Doc, how can that be? You've been in the Navy for years!"

"One word, Vietnam, that's the only place I've been to, baby, and it was no picnic I can tell ya' that. Remember, I was a corpsman with the Marines up near the DMZ. No ships there."

"But you've been at HS-10 for a long time, how'd you manage that?"

"It's really personal but no big secret, so you should know. I have three daughters; I'm divorced too, you understand, and one of my girls is real sick and probably not going to get better. She was born with a heart problem that can't really be fixed, though God knows I've tried. I've got humanitarian shore duty, at least until, until..." He began to tear up and stare at the ground, so I switched the subject.

"So, have you ever seen a Sea Bat?"

"C'mon, Manthos, they aren't real, are they?"

"Guess I'll find out, Doc; sooner or later I'm headin' out on a WestPac."

WestPac: Western Pacific deployment. That meant the South China Sea.

Training progressed, my flight syllabus was getting filled in and my motorcycle finally made it to Imperial Beach. I was a free man. But not for long. SERE survival school was approaching fast. It was finally scheduled and I was set to go, whether I was ready or not.

I had *not* been ready for SAR swim school, administered by the H-2 training squadron, HSL-31. All my bluffing came home to roost on the first day in the pool. We were to do the 1st class swim test for starters. Oh god, not that again, I thought.

There were instructors everywhere, and with just a handful of prospective rescue swimmers in the class our every move was watched closely. They liked to wash guys out, better there than failure in the open sea with lives at stake.

I washed out. All the anxiety that had built up since I got my orders to helos sank in the deep end of the 32nd St. Naval Base pool. It was over. I had visions of the *Hancock* slowly pulling away from the dock as they tossed me and my seabag aboard.

But a remarkable thing happened. A second chance. Chief Lawson pulled me aside when I returned from the first day's swim. "Manthos, are you a quitter? I've got to know you pretty good over these last few months; I've been watching you, and I don't think you are. You wouldn't have gotten this far if you were. We want you to finish the training, to complete SAR swims, to become a helo AW. Here's what I'm gonna' do, young man. We're pulling you out of this SAR class and sending you to SERE instead. After SERE you will work with Petty Officer Wagner on your swimming, he can help. Then, we'll set you through again if you make progress. Anything else is not being considered. Are you with me on this?"

Well goddammit. I may have lied and bluffed my way that far, but the chief was right, I wasn't going to quit. "OK Chief, I'm in."

"Don't let me down. And remember, if I could do it, you can too."

Somehow I couldn't picture the chief's nose-tackle build squeezed into a skintight wetsuit, but I believed him. And I sure as hell didn't want to let him down. I had quit sports in high school after a few years; my heart wasn't in it at the time, but I wasn't going to quit again, even if I drowned trying.

I boarded a big gray bus once again and headed for NAS North Island and the legendary SERE school. The *Hancock* deployed to Vietnam on May 8 without me.

SERE: SURVIVAL, EVASION, RESISTANCE, ESCAPE. Day one, zero dark-thirty. "No breakfast gentlemen, and empty your pockets of any 'snacks' you might have brought along. Until we say so, no food is to be eaten except for what you catch."

I knew that was part of the deal but I was already dreaming of a plate of sizzling hot eggs right off the griddle, with hearty sides of hash browns, crisp bacon and buttered toast. No such luck.

Bussed down to a jetty after morning lectures, we were to simulate washing up on shore and instructed on how to make shelter, crab nets, fires, and shown the glories of multifilament parachute cord—like we carried a parachute in our helicopters. I knew we didn't have them, I looked, much to Doc's amusement.

Broken down into two squad-sized units, each squad hurried to set up tents, make crab nets and get a fire going to cook whatever might be caught.

There were five SEALs in the class and we ended up with a hulking guy named Esterlund in our squad. Everyone looked to those guys for something: leadership, courage, poise, whatever. Esterlund did not disappoint. He was a wizard with the crab net, and bellowed out to the rest of us to get our hole dug for the fire. Lined with seaweed, we would cover our catch with sand to bake. The squad next to us was engaged in the same event, and a friendly competition started.

Once our substantial catch of crab, courtesy of Esterlund, was in the pit, we covered it and sat back, enjoying the twilight beauty of the San Diego skyline. We had a rough idea of how long to cook our little crustaceans, and waited patiently.

Not so our neighboring squad. They were having a hard time controlling their hunger and went a digging. There's nothing more pissed off than thirty half cooked, hot as July asphalt little crabs turned loose on the beach. They came charging out of the pit at a scuttling race of a pace, claws snapping in the cool night air, scurrying toward somebody, anybody, who was responsible for their predicament. Once water was sensed by those hot little numbers they made a bee-line for the surf, steam rolling off their shells, hissing and spitting as one by one they entered the water.

We were laughing our asses off. Grown men chasing after little hot and angry crabs, trying to grab at least a few to cook some more while their half baked dinner hustled back from whence they came, made for comic relief. Most of their crabs made it back into the relative safety of the rock jetty, perhaps to be caught another time by some other hungry SERE student. It was only the first day, and showing some compassion for our neighboring survivors, we shared our catch, after a lengthy wait.

There would be little humor for the rest of survival training.

After the night of the restless crabs and a restless sleep, we arose with the chilly gray dawn of the West Coast morning. A big bus the same color as the sky was already waiting to take us inland to Warner Springs. Those two words struck trepidation into all of us.

Nestled near Cleveland National Forest, Warner Springs was an isolated spot edged against Highway 79, marked as a scenic drive on a road atlas. Once we turned off the road onto the dirt drive it got very quiet on the bus. Remote control cameras on the gate were scanning us from numerous angles, and I made a mental note of that, just in case. Just in case what? Like I was going to storm the gate and liberate the mock POW camp we were destined for? Fleeting fantasies of heroism gave way to hunger and apprehension. Stories of beatings, torture, psychological torment, and most feared, the water board, circled in my head.

We were dropped off at a Quonset hut and greeted by the staff, who filled us in on the syllabus. Our week was shaping up: five days in the bush learning the ropes of survival techniques. The first letter in SERE stood for Survival. Then, on our last "free" day we would embark on a cross country navigation exercise. Map, compass and weary sailors would fan out into the barren countryside. Once at the destination, a little rest for those who managed it briefly precluded the next cycle, the next letter in SERE, Evasion. Capture was assured, and "R," Resistance, was taught the hard way. Carted off to the POW camp, "E," Escape was expected, or at least the attempt encouraged. I would take it one day at a time.

We had lectures in the morning, many focusing on Dieter Dengler, the naval aviator who was shot down over Vietnam early in the war. He was captured, escaped, and lived to tell a remarkable story of survival, will power, and endurance. He was our model to study.

In the lecture room were display cases of survival gear, improvised tools and weapons plus my favorite, a can of dehydrated water. The instructions read "dehydrated water—just add water." If you still had your sense of humor it was pretty funny. There was a large banner that read: "Here there are tigers."

Afternoons were spent foraging for food, gathering firewood and working on getting a diverse gaggle of sailors from specialized fields, all with big egos, to work together. We could eat anything we caught or dug up. The instructors warned us about the tadpoles in the swamp, they just didn't have enough protein to bother with. Road kill could be traded in for a more sanitary cut of meat, if you made it to the road at all. There was a big towable water tank since there was no potable water available. Some small concession to our survival, the water was hot and tasted like the inside of a gas tank.

That first evening we paired up, two to a pup tent. It was March, and at that altitude it got cold at night that time of year, so one of the lessons was the value of body heat. This was an uneasy thing, to pair off with a stranger and get close, real close, just to stay warm. I would have bet all of us slept back to back.

I slept soundly after roaming the hills for something to eat. We were allowed to bring a knife, and I dug for Indian Potatoes, an onion-like bulb that formed about five inches underground. You had to follow the green stem carefully, if you accidentally broke it off you would never find the bulb. It was one of those tasks where you could easily burn more calories digging than gained by eating the fruit of your endeavor.

The biggest problem was that the school had been held on the same acreage for years, and anything edible with legs or wings was long gone once they heard busses arrive. I did cross paths with a spindly little jade colored lizard. As he sat on a warm rock doing those funny lizard push-ups I skewered him with my knife and tossed him into the communal stew pot back at camp. Along with mustard greens it made for a mix that would gag a maggot.

Halfway through the survival phase we were paid a visit by the compound CO. A full commander, he strode into our little bivouac with a determined gait; it was clear he was in command and had something to impress upon us. He also was carrying a cardboard box with a few odd items in it. Tossing the box down in the middle of our camp he bellowed out his disapproval.

"All right you motherfuckers listen up, I'm not going to repeat myself. I'm pissed and am about ready to kick everyone's ass and toss you back to the training command where your sorry butts came from. I have no tolerance for bullshit, you knew the rules, they were broken and now you are going to have to live with it. We *were* going to give everyone a bowl of rice, but forget it. Whomever is the senior officer here, front and center. Here commander, you divide up what's in this box, that's it, nothing else, and I hope it pisses you off because the stunt that got pulled sure pissed me off. And I'll remember this in a few days. Good day gentlemen, and good luck, you'll need it." His neck was red and veins were standing out from his prominent forehead. What a speech; I was impressed. He should have gotten an academy award for that, I felt, very convincing. I figured the whole thing was SOP, just a midweek asschewing to keep us on our toes.

The box held a loaf of bread, a tin of tuna fish, and a can of peaches. Our senior officer divided it up, which didn't amount to more than a nibble per man. While savoring my bite of peach I noticed we were missing someone. We would not know the full story until after the POW camp phases of Resistance and Escape were played out.

After five days of scrounging for nothing to eat and shivering in the night cold, our free days came to an end. The first E in SERE stood for Evasion, and it was time to evade.

The day began by rolling up our pup tents, policing the bivouac area and teaming up for the navigation phase. Compasses and crude maps were issued to each squad and we were set loose upon the dry brown hills.

After a hot hike in the sun we came to a "discussion" as to where we were and what should be done next. My suggestion was to head to the jeep on top of a bluff overlooking the course about a quarter mile away, which turned out to be right. Once there we were encouraged to rest as much as possible, the real fun and games were soon to begin. At the signal we were turned loose and encouraged to make it to the safe compound, where a sandwich and cool drink awaited us. Not as easy as it sounded. Between us and it was a huge wash that hadn't seen water in a millennium, covered by scant scrub brush and crisscrossed by dozens of trails left by thousands of previous "guests." On the right flank was another bluff and on the left was a prison. Being a medium security jail it housed drug dealers, petty thieves and all around losers. They roamed a large fenced-in area which ran for hundreds of yards alongside our evasion course. This afforded them great sport, which consisted of telling our pursuers just where we were: "Hey, over there, there's two of 'em by that bush," or "One just ran by here a minute ago, headed that way."

We would be hunted after what seemed like a split second of time. We scattered like an upturned bag of scared rabbits, some heading in a determined direction, others wandering aimlessly looking for god knows what. I sprinted for a hundred yards and then went low to the ground, as low as I had ever been. I crawled like a centipede, I slithered like a snake, I was one with the dirt. After what seemed like an eternity I felt I wasn't making any headway, so I hugged a small bush, curling around it to hide and rest. At one point my sixth sense told me someone was very close by, and if I looked up that would be the end of it. I suppressed the feeling.

At the time limit if you weren't either captured or home free you had to turn yourself in. An armed deuce and a half truck rumbled along the dusty road, the gunner firing a .50 caliber all around the area. A siren blared signaling the end of the evasion sequence and as I slowly rose up a bunch of dirty, nervous heads popped up in unison, like startled gophers looking out of their holes. A squad of nasty looking "bad guys" in khaki uniforms replete with big red stars on their pith helmets were spraying AK-47 fire and yelling at those not yet captured to get to the truck or be killed. I knew they couldn't really kill us, but the gunfire registered deep in my psyche.

Once at the truck I was pushed, shoved, hit, and a bag was placed over my head with the threat to not look out from under it unless I wanted to be beaten severely. I managed a peek and saw my classmates on benches in the truck bed, each with a bag over his head.

"No talking, Imperialist swine, or you die!" OK, that was the tack, I thought; I'm in some surrogate Communist gulag. Mock executions could be heard nearby.

We were kicked off at a holding area where madness was in charge. My hood was removed as we were herded into groups and beaten. The higher the rank, the more abuse one got, a rare time I was thankful to be just an E-2. A young Lt.j.g. was repeatedly thrown to the ground with swift judo moves; each time he got up they threw him down harder. He was holding up OK, but pain was showing on his face. A line of men led into a shack. A wet, drowning hell was inside. I heard sounds piercing the air I didn't think a human could make. Part of the psychological torment was listening to what others were enduring.

The shack housed one of many waterboards, the most feared torture technique. Amazingly simple in principle and design, it was comprised of a door-sized plank with straps for your wrists and ankles. Once strapped in, your head was lower than your waist. Then two interrogators went to work. One straddled your head, holding a cloth tight over your face, while the other one poured water down your throat. You can't hold your breath forever, and when they clamped down on your nose that forced you to breath through your mouth, inviting more water to be poured in. You thought you were drowning, dying, hallucinations flashed through your mind, you struggled against the straps and they would just laugh.

"Individual!" That was their favorite word. "Individual, tell us what we want to know, or you will stay here for hours and hours. We have plenty of water for you, individual!"

My turn was coming as we were processed through the shack one by one. With several guys ahead of me a reprieve came. We were hooded once again and herded back onto the big truck and hauled to the next destination. The prisoner of war camp. R. Resistance. Time to get it together because the fun and games were going to be ratcheted up in a big way.

Chaos was king. That was part of the plan no doubt; still it was hard to ignore screams, machine gun fire and death threats. We were ordered to strip while still wearing the canvas bags over our heads. One man came by and grabbed my hood, shoving a hose in and spilling water into my mouth. I resisted, I didn't know what it was, even though it was a chance to get a precious drink. A big man—at least his footsteps sounded big—tried to scrape off my new dragon tattoo. "Why do you have this, individual?"

"To honor myself," came my improvised reply. No retort, maybe I caught him off guard. Shoved into another line I was soon at the commandant's office. Yelling was constant as two big goons threw me down on the floor before him. I was staring at a jackbooted official wielding a braided black leather riding crop. He slapped it against a finely polished boot as they had me kneeling, legs crossed at the ankles behind me. I couldn't move.

"Why are you killing our people? Why do you wage war against this peaceful country? Why are you here?" The commandant spit out interrogatives like rounds from a .45 semi-auto. The questions tied themselves into an accusatory Gordian knot.

My peripheral vision was filled with classmates being hurled up against a wall or thrown to the floor. The commandant regained my attention. "You, you who come here and kill my people, bomb my villages, poison the minds of the masses with your capitalistic propaganda, you who rape our women turning them into whores, you are a war criminal. You are war criminal number 113. You have no name. You are known from now on as war criminal 113, that is what you will respond to, that is how you will identify yourself, that is who you are. There is no Geneva Convention here. You have no rights. You think you are a prisoner of war? You are not. You are a criminal. You have committed crimes against my freedom loving people and against my free country. Now, tell me what ship you came from and what your mission was."

"My name is Jeff Manthos, my rank is Airman Appren ..."

"Stop! That is not what I asked. If you insist on this stupid code you and your countrymen allege to go by, you will die here. I already know who you are, Airman Apprentice Manthos from Colorado. I already know you fly on those big white and gray helicopters that come to kill us. Do not play these stupid games with me. You cannot prevail here. No one ever does."

I was getting an earful. A quick glance aside showed Esterlund being carried on a stretcher. Fuck, I wondered if he was hurt, if they hurt him, or if it was part of their plan to take out the natural leaders. So much was happening all at once, I could hardly take it in. I was snapped back to the moment.

"You are being uncooperative, individual. Take him, comrades, and do what you must do. He brings it on himself; it is his fault we must do these things to him."

My head was snapped back by a handful of hair in a tight grip as he spit in my face, a parting gesture of contempt. The two brutes pulled me off the floor and dragged me to the wall. We had been lectured to make them work for it; drop your center of gravity, force them to pick up dead weight, don't make it easy for them.

Bam—up I went against the corrugated steel wall, bambambam as they threw me over and over again. It didn't really hurt; it was more of a shock to the senses. They tired as I let my 165 pounds sag toward the Earth's core. Soon I was shoved outside. As I stood I heard the wall sing a metal song, like a giant saw blade was being flexed with men's bodies.

The warm California sun set among the tall pine trees as early evening coolness crept in from the woods. California? Was that where I was? Without the hood I took a look around. A tall barbed wire fence enclosed the compound, which was dotted with squat buildings. A tower stood menacingly at one end manned by guards sporadically firing a big caliber machine gun. The camp cadre wore pith helmets sporting that large red star. With night approaching the guards grabbed us and led us to rows of dog house sized boxes. Tiger cages.

"This is where you will stay, individual! Slide the door up like this, now, crawl in! The tin can is your honey pot. Go in, go, you will fit if I have to cut off your legs. Do you want the water board, individual? You will fit, yes?"

Yes, I fit. Sitting hunched over, my legs drawn up under my chin and wrapped tight with my arms, I took up the whole box. I couldn't stretch out, sit up, lie down or recline. It was cold, just thin plywood between me and the crisp mountain air, but we were given back our field jackets which afforded some insulation. There was hardly room to shiver. The coffee can that served as a waste collection device sat at my feet. I didn't know if I could have maneuvered inside enough to have used it, but by that time my body had nothing to give.

Occasionally a guard would rap his baton against the hatches and you could hear responses coming from other "war criminals": 110, 99, 132, 145, on it went. We were to sound off, a bed check for the bedless. "War criminal 113." I sounded off. We were encouraged to try to escape and night would have been a good time to try, but I was exhausted. I fell asleep dreaming of burgers and fries and cherry pie and ice cream and hot coffee.

An uneasy night's rest and foggy minded morning was broken by tiger cage hatches being thrown open. The camp was bombarded with propaganda blaring from trumpet shaped speakers mounted high on the fence, a cacophony of noise greeting us.

We were broken down into work groups. My unit was tasked with raking gravel with our fingers while on hands and knees. The guards entertained themselves by walking through our freshly hand-raked rocks, kicking and shuffling their feet. "Start over war criminals, or we will shoot!" As the big gun fired from the tower my finely spitshined flight boots were getting the toe leather ground off in the gravel. My fingers would heal from the abrasions but those boots were beyond help.

Since I was only an E-2 I was insulated against the harshest punishment. The ranking officers got the worst treatment, and the prisoner chain of command was tested. We had been lectured on that back at the Quonset. "They will try to break you any way they can. They will take the leaders, the officers, the ones others look up to, and brutally remove them. They will attempt to render you leaderless and thus unorganized. As individuals you will be less effective and more vulnerable. It is of the utmost importance to maintain the chain, as officers are removed the next ranking officer will take his place. You will step up and fill in any void left by the elimination of another who is your immediate senior. After all the officers are gone, enlisted will take their place by rank until you're down to the last two friggin' seaman recruits, and they better decide who sewed on that little stripe first. For those young men who think rank is all privilege, watch what happens to the officers."

They got the crap beat out of them. In formation for more propaganda and harassment at midday, our ranking officer stood at the front of our group. He had a function—to pass on information, to issue orders, to be a figurehead, to lead. The guards took him and threw him down repeatedly until his face was red and his breathing rapid, a wince shyly gracing his middle-aged face. Once he was thoroughly whipped, they dragged him up to the waterboard placed above bunkers. Interrogators strapped him down and started the water torture. Holding his mouth shut didn't work; they just pinched his nose until he had to open his mouth to breathe. It was his choice, a terrible choice, to hold his breath or try to gasp for air only to feel like he was drowning. He gurgled, coughed, screamed and gasped,

SEA KINGS | 49

all guttural sounds muffled by the wet cloth stretched over his face. His arms and legs jerked at the restraints, and his body tried to buckle from the visceral reaction to suffocation. Somewhere in his rational mind he knew they couldn't drown him, but that part of his cortex wasn't being used at that moment; it was the deeper reptilian-like brain stem that was in charge, and it was telling him he was going to die.

The camp commandant strutted before us, laughing. The guards pouring the water were laughing. The tower machine gunner was laughing. As the commandant turned his right side to me I saw a rosewood handled .38 revolver perched on his hip, tucked into a tooled leather holster. I seriously considered making a try for the gun, a heroic move to grab the revolver and take the commandant hostage, take control of the situation, change the course of events.

I didn't. All the things that could have gone wrong flashed through my mind: it was loaded with real bullets and I accidentally shot him; I failed in my attempt and it was me up there, after they got through with the commander. As those alternate realities faded to black, I instead thought back to my 4-H days when I learned how to tool leather, thought how someone had made that nice holster and put hours of work into the intricate patterns embossed in the hide. I was so engrossed in my daydream I momentarily lost track of the gurgling screams.

The interrogators finally tired and set the commander loose. He weakly stumbled down the steps as they led him away. Then the interrogators set upon the lieutenant commander who had taken the position vacated by his superior. After the perfunctory beating he took his turn on the waterboard. The process repeated itself through a handful of officers until the commandant yawned deeply and dismissed us with a flick of his riding crop.

As I turned to reform with my gravel landscaping crew I was culled from the group by a big paw of a hand grabbing my fieldcoat collar. "Individual, someone wants to talk to you. But first, we cannot allow you to see." The canvas bag was positioned with a whump over my head. I got a strong whiff of an odor like the inside of a moldy old canvas tent. As I peeked down I saw two bare legs with scuffed flight boots attached. I wasn't really sure it was my body anymore.

I was led into a wooden building—at least the porch and floor were wood, that much I could see. Seated, the hood was removed and I was staring eye to eye with a character right out of an ersatz James Bond flick. The tan pith helmet sat squat on his head, brim down across dark glasses. He was sitting on the edge of a desk, his legs hanging over. He held a burning cigarette in his right hand between his index finger and thumb, palm in, thumb pointing at me accusingly. His left hand rested on a button on the desk.

"So, war criminal 113, tell me all about how you got here. I know, I know, you've already spoken to the commandant. I know he can be harsh, I know he can seem impatient, but listen, you and your fellow criminals make him that way. It is not his fault, it is not his wish. All we need to do is have you answer some questions and you can be on your way. Good prisoners will be rewarded, bad prisoners will be punished. You know how we punish bad prisoners, don't you? You saw what we had to do to your leader earlier today. He wouldn't talk to us. We already knew what squadron he was from, where his hometown is, what his wife's name is, but he wouldn't cooperate so we were forced to teach him a lesson. He of course has talked to us since then. He has abandoned you. He is enjoying a nice hot shower right now, and then we will give him warm clothes and a hot meal. He hasn't told us anything we don't already know; he is just being a good prisoner. Now, will you be a good prisoner?"

Goddammit, a hot shower would have felt so good. But I didn't believe him, I didn't believe anyone from our group had given in and was getting a hot shower much less food. But he had planted that idea and it was distracting.

"My name is Manthos, my rank is Airman Apprentice, my serial number is ..."

"We don't care about that; we already know that you are just a number to your own government. See how little they care about you? Now, just tell me how many men were in your group."

I hesitated. What the hell, just make up a number. "50."

"Very good, Now, what is your job?"

"Dishes. I wash dishes." Clever of me, I thought.

"How many hours a day do you wash dishes, individual?"

"10."

"Do you enjoy your work?"

"Yes."

"When do you want to go home?"

"When I can."

"Well individual, you did very good. Now, let me show you what we will have you say to the oppressed freedom loving people of the world."

He sauntered behind the desk and set a tape recorder on top. Rewinding the tape back onto the feed reel, he flipped the big lever and the tape came to life. I heard his voice and I heard mine, but something was terribly wrong.

"How many of our children did you kill, war criminal 113?"

"50."

"How many villages did you destroy?"

"10."

"Do you enjoy killing innocent people?"

"Yes."

"When do you attack our peaceful country?"

"When I can."

Fuck. My head was reeling. They had ten minutes of my answers all turned around so anything I had said was sounding like I was a war criminal. I had no idea. They sure did. I really wanted to punch the bastard, but there were rules, and one was we could not attack camp personnel. It was such a strange mix of unrealities and rules.

"Now, individual, go back to your tiger cage and think about what you have done to advance our cause." He snickered and smugly turned his back on me as I was led away.

By that time it had turned cold and dark. Stuffed back into my cage, I sat hunched up and shook; it wasn't so much the cold, it was my monumental fuckup. They gave me a lot of time to think it over.

Sometime that night they came for me again. Trying to outwit them wasn't going to work, that I had been shown. Resolving to give them nothing was the only answer. I had made that decision hours before.

Half asleep when they pulled me from my tiger cage, I was led through a crackling-hot campfire. Embers burned my bare legs like hot needles. More laughter. Those guys were sick fucks.

I was seated on a hard bench inside a hut facing someone I had not seen before. Behind him was a mirror, one way no doubt. I noticed my reflection and how tan I had become, my dirty face filling in with brown stubble. Off to my right was that bastard from the interrogation session. He was smoking again, a depraved grin spanning his face. I hoped he had smoker's cough. He stared at me from under his pith helmet, cigarette smoke curling up around a bare light bulb suspended from the ceiling. Other faces remained half-hidden in the dark recesses of the room.

The man before me broke the silence. "OK, Manthos, listen up. I'm speaking to you in this moment as an instructor, not an inter-rogator. This is a 'time-out' as it were. Look, you know it's a game, I know it's a game, but you talked too much at your last session. I know thinking that off-handed and maybe stupid responses might be harmless but you found out they're not. Propaganda is a tool that will be used against you and your country, using your own words. You have to learn that, and learn it the hard way, apparently. They will be coming for you again; that will be your second and last chance to get it right. I suggest you get some rest if you can."

Juggling multiple realities was never easy, and here was a real-ity embedded in a separate reality out of context from its ground-ing in what I left behind a week ago as the only truth I knew. Or maybe I was just exhausted and hungry enough to let my mind bounce around. I had to play it as if it were real, even if there were rules preventing me from doing just that. It was all inward, the dis-cipline and motivation; all you could do was temper yourself to cope without striking out against your captors who, in a few days, would transform themselves back into your advisors in survival techniques from a pedagogical vantage point. It was all, of course, for my own benefit should the unthinkable happen.

As soon as I was out the door, the game resumed. Led back through the campfire once again, I was crammed into the cold dark cavity of my tiger cage. With no watch or clock anywhere for the last week I had lost track of time. They banked on that. It was still dark and a lot colder when they came for me yet again. My favorite detractor was waiting in the shed. And smoking. We both knew it was time to cross a vital point, and it was up to me to define when and where that was going to be.

"Individual, you were so cooperative last time, you helped our cause greatly. Now, all I have are a few simple questions and we can be finished. Where is your hometown?"

"My country does not allow me to answer that question." That's what we were supposed to say. Made sense, our country could bear the burden more than any individual.

"Insolent fascist! I know you are from Colorado, you attended Colorado State University. I know all about you. You serve the petty bourgeoisie in their quest for world domination by invading other countries to further the moneyed interests of your elite class. And yet look at you, what do you have? You are a lowly enlisted man who only has what your government wants you to have. So why do you behave like this? Just tell me a few things and you can go back and sleep. Now, once again, where is your hometown?"

"My country does not allow me to answer that question." I braced for the slap across the face. It came. Hard.

"I have no time for this, individual. You are not cooperating with us. You leave me no choice, I must be forced to punish you until you learn that you can help yourself by helping me." He grabbed me by my coat and pulled me to my feet. I sagged as best I could but he was strong, rested, fed and eager to play with my mind. Two more reprobates materialized and I was hooded and unceremoniously led back out into the cold night.

It couldn't have been more than twenty paces before we stopped. I was unhooded and stripped of my coat. Standing in just my dirty skivvies and scuffed flight boots I was feeling extremely vulnerable.

"Individual, you need punishing. Lie down on the board and buckle yourself in."

The waterboard. My time had come. And they made me strap myself in. The buckles resembled the harness gear in the helicopter; the freezing cold aluminum latches almost burned as I secured the web strapping around my ankles. I couldn't do my left arm, so I relented to them finishing the task. As they buckled my remaining free limb I stared up at the brilliantly clear night sky littered with millions of stars. No wonder the Palomar observatory was placed not far from there; the sable canopy above revealed wonders of the heavens with a welcoming gesture. It was pristine and secure from the madness that raged on our planet. My mind walked among the stars.

I almost didn't hear my captors. "Individual, one last time, where is your hometown?"

My words spoke themselves as I relented to the events unfolding under the dazzling night sky. "My country ..." and that's as far as I got. Freezing water shot out of a hose and they soaked me like I was a newly planted tree. It took my breath away and my skin contracted as pores snapped shut, trying to hold on to any heat my body retained. I shook and shuttered in the frigid night, convulsions rattling my bones. But I did not talk. My arms and legs strained at the nylon webbing holding me in place. I couldn't move but half an inch, but my body still tried to free itself from the board. My mouth was filled with cold water as I gasped for air, ice water ran into my nose and chilled my sinuses to the bone. I could have bent rebar with my teeth they were chattering so badly. As my eyes glassed over, the stars faded into a blur. After a while I couldn't tell if I was being soaked or not as hypothermia lurked in the darkness. I could feel life-sustaining heat leaving my frame, abandoning me to the hard wooden board and two sadistic keepers who laughed throughout my ordeal.

I didn't know when it stopped; time stretched into a long thin thread of ice. I saw the guards' breath in the night but not my own; it felt like nothing was escaping from my shallow gasps for air. They let me shiver and rattle against the restraints until they got bored and accepted that I wasn't going to give them any information, not even something they already knew.

It was still dark when they finally let me off the board. The field jacket was returned and although it was cold and stiff from the night it felt wonderful. Hooded and led back to my cage, I would have given anything to be led through a campfire. It didn't happen. When I finally fell asleep in my small box I dreamed of the big walk-in freezer we had at the Safeway store where I once worked.

Morning broke to the sounds of more propaganda blaring from the speakers. As my door raised I was greeted by a fellow prisoner. He was collecting honey bucket contents from all the cages. I had nothing to give but felt sorry for the guy, not a job I'd want; I'd rather rake gravel with my fingers.

We were formed up in ranks once again and watched as the enemy flag was raised on the tall pole. I had time to reflect on the night before. With no food for days I had no way to replace the calories, units of heat, I had lost except from my own body. I was pretty lanky but had some fat somewhere to draw on. But I didn't talk, I had passed the test.

The day was a repeat of the one before. Had it only been a full day? Time was a blur. We were ordered to bow before the enemy flag. We didn't. Our new CO, a man who had filled the gap in the chain of command, bowed for us, after a severe beating. More water-board demonstrations punctuated by air raid sirens and mad dashes to the bunkers by POWs filled in the morning.

I tried to check out the camp perimeter as best I could. There was a small building just outside the wire; that must be the commandant's place. Guards were everywhere.

We were once again broken down into small squads to perform menial and degrading tasks. More finger raking of gravel. We created Zen garden-like patterns in the rocks, again to be destroyed by the guards. Maybe there was a deeper message. My poor flight boots were a wreck, at least the steel toe-caps protected my feet. Air raids again sounded and we were crammed into the bunkers until the all-clear was given.

By day's end I was actually looking forward to crawling back into my tiger cage; at least I wasn't being harassed in there. I plotted my escape in deep REM sleep.

By the next morning things were routine. Form into ranks, beat the CO of the hour, torture select prisoners with the waterboard as we watched and listened in disgust. Then the raising of the enemy flag. But this time was different. Two prisoners were led outside the wire carrying something cradled in their arms. They stood at the base of the flag pole and as the national anthem, our national anthem, was played over the PA system, the American flag was raised. Simultaneously and without hesitation we all stood tall and proud and as a man saluted the flag. Our flag. It was over.

Spontaneous whoops and hollers went up into the crisp mountain air and we felt once again that we were just in Southern California. It had taken less than a fortnight to graphically illustrate what we might encounter and how we might respond, and what we might find within ourselves. It was just a hint, but one worth listening to.

We were allowed to leave the camp through the open barbed wire gates. We took a brief stroll down a dirt road and found ourselves back at the Quonset where we started, not a ten minute walk from our little hell. Greeted by the staff, we were treated to the coldest, freshest milk I had ever tasted, all we could drink. It never tasted as good since. Somehow the "dehydrated water-just add water" display was even funnier.

The camp commander filled us in on the food episode from the week before. "Gentlemen, first of all, I congratulate you for completing one of the toughest schools the Navy has to offer. Not everyone makes it through, as you all know. Last week we pulled a student from the course. You probably remember him, he was an officer from a special warfare unit. He didn't play by the rules and he didn't give a rat's ass about any of you, breaking a cardinal rule of survival and teamwork. He dishonored both his rank and his profession. He thought he was smarter than us. He wasn't. Here's what he did, just so you know. He had his wife drive up and leave food for him on the camp perimeter. He snuck out, or rather he thought he snuck out, and ate while you went hungry. He didn't share, he didn't play fair, he was stupid and he paid a price. The food I brought down was what was left after we figured out what he was up to and caught him in the act. I didn't know at the time who else was in on it with him, but as you are well aware by now we have ways of finding out whatever we want to know. He has been reassigned, and I doubt any of you will run into him anytime soon.

"Here's a little tidbit you'll find interesting. By now you know how awful the waterboard can be. We didn't want to tell you at the time, but the man holding the rag over your face was a corpsman and the man pouring the water was a full blown M.D. So, you were in good hands. Even though they meant to take you as far as you could go, they were alert to medical problems that occasionally surface. And, they're really nice guys. Now, I have the honor of presenting each of you with your SERE certificate."

After we all downed a few more glasses of milk he wrapped things up. "Gentlemen, please board the bus which will take you back to FASOTRAGRUPAC at North Island." The Navy jargon sounded like music to my ears. Talk of food and families and torture peppered the air as we rode down the mountain.

I never did find out who was behind the one way mirror.

Chief Lawson took one look at my flight boots when I returned to the training squadron and went ballistic. "Manthos, what in the hell have you been doing? Those boots are not satisfactory, no way, no how. Explain to me just what the fuck you've been doing to them, and it better be good or you'll pull extra watches and field day the entire area."

"SERE, Chief."

"Oh. OK. Well, do the best you can polishing them, then."

That's all it took, that little acronym. Being on the other side of SERE carried with it a great deal of pride and some weight—it proved you could hack it. But I was due for another challenge, one that had dogged me from the beginning of my aircrew training back in Memphis. I still couldn't swim.

I HAD TWO WEEKS to recover from SERE and get ready for SAR Rescue Aircrew Swim School, run by HS(L)31, the LAMPS—Light Airborne Multi-Purpose System—training squadron. Running, swimming lessons and eating to bulk back up prepared me for the school, as well as NATOPS study and training flights needing to be taken care of to continue my flight syllabus. I had lost some weight during SERE but quickly gained it back. I was able to run around the base on lunch break, and it was starting to feel good. I was never a natural runner and my skewed left leg, broken in a skiing accident ten years before and healing out of alignment, didn't help. The swim lessons did help, even if they were at the instructor's apartment pool.

I had my second chance, and I wasn't going to fail again. Chief Lawson and Doc Bliven had faith that I would make it, if for no other reason than I simply would not quit. They knew that much about me. SAR was not about being graceful; it was about being in shape and developing a second nature in the water. Conditioning was an integral part of the SAR day starting at dawn. NAS Imperial Beach didn't have a decent swimming pool, so after a fast breakfast at IB's chow hall we were bussed over to the 32nd Street Naval Base pool. The base sat at the foot of National City, Iwo Jima Eddy's town.

We did sprints and calisthenics until we were well warmed up in the cold bay air before we hit the pool. We swam in our bootcamp issue trunks, apparently designed by a committee, because they were neither stylish nor functional. Baggy and clinging to wet thighs like waterlogged canvass, they impeded efficient leg movement in the water. But we wore them, and huge black rubber fins and a big oval shaped mask and a rescue harness strapped around our chest. That harness was our way out of the ocean; it was strong green nylon webbing with a hook folded into a pouch closed by Velcro. We could pull the hook free with one hand and attach ourselves to a rescue hoist and be lifted from the water in a single swift motion.

The first order of the day after a dry-land workout was laps, and more laps. This would be followed by relays with teams on either side of the pool. One lap might be with a towel in each hand, fins held in teeth and flight boots on. The next lap may be a wet towel in your teeth and a boot in each hand; the next logical step would be boots on your feet and a heavy fin in each hand. It was a mix-and-match relay designed to exhaust you within seconds. It worked. This could go on until the instructors were satisfied you were tired deep to your soaked core. I once dared look aside at the big clock that ticked seconds off, and I swore the hand did not move. I was thrashing the water with the bulky fins held tightly in my hands, dragging them through the water like broken oars. I swallowed water like a shower drain as the towel in my teeth held my jaw open enough to siphon off water as I gasped for air. But I got to the other side as the next swimmer took the return leg.

A break for some rescue gear instruction would allow us to regain some strength. We would need that and a great deal of self-control for the next phase. Doc Parsons, our first aid instructor, would announce it. It all started so peacefully; we would simply swim around in the pool in our rescue gear. And wait. And wait some more. It was about being caught unprepared, surprised, attacked. The instructors would suddenly leap into the water, jump on your back, scream, yell, pull off your mask and fins, push you down, force you down into the deep water, stand on you if they could, make you think you'd never get another breath of air. Another limit being forced to its breaking point. Gathering your gear off the pool bottom you would don it again in the water and swim some more, and wait for the next attack. Inevitably it would come.

"Welcome to harassment swims, gents," boomed Doc. Over time they backed off that little exercise once they culled the sailors from our pod of would-be-rescuers who couldn't handle the stress of feeling like they were drowning. One final attack would follow, a solo performance with the whole class looking on. We would, one by one, tread water in the deep end as an instructor would swim up behind and with a war-whoop jump on us and come as close to drowning us as he could. We learned how to work away from a frantic, hysterical man and get him under control, bringing him to safety. It was underwater wrestling—right up my alley.

A catwalk was suspended above the deep end, and we would practice our open ocean jumps from there. That's how we would get from the Sea King into the sea, by jumping. Ideally we would be jumped from the helicopter at ten knots and ten feet of altitude, a very manageable speed and height. But since the swimmer was not plugged into the ICS and judging altitude is very difficult over water, he must take the jump command from his senior crewman. Three taps on the head was the signal to jump, and not under any other circumstances.

We were sitting on the catwalk in our gear, listening to one of the instructors talk about the importance of all that. I looked down and saw Parsons paddling about, his one piece face mask framing his round, middle-aged face. We locked eyes. He looked so trustworthy. He gestured to me to jump. "Come on down" his hand signal said, urging me to join him in the pool. He must have had a good reason—he was the instructor after all—so I jumped. My solo entry into the water made a resounding echo in the indoor poolhouse, a splash worthy of notice. I was rather proud of my entry, my head was up, my eyes on the horizon like they taught so I wouldn't tumble head first into rock-hard water. It was textbook. Except for one thing. I didn't get three taps on the head. I got a come-hither gesture from an alleged survivor who did not have my best interest at heart, who had no idea what my "helicopter's" altitude or airspeed was. I was made an example of, and was introduced to flutterkicks. Poised on my butt on the edge of the pool, my legs over the water and supporting very heavy fins not meant to thrash air, I scissorkicked while counting repetitions. Not so bad, a little hard on the abs but I was also wearing my swim mask, filled with water. That made it all a bit awkward, trying to count out loud while water ran in my nose and down the back of my throat, chlorine stinging the whole way. Doc made his point to me and everyone else, and that took care of any more ill-timed jumps from eager to please swimmers, try that they did to catch another of us. It also showed me that I was gaining confidence in the water; maybe I was going to make it through this time.

The catwalk was also used for parachute work. Since there was a high degree of chance we would be rescuing pilots, parachutes were problematic. They float like gigantic jellyfish on the water's surface, and yards of shroudline will entangle anything nearby. Very dangerous. We carried shroud-cutters, a curved knife blade designed to slice on the pull stroke and not puncture flotation devices or pilots.

They had us jump right into the floating parachute, letting it enclose us like a cocoon of ripstop nylon. It encapsulated us underwater. We were trapped. Keeping a cool head was vital as we would slowly work our way out of the 'chute and shroudlines, pull the pilot free and disentangle him from his rig. Breathing almost became incidental as our confidence grew.

After the tiring mornings we had a quick lunch break with time to shower and get into some dry dungarees, ready for afternoon lectures on first aid. The first rule of first aid: stop serious bleeding. We learned how to place a tourniquet on a neck wound without strangling the victim. I never thought I could do CPR on a survivor while hooked to a rescue hoist, but I learned. We learned the rule of nines for burns, determining the percentage of skin damage. We learned about shock and how to detect it and prevent it from killing. And we did push-ups if we became drowsy in the hot, stuffy classroom.

As the weeks passed we whittled down the phases of conditioning and water confidence. Drown-proofing, a technique designed to allow a swimmer to ride out almost any sea state, was practiced near the end of the swim day. If done correctly it was a chance to relax. And that was good since the final activity was the whistle drill. It was the way out of the water. It was brutal. It turned us against each other in a mad scramble to get out. A whistle was thrown into the deep end and the first one to find it, rise to the surface and blow it three times could get out. It looked like a Hammerhead shark feeding frenzy. Altruism sank faster than the fucking whistle. The lucky bastard who found it quickly became the target of a dozen robbers, everyone else trying to steal it away and get out three blasts. One was easy, two lucky, three blows on the whistle almost impossible. Once we conspired to not play the game; it was getting nasty and genuine fights were brewing. We didn't go after the whistle. They were not amused. We had an extra harassment swim.

Towards the end of the course Doc made an announcement. "Tonight you meet Harvey the Mudman. He lives deep on the bottom of San Diego harbor. You will go a knockin' on his door." It was time for our night ocean swim.

Boated out to the center of the bay at dusk, we jumped into the cool water and were strung out in a line. Our custom wetsuits helped insulate us from the cold, and a classmate said just piss in your suit if you get too cold, that will warm you up. I wasn't sure I could do that.

We popped flares and smokes, all designed for us to be found in the darkness of the open ocean. After survival training we were finally ordered to go meet Harvey. The Mudman. On the bottom of the bay.

"Gents, dive down to the bottom and bring up a handful of mud. You can throw it at me if you want, that might be incentive enough, but bring me mud, and do it now!" Doc floated contentedly as we went to meet Harvey.

The water was dark. Pitch black. The ocean was filled with slimy, spiny, hungry, toothed and gilled demons, all circling our psyches, ever closing in around our tender land-dwelling flesh. The antitheses of fish out of water, we were landlubbers out of our natural element, and nothing made that more clear than the inky black water enveloping us. We had to penetrate that dark world as blind men, entering that domain as sightless creatures who would soon find that up and down were not absolutes. Our wetsuits added a lot of buoyancy, and swimming down was hard work. Trying not to think of some clammy scaled denizen of the primordial ooze awaiting our bare hand was even more work. We all knew they were down there, in the complete darkness, that's what our collective unconscious told us. We had evolved as a species from that very ooze, and we really didn't want to return to our ancient origins, not even for a brief moment. But we did.

I swam to where I thought the bottom was; there was no way to tell up from down in the darkness. If you stopped to float up and get your bearings you lost ground, or water, in the search for Harvey. I kicked my big fins hard with my arm extended; I didn't want to get any closer to the mysteries on the bottom than I had to. I had no idea how far down the sediment was, but my hand finally struck muck. Slimy gooey muck. But just muck, as far as I could tell. Not waiting for a sleeping beast to awake from the abyss and tear my arm from its socket, I reversed direction and scissorkicked my way back to the surface. Heads popped up all around Doc as he was treading water in the center of the circle. My mud missed him but he saw it, that was good enough. A few unlucky souls either didn't get enough and lost it or never made it all the way and had to keep at it until proof positive was shown.

It was all about conquering fear: fear of the unknown, of the abhorrent, of the repulsive, fear of what lay below every ship and sailor on the high seas, and fear of what lay below the surface of our minds.

I wasn't sure who was the most terrorized that night, us or the poor sea life in the bay. We all made it back aboard the little launch with limbs and psyches in tact.

Rescue swims graduation work consisted of four phases: a six mile run, night parachute rescue work, a 2,000 meter timed swim in the ocean and a first aid test. I passed them all. Another certificate made its way into my service jacket.

It had been a long road from the day I failed the 1st class swim test and lied my way out of it. The master chief at Memphis was right; they did teach me everything I needed to know. And Chief Lawson was right, too, I wasn't a quitter. All he said to me when I got back to the training squadron was, "Now, get yer ass over to sonar school, you're still a long way from gettin' those wings."

———◆———

MUCH HAD HAPPENED OVER the previous month. SERE and swim school were over. And I had bought a brand new Honda 750 cc road bike. It was chestnut brown, a warm color to go with the warm California sun. I traded in the Triumph and rode off on the big four cylinder wonder. It was a smooth running machine, I could stand a nickel edgewise on the engine block and start it without the coin falling over. If I had tried that with the Triumph it would have made change.

I got my ass over to sonar school like Chief Lawson suggested. It was a nice break from the physical exhaustion of SAR swims and mental stress of SERE. The instructor was AW1 Hatfield, a pleasant man who may have very well descended from the Hatfields of the famous feud with the McCoys. I couldn't imagine anyone not getting along with Hatfield. He handled people well and was able to get us to comprehend the complexities of dipping sonar, something that seemed counterintuitive at first. The SH-3 carried a sonar system that would deploy a transducer—or dome—into the ocean from a hover. Any other mode of flight with up to 500 feet of cable attached to a big transducer in the water would prove disastrous.

"Class, do not confuse the sonar dome with an anchor, but it will function as one if you don't keep the helo centered over the cable. There are sufficient gadgets available to you to accomplish this. Anchors and flight are inherently contradictory; do not try both at the same time. The Sea King has onboard computers to keep it in a hover, even at night, with just a little help from the crew. Forty feet spans the distance between your helicopter hover and the deep blue sea. Try not to get any closer."

He filled us in on the sonar equipment, to the untrained eye looking like a black paneled collection of odd shaped knobs, meters, whirligig handles and a yellow tinted seven inch scope. It was just like in the old movies; the sonar would let out a ping and the sound wave would writhe its way across the scope, out towards perhaps nothing, for thousands of yards. Hunting subs was a cat-and-mouse game, and they could hear us looking for them at a greater range than we could get a fix on them, so surprise was paramount.

We could also listen passively for any sound, whether it be a Blue Whale or Soviet Whiskey Class sub. Such an odd setting, a four man crew sitting in a hover, a cable seemingly holding everything up in a delicate balancing act, while two men probed deep waters with sound. Subs were all about sound; it was their eyes and ears, they lived and died by it, but a helicopter with sonar was just odd. Still, it worked, and the Sea King could carry multiple torpedoes that would search and search until they found their mark.

Hatfield said his goodbyes as he handed out the certificates after three weeks. "Ya'll take care now, hear? And the Navy makes the world a small place, maybe we'll run into each other someday, happens all the time. Until then, here's your certificate, add it to your growing collection. It's proof positive you can tell the difference between a submarine and a whale fart."

Mastering helicopter sonar enough to pass the school, I was sent by Hatfield back to HS-10 and Doc Bliven. I still had lots of flying to do.

<hr />

MASSAGE PARLORS. NO PORT city would be complete without them and San Diego was the quintessential port city: Navy, commercial fishermen, other country's navies, shipping, if it floated it came to San Diego. If it was manned by young men, much of its crew sought female company. Sex to be exact. Euphemisms abounded for the arrangements: escort services, massage parlors, it was all in the name. They dotted the area like fast food joints for a different hunger, usually scattered along Broadway with used car dealerships and pawn shops. Iwo Jima Eddie's National City had its share. I made the rounds. The chances of finding willing female company was next to nonexistent. Had I a young daughter I would have warned her away from the likes of me.

"WestPac widows," wives of sailors on deployment, were available if you knew where and how to look. I had been so busy with all my training I hardly had time to look for someone to date much less randomly meet a woman my age. My haircut—trimmed short and inspection ready—set me off as a sailor and that alone would scare women away. So I drank weak beer at the EM club, climbed on my 750 Honda and roared off to some establishment catering to my needs. It was never fulfilling, sometimes disappointing, often bleak, but I was a healthy twenty-year-old under the control of Darwinian forces propelling me towards an unsatisfying rendezvous with a hired hand.

The world seemed a tense place that summer. The Watergate scandal had been increasingly in the news, and it looked like Nixon was involved. Food prices were rising fast and meat portions were rationed at the chow hall—no more "all you can eat" of the main course.

I managed a glance at the news on my rented TV. It mentioned that the Senate Armed Services Committee started hearings on the secret bombing of Cambodia. It was a secret to me, but not likely the Cambodians.

The Middle East seemed poised for a conflagration. OPEC was playing stingy with its product and Israel was preparing for war with its neighbors, who seemed eager to fight. Gas was around 40¢ a gallon and going up with no end in sight.

The base was periodically put on alert, which meant more ID checks at the front gate. I couldn't fathom who would want to sneak on to our little base, but the tension was tangible. And behind every world conflict there seemed to be the Soviet Union and us. My job was going to be a part of that confrontation.

My grades had not been great in A school or sonar school, but getting in a Sea King helicopter brought a whole new world to me and I donned that green Nomex flightsuit like a second skin. I was in my element.

Sitting in a sonar hover at night in hot weather was a sweat-drenched, claustrophobic experience. In cold weather aircrew had to wear their SAR wetsuits in case of "water entry" to protect them from hypothermia. Wearing a wetsuit under flight gear in a stuffy helicopter cabin was stifling. Whatever the weather, hot or cold, we seemed to swelter.

I much more enjoyed the rescue scenarios, the cargo and personnel transfers, the medevacs. The Sea King was big enough for me to walk around in almost standing upright; I just had to bend my helmeted head a little. I was also thrilled to be able to, on occasion, strap on the gunner's belt and plug into an ICS extension cord and stand behind the pilots' seats. This not only put an extra pair of eyes up there but allowed me a panoramic view through multi-paned Plexiglas. The aircrew seats, abreast behind the sonar detection gear, had but a small starboard side window to see through, or egress through, if necessary. It never looked big enough to me, and at times seemed to shrink. I hoped I never had to find out if I could get out of a sinking helo through that tiny opening.

I was accelerated through the flight syllabus which brought me ever closer to graduation and the coveted gold wings. Dad and I had talked about him coming out to pin them on. It was a sort of atonement for the difficulties I had caused growing up. There might have been greater difficulties had I been caught doing any number of things as a young teenager but I hadn't. I felt giving him the opportunity might make me stand a little taller in his eyes. I wasn't sure he could make it. Back and forth between Colorado and his home state of Texas, Dad searched for a place he felt comfortable, at ease, at home, which was never the family house. I didn't know where he would be come graduation in September, but I made the invitation and thought he would enjoy the ceremony. I wasn't an officer or pilot, and in many ways was glad there wasn't that more direct comparison between us, but I was sure he would have liked me to have followed in his footsteps. Still, I was getting wings and flying; that would suffice for him to tell his war buddies about down at the bar.

<hr />

INTELLIGENCE WAS AN IMPORTANT part of antisubmarine warfare—we had to know our adversaries. This required getting a secret clearance and I had visions of FBI agents questioning my high school teachers and counselors, old friends and the occasional nosy neighbor. I never knew what was done in my background search but nothing terribly compromising was found since I was granted secret clearance.

Secrecy was interwoven into our training from A school on, and we were cautioned to not talk to strangers, especially women in bars, about classified aspects of our work. I longed to know what a sultry female Soviet spy would look like; what would she say, or do, to get secret information out of me? Would I break under that kind of seductive interrogation? Perhaps I had seen too many James Bond movies.

Our knowledge of the Soviet Navy was extensive. I knew every detail about every Soviet submarine down to the gear-reduction ratios of their propulsion systems. I knew what weapons they carried, what their defensive tactics might be, what port they sailed from. It was ironic that I knew less about our own sub fleet than I did the Soviets', just enough to tell the difference. It was all based on a "need to know," regardless of one's clearance. I knew the armament of their surface ships and how to identify each class by distinguishing marks. I also knew they deployed small boats that poorly passed as fishing vessels, called AGIs, to trail carriers and pass on vital information; I didn't know to whom but certainly it would end up in Moscow and perhaps Hanoi as well. These AGIs would prove to be a constant bother, like an annoying, yapping mutt that nipped at your heels as you walked your neighborhood. There would be protocol; we couldn't harass them much less sink them, but we monitored them as closely as they us.

Part of the AW's job was photo reconnaissance, every helo had a 35 mm single lens reflex camera on board as standard equipment. Our job would be to film ships of all kinds, and Soviet vessels got special treatment.

The Cold War was a tense standoff using military power of untold abilities, and naval ASW was a centerpiece of that impasse. Capable of carrying a nuclear device, the Sea King could be commissioned with what would amount to a suicide mission if it were tasked with deploying one. Mutually Assured Destruction was taking on a whole new reality.

I would struggle with my new-found responsibilities when it came to nuclear weapons; I honestly didn't know if I could partake in dropping one, and I would have to make that decision long before it would ever become a reality. The master chief back in Memphis had asked me if I could help drop a torpedo on several hundred submariners and I bullshitted even myself and said "sure." Anything for a chance at an A school. But when it came to megatons of nuclear energy I didn't know how I would answer.

Dad wrote and said he wanted to pin on my wings, and that of course he had an old uniform tucked away. His Air Force blues still fit, his shoes spitshined like he taught me when I was a five-year-old. He even had his Air Corps flight jacket from his P-51 Mustang days in WWII, emblazoned on the back with his personal motto "Mad Pappy." He had altered his birth certificate to show him young enough to be eligible for flight school, but he was still older than most of his fellow Mustang pilots. I was a little older than many aircrew candidates but not the oldest. The fewer parallels between Dad and me the better; I really wanted to avoid comparisons.

I had arranged to borrow Doc Bliven's car to help get Dad around, since all I had was my Honda 750 and its ever-increasing odometer reading. I couldn't see Dad riding around on the back of my motorcycle, especially wearing his dress uniform.

All I had left to do by September was pass a final checkride. Eleven months of at times rigorous training had gone into a journey not sought but offered, and taken. I hadn't given myself credit for being able to do something like attain aircrew wings back in boot-camp, when we made choices about our futures. I quit football in high school the year the team won the state championship. I wasn't going to quit, ever again. Attrition had taken its toll; many had quit or were dropped from the program, for whatever reasons. But god-dammit, I made it.

One of the aircrew instructors was a young 3rd Class on his first enlistment. Graduates could go to one of five squadrons—four were carrier deployed. The remaining was the training squadron, HS-10, which was always based at NAS IB. I envied that guy; he was land-locked, he had an apartment "on the beach," meaning off base and off ship, he knew women, he had a regular schedule and best of all, he never went to sea. I shared my envy with Chief Lawson.

"Manthos, trust me, he may look like he has it made, but he's never gone anywhere, never seen the South China Sea, never walked the narrow back alleys of Hong Kong, never seen sea snakes. He ain't been anywhere but here, ain't had any great adventures, don't have any sea stories to tell, to nobody. Do you see any cruise patches on his flight jacket? Those G-1s are roadmaps to a life at sea, and his is as naked as an egg shell. I swear to God, when you get back from your first WestPac he'll envy you."

Graduation was set for September 20. As Chief Lawson would say, it was all over but the screamin'. My time in grade for E-2 had been met at one year from my enlistment, and I was unceremoniously promoted to E-3, Airman, on September 15. No more "Recruit" or "Apprentice" attached to my meager title. I could actually pull rank, if not very often.

I was destined for one of four squadrons, even numbered ones being assigned to the West Coast. It was either going to be HS-2, 4, 6 or 8. We didn't have a choice and I wouldn't have known which one to pick anyway. The squadrons would rotate deployments and the constant rumors about which one was going to Vietnam next was standard training squadron gossip. The war had all but ceased for American ground forces, but the 7th Fleet still maintained a healthy presence in the Tonkin Gulf and the fighting between Vietnam's north and south wasn't over. No winner had been decided, no political outcome voted for, or stolen, or taken by force. And tensions had spread. The two Vietnams, Laos, Cambodia, the whole region seemed to be tearing itself apart. Whether it was the Communist expansionist domino theory, or wars of liberation, or something all together more complex and misunderstood by Western minds, those small countries were coming undone. And yet, even as China supplied Vietnamese Communist forces with materiel, they had been enemies for a thousand years. A prominent Cambodian Communist leader would say that once China was done with him they would spit him out like a cherry pit. The Soviets also supplied North Vietnam and they and China had fought each other in border disputes. And sooner or later I would be heading that way, to South East Asia and the South China Sea. I wondered what patches might find their way onto my flight jacket.

Dad made it out to IB a little early as was his way. I got him settled into the Travelodge Motel on Palm Avenue and made arrangements to pick him up in Doc's borrowed car for the ceremony.

The twentieth was a busy day. It started off with my class being called into a room by a Lt.j.g. We had no idea what was going to happen but as far as I knew none of us had messed up anything beyond repair or repentance. I had not seen the j.g. before; he wore aviator's wings so he was a helo jock, but he held a stack of papers making me think admin duty struck while he wasn't looking. I would find out all on my own how many collateral duties could be thrown a crewmember's way, but it was his turn. Pater, Turner, Diaz and I looked at each other and slumped in our seats, anticipating something smelly rolling downhill.

"Greetings men, I am Lt.j.g. Storvich and I have the pleasure to inform you of some unusual news."

Unusual? The heads needed another field day before we could graduate? What pleasure could he possibly get out of telling us anything?

"The aircrew chief and skipper of HS-10 have decided to do something out of the ordinary for your class. They've been watching all along, the four of you, and arranged for the unprecedented award of 4.0 quarterly marks in three categories for this report period. This does not happen, not for new E-3s, not until now. Seems you all made a good impression. Now, if you look at your performance evaluation pages—here you go, each of you gets his to look at—you'll see that at opposite ends of the categories there is an asterisk, denoting further explanation as to why a sailor is graded at that extreme. Read the comments if you like, there is a language all its own for quarterly marks but these speak for themselves. You all have done well so far. The bad news is now that this has happened your respective squadrons will be expecting a lot from you, and you likely won't get 4.0s again for some time; it just isn't usually done for non-rated sailors. Now, sign at the bottom, right there, and you're free to go. Enjoy the day, I hear there are four sets of wings waiting for you."

As he left we all exchanged a look of surprise. We sat a lot taller in our seats for the quiet moment we took to let it soak in. We were cut loose to get ready and I hopped in Doc's car to go get Dad. Back at the base I gave him a tour of a Sea King, and I could see his eyes wistfully scan the instrument panel. I knew how much he missed flying; he might have even been willing to fly a helicopter if it meant getting back in the air. But his aviation days were over, heart problems grounded him a dozen years before.

Dad's old dress blues fit well and his WWII and Korean War ribbons under his Command Pilot wings told his story. As we walked to my barracks so I could get dressed in my Tropical White Long uniform it took me by surprise to have men who outranked me saluting Dad. After being an Air Force dependent and living near air bases and around jets most of my life it was all brought home in a very solid way that morning. And my turn would come to salute him later that day. One time, worth twenty years of waiting. For both of us.

At the HS-10 hangar Dad was treated to coffee and a meeting with the squadron CO as I readied for the big moment. The whole squadron was assembled for an inspection; our little ritual was—for most sailors—a mild inconvenience as they waited to be inspected and released back to a normal workday.

Once assembled, the four of us awaiting wings stood in front. The CO of HS-10 pinned on three as Dad stood ramrod straight, waiting his turn. Once given the go-ahead, Dad strutted out, cutting crisp cadet corners on his way, until he stood before me. A few inches shorter, his eyes lifted to mine. I summoned my best salute, the one and only time I would ever pay that tribute to my father. He returned his best, as was protocol and a father's pride. He took the gold wings and placed them on my sparkling white uniform, and uttered a single sentence saturated with implication and sentiment, as best he could ever express emotion. "I now pass command to you." Six words symbolic of a change of command ceremony, meaningless in that context but clearly defined between us. The wings were a bit crookedly placed, his eyes not the keen sensors once used to spot Messerschmidts or MiGs, but I would feel his fingers delicately placing them for years to come.

After we were released from the inspection we commenced our celebratory bash at the EM club. It was a dark, beer soaked into the worn shag carpet kind of place, but it was the only club we could go to. They served diner type food and the ubiquitous 3.2 percent beer by the pitcher full.

We graduates and a host of aircrew training personnel congregated at the club to start the party. Dad stayed as long as he could bear. As afternoon turned to early evening, the stage gathered the clutter of a local garage band ready to wail the sounds of Jimi Hendrix, Led Zeppelin, Three Dog Night and any other group they managed to pick up rhythms and lyrics from. Once the chest-high speakers were plugged in Dad said it was time for him to go. Had it been Crazy Otto plinking away at "Red Sails in the Sunset" or "Big" Tiny Little playing "Peg O' My Heart" he might have stayed, but I knew he couldn't tolerate one refrain of "Whole Lotta Love" much less the sound check so I whisked him away to the relative quiet of his motel room. I stayed a bit but he knew I wanted to get back and enjoy the remnants of a great day. Plus, there was more thin pizza and weak beer to be consumed before last call.

Back at the club and well lubricated by drink, I decided to enlighten Chief Lawson on my civilian drug habits. Any of my statements could have been grounds for losing my secret clearance and hence my aircrew status, my new wings and my new future.

The chief wasn't writing anything down. "Don't be tellin' me this shit, man, I don't want to hear it. I know you've had some beer, here, let me fill up your glass, but listen, just keep all that to yourself, ya' hear? I know what you're saying, that you're proud of what you've done and you're putting your past behaviors behind. Just let that be understood between us, and forget it. And, forget about that woman you keep thinking about, I can see it behind your eyes. Forget her, she's history. Now, let me be the first to tell you where you're headed—HS-4, the Black Knights. They know about your quarterly marks, they know about your swimming ordeal, I filled 'em in on it all. Just keep doing your best and you'll be fine. They ship out before year's end, so don't get too settled into your new barracks, you'll be going to sea almost immediately. You finished that beer already? God, Manthos—here's two bucks, go get another pitcher and tip the change."

I didn't know where chiefs got their extrasensory ability, but it seemed like most of them I ran into had it to some degree. Lawson could tell I was still pining away for Marsha, hoping she would rematerialize into my life. He saw a lot of things. I was beginning to wonder if there was anything a Navy chief didn't know.

September had been a full month. Marxism and Fascism had collided once again, this time in Chile, where General Pinochet took power over an elected president in a coup. The Middle East was still gaining momentum for war. Things seemed quiet over in South Vietnam, for the time being.

George Foreman TKO'd Jose Roman in the first round. Brady wouldn't bet me on that fight. Foreman seemed unstoppable.

And I had bright golden wings on my dress uniform. Still pretty bare of other accolades it was a major accomplishment, taking one year and five days from when I went to San Diego the first time and to my bootcamp company. Two more certificates were added to my service jacket on September 20, one stating I had completed the Aircrew training syllabus, the other designating me as an Aircrewman. And those certificates elevated me from my previous code of 0000 to 7881, an actual code that meant I was qualified in something besides spitshining shoes and mopping floors. All the study, hard work and training, on top of all the late night watches, finally added up to something. Now it was time to put all of that to work in my new, real Navy sea-going squadron, HS-4. The Black Knights. I wondered how they got that name.

Looking back I couldn't help but wonder what might have been had I made different choices; had that young officer back in Memphis not pulled my service jacket and offered me A school. If I had wrestled for NAS Millington I might be somewhere else, impossible to say where, but where I was seemed to be making sense. I never set out to be at that place, it all just happened, in spite of my failures in swimming and poor academics. And I would soon be in the fleet, putting all that training into play. My new squadron awaited.

5: BLACK KNIGHTS

NAS I.B. sported several new squadron spaces: double-decked cinderblock buildings with cavernous indoor hangars accessed by huge sliding doors over two stories high. But HS-4 was not in one of those well lighted and spacious buildings; it was down the street in old, dark, one-story wooden structures, hangovers from WWII. It was a short walk to my new squadron. All their aircraft were parked in the open, sporting the numerical sequence assigned to the Black Knights. In big block form on each flank, as well as the nose, were numbers from 720 through 754. They weren't sequential, but ten helos each had its own number, sounded individually, as in "seven-two-zero." High on the tail were two letters in the same block form denoting which air wing HS-4 was assigned to. NH, "November Hotel," was Air Wing 11—wherever they went, HS-4 went. That meant the aircraft carrier *Kitty Hawk*.

A handful of helos were in various stages of maintenance. Some had missing rotor blades; one had gaping holes where the gearboxes went. Perhaps the gears had set off a chip detector light on the instrument panel. Those little lights indicated a high degree of potential in-flight disaster—they could detect metal fragments of disintegrating gears and extreme heat. As NATOPS said: "The presence of these conditions could cause excessive wear and/or premature failure of the gear boxes." Premature failure, ergo, "land immediately." That took me back to Doc Bliven's assignment. I was already thinking about having to land at night in the open ocean in bad weather 100 miles from a ship I wasn't even on as a member of a squadron I wasn't initiated into yet.

Standing at the aircrew door with my check-in sheet rolled up in my hand, I would be an official Black Knight within minutes.

Marsha bartended at the Black Knight Inn. I wondered if she would care at all where I was headed, see any irony in it, give a damn.

Life shifted into a whole new gear. HS-4 was the real deal. Officer's khaki uniforms displayed rows upon rows of medals. Enlisted working uniforms had no such display, but I got the feeling most of those guys were salty dogs. If one was an E-4 or above chances were he'd been overseas, and on the West Coast overseas meant deploying to Vietnam.

The squadron was buzzing with activity. The aircrew division had its own separate section where, well, where what? I didn't even know what aircrewmen did when they weren't flying. I saw a few gray steel desks with Royal manual typewriters squatting heavily on them—that hardly seemed like aircrew stuff. And I saw Chief Hatch. Or rather, he saw me as I entered the building looking more than a little out of place.

"You must be Manthos. Where the hell have you been? And where the fuck is Turner? He's supposed to check in today too; no goddamn way to start off with me. If you're on time you're already late. Your first assignment is to go find this Turner guy so do an about face, march out that goddamn door and go find him. What, you're still here?"

My eyes filled with a starched khaki blur. I felt dizzy. The chief was about my height with stooped shoulders supporting a balding head and small eyes that stared at me with a blue flame. Before I made it back out the door he had a parting question. "What is the rotor brake pressure supposed to be when the number one engine is started?"

I mumbled something about 320 psi as I backed out and made my retreat down the sidewalk looking for Brady. I knew he had orders to HS-4. He had been in bootcamp with me and all through the pipeline since. Now we would be in the same squadron. If I could find him.

I did. He was about halfway between HS-10 and our new home. "Brady, we need to get our asses in gear; the aircrew chief is not only expecting us, he's waiting for us. His name is Hatch. And he isn't in a good mood." I would find out he had only two moods: neutral and malignant.

Back at the squadron, Chief Hatch was grumbling about clouding up and raining all over us as he passed Brady and me off to an affable 3rd class by the name of "Papa" Gire. The day was looking up. "OK you two, I'll take you around and introduce you to aircrew; let's start with Bailey. Hey Teddy Bear, check out the cherries."

"I don't have time to check out nobody; I have a NATOPS checkride in an hour, all the navigation bags need new approach plates and I lost the fuckin' key to the supply locker. Other than that, everything's copacetic, so, later."

"Teddy Bear's cool, just a little stressed right now. And he's a rent-a-crow but I wouldn't rub that in; he just might find some shit-cans that need cleaning—by you. Alright, this here is Little Green Sprout, but don't call him that; he's small but so is a bobcat. He's cool too, and a short-timer like me. Ain't that right, Sprout?"

"Fuckin' A. Got my short-timer's calendar already started, see?" The dark haired, wiry crewman held up the calendar, an outline of Vietnam with a foxy chick stretched across it divided into 365 units, one for each day of the last year in uniform. "The plan is to get assigned to a beach detachment, you call that a 'det,' in the PI, then an early-out so I can start college back home. Where there ain't any ocean. Or Chief Hatch. Welcome to HS-4 you guys, guess you're hell-bent on dying in a helicopter." He smiled sardonically, his voice betraying Brooklyn roots. "You know why we're called the Black Knights? Black Knight-black night, get it? The H-3 is all-weather and nighttime capable and we prove it all the fuckin' time. You'll be flying in pitch black nights where you can't see your hand in front of your face, in lousy weather, far from the ship, probably low on fuel, all by yourselves." He opened the small black book held in his hand. "Look here in my log book; see all that red ink? That's night time logged in. Now it's your turn in the barrel. Have fun. I can't wait to get back to school: normal hours, lots of women and no chiefs to hassle me. FTN." He chuckled as he waved over his shoulder, sauntering down the hallway.

Gire rolled his eyes. "It's a disease—short-timer's syndrome. It's where you start to realize you just might make it out alive but you're not done with flying yet and something deep inside you starts to come to its senses and tells you to stop taking risks. As in climbing into an H-3. Don't worry, you won't get it for a few years, but it's all around you. A lot of these guys are short; they don't give a fuck, but don't let that get to you. You can't afford to cop that attitude just starting out; it will kill you as quickly as a thrown rotor blade. Now, let's go meet the rest of the gang."

AW3 Allen, also a short-timer, wanted to be a journalist. His big aviator-style glasses seemed to be perpetually sliding down his nose. "It's inevitable that my service contract will expire. Once done with journalism school I shall embark on my true calling, bringing world news to the common man, and in a fashion, I suspect, that will engage the reader and call to order his or her curiosity to find out more. But I have a few months left, so, until we meet again, adieu." I shook my head, feeling like maybe Allen should start his own university.

AW2 Taylor was short too, and planned on being a truck driver. But some guys just seemed at ease with the Navy and he was one of them. Perhaps he would re-up once they dangled a big bonus in front of him. I had no idea what I would do if they offered me a big bonus; that was too far off to consider.

A handful of guys had been there for a bit but not yet on a West-Pac. There was another aircrew chief but he seemed in his own ghost-like world. I had to keep looking at his name tag to remember who he was.

HS-4 was going to lose a lot of crewmen over the next year to reenlistment or discharges. I was surprised all four in my class didn't get orders to the Black Knights. Pater and Diaz went to HS-2, up the street. But more bodies were going to show up at HS-4. A sister squadron, HS-8, was loaning us a handful of "volunteers" to augment the ranks, plus a few more guys were coming down the pipeline destined for my squadron. It *was* my squadron, I was already feeling that.

I was assigned to "Clyde Dog" Traynham, a 3rd class who had been in HS-4 long enough to have a feel for things. It said "Steve" in his records but nobody called him that; it was always just Clyde Dog. A tall, solidly built man with broad shoulders and an easy wide grin, he planned on getting back to college to play football in his home state of Kentucky, but not for a couple of years. Until then he was going to help break in the new guy: me. He introduced me to one of the Royal typewriters. "Now, I need you to type out the flight schedule. Here's yesterday's so use it as a guide and, no, don't do that, take that paper out, this is for a mimeograph machine, you need a stencil..."

"But Clyde Dog, I don't know how to type much less make a, what is it, a stencil? As close as I ever got to this was walking past typing class in junior high. Shit, I have no idea what to do, I mean, we're supposed to be flying, right, not doing office work?"

"You think the Navy is going to pay a yeoman to sit here doing work you can be doing when you're not flying? Welcome to the fleet, dude!"

"So, when I'm not using all the training I just went through over the last year I'm a fuckin' secretary?"

"No shit, Sherlock. There's a lot to do in the division: the flight schedule, logs and records where we process the yellow sheets for pilot and crew data, navigation and photo recon, aircrew training, supplies, the comm office has work plus classified messages need to be typed and you need a secret clearance to even see that stuff and that would be us aircrew, so get comfortable. And figuring out how not to jam the mimeograph machine is an art form all its own, but we'll deal with that when you're done typing."

As I settled into the gray, steel-framed chair and started my two finger search for keys Chief Hatch sauntered by with his ever-present coffee mug. My typing sounded like a slow drip into a steel sink. "Get out the extinguisher, Manthos is going so fast he'll set that paper on fire."

The world situation continued to evolve in the weeks since I'd checked into the squadron. War erupted in the Middle East on October 6, and we were put on alert on the twenty-fifth. Mixed messages from the Soviets about military intervention in the crisis intensified the atmosphere on base. The Watergate scandal continued. Vice President Agnew resigned under corruption charges.

HS-4 was gearing up to deploy on a WestPac, meaning we had some short shakedown cruises before we left for eight months. As a rookie to the squadron I had several checkrides with Chief Hatch. I was very well behaved. No sense waking a dragon. He usually flew with the commanding officer, or CO, Cdr. Pearigen, a career officer just short of his retirement. It was Pearigen's final command, his final deployment, his final flights as a naval aviator. The same went for Hatch. If I was with Hatch I was likely with Pearigen—just a little pressure flying with the senior crewman and senior pilot. They probably had more flight hours in a week than I had total. Lt. Leo Rolek often flew as the CO's copilot. He was an Academy man, big ring and all, and was friendly and liked joking with everyone. He and I got along well, under the watchful eye of Hatch and the CO.

Air Wing 11 had a distinctive unit patch: a pair of dice showing a five and a six on a five-pointed star background. It looked great on a flight jacket. Too bad I couldn't lay my hands on mine. It had been stolen weeks after getting to the squadron. The aircrew lockers were gray steel free-standing double door units. Years of use and abuse had loosened the hinges and latches to where some bastard had been able to pry the doors open enough to stick his arm down and grab whatever he could from the guys willing to risk their lives in the air. I was dumbfounded that a squadronmate would steal something so intimate as a flight jacket from one of his own. They had great resale value and everybody wanted one, especially those who hadn't earned the right. I was a naive young man from a small town. I would learn that not only were the criminals avoiding jail doing fine in the Navy but that aircrewmen were resented by some. I didn't know what to do about it and I didn't report the theft because I was embarrassed. But I was also without my hard earned G-1.

The USS *Kitty Hawk*, CV-63. It was a true supercarrier, not a converted WWII straightdeck rustbucket like the *Hancock*, but built as a supercarrier from the keel up, angled deck and steam catapults included.

The ship's statistics were staggering: the displacement was over 80,000 tons. The flight deck was 1062.5 feet long, something that would seem to shorten as time passed at sea. Everything seemed to be made of dense steel; the anchors weighed thirty tons each, held fast to the bitter end by an enormous chain over a thousand feet long, each link weighing 360 pounds. Four propellers measuring twenty-one feet across were powered by eight boilers producing 280,000 horsepower.

The ship could store more than 2.2 million gallons of fuel oil for propulsion plus 2 million gallons of fuel for aircraft. Add thousands of tons of ordnance and the ship was a floating steel-encased explosive operated by almost 6,000 frail, soft bodied beings.

Sixty-one feet of salt air stood between the flight deck—4.1 acres of flat, rough-coated steelplate—and the water below. Four catapults, called "cats," were embedded in the deck: thin rails with hooks that slung aircraft—some weighing as much as 62,000 pounds—into thin air with enough force to make them fly. Fortunately helicopters didn't depend on that sophisticated mechanism to get airborne. Unfortunately that also meant we would fly when the fixed wing weren't able. I would learn that as a rescue helicopter crewmember; we would be first off the flight deck and last back on, regardless of the situation, for every cycle of air operations. If there were Mach 2 fighters or lumbering reconnaissance planes in the air, we were there first. I would eventually take some pride in that.

The mission of providing that rescue capability for air operations was called "plane guard." The rescue helicopter would take up a position on the starboard side of the carrier and fly a racetrack pattern, hence the location name "starboard delta." It was a position of maximum readiness. Should something go wrong on the flight deck or in the air the crew with its rescue swimmer would be able to prosecute a fast pickup. Things would go wrong but mostly it was a mind-numbing four hours of flying in a circle trying to stay alert. Much like guard duty, one needed to be prepared to deal with any contingency but much of the time nothing happened. Planeguardinstarboarddelta, planeguardinstarboarddelta, it would become a mantra. And yet we thrilled at making a rescue; they were the best missions. Every swimmer wants to jump like every golden retriever wants to catch that Frisbee. Mostly it was a matter of being suited up in rescue swimmer gear, sweating and waiting.

A small detachment would be aboard the *Hawk* for plane guard duty during shakedown cruises. I pulled several of those short deployments and decided to take a book along on plane guard hops, just to keep my mind busy. I wasn't a big reader but I felt pulled toward a recently well received Russian author, Alexander Solzhenitsyn. I could have started off with something less cumbersome but I nestled his *August 1914* in my helmet bag along with my checklist, flashlight, kneeboard and other assorted necessities. The book was 714 pages of tiny print, tongue twisting Slavic names and historical settings, but we would be leaving for the South China Sea within weeks and not returning for almost nine months. I figured I should have it all read by then.

The *Hawk* was moored at NAS North Island, ten miles up the Strand from Imperial Beach. We were scheduled to leave from there on Friday the twenty-third, and the last weeks had been a frantic but calculated on-loading of equipment. Collapsible metal crates called "cruise boxes" were the standard container for gear of all kinds. Once emptied they folded on hinges for easy storage. When full of tools or manuals they were extremely heavy.

It was a monumental task and with eleven squadrons all loading their aircraft, tools, parts, paperwork, people and other assorted items it was a circus, especially on the hangar deck. Covering over one and a half acres, it was a cavernous open space used for storage and maintenance of aircraft. As the main deck it also housed the quarterdeck, which meant all personnel boarded and departed the ship on gangways called "brows" at that level. Enlisted boarded aft, officers toward the bow, both on the starboard side.

I tried to call Dad Thanksgiving night from a dockside phone booth missing its door, just rusted hinges supporting night fog. He was somewhere in Texas, where he had retreated from whatever it was that drove him south. I tried the two places he could have been with no luck. I had no idea when I'd speak to him again.

Wearing my Bluejacket in the cool waterfront air, I boarded the *Kitty Hawk* and joined 5,800 other sailors. We were heading west, sailing 8,000 miles to join Task Force 77—the Tonkin Gulf Yacht Club—in the South China Sea. Chief Hatch had his 2¢ worth. "We're leaving our families and going to see our loved ones."

6: WestPac

Our departure was in the dark of night, as if we were secretly stealing away. Those left behind at North Island might not have noticed the gaping hole left at the pier. In the hours before we left I had watched thousands of sailors pry small kids from themselves and kiss their wives goodbye. Thousands of others hugged and groped their girlfriends. I stood in the flight deck catwalk feeling for once content that I had no one to yearn for. I missed Marsha but in a longing, unattainable way, not as if she had been standing on the dock embracing me, crying, telling me she would be there when I came back. She wouldn't, no matter what stories I allowed into my imagination.

The idea was to get to South East Asia as quickly as possible so we didn't have much of what would become hectic and at times dangerously frantic air operations. Once at sea we did have pranksters at work, however. It didn't take long before old salts had new guys looking for buckets of relative bearing grease or six feet of waterline. A favorite was the sea bat hunt. The huge hangar deck was a good stalking spot. After some time spent hunting, a sailor in on the prank might produce a sea bat captured in a shoe box. It could get pretty elaborate; the "bat" would flutter and make all kinds of commotion inside the box, and if you wanted to see it all you had to do was look through the hole in the end. That would be the final insult; with a whack on the ass you were initiated into one of the oldest jokes in the Navy. The bat turned out to be a contraption of a stick, rubber bands, loose paper and a trigger to make it all move inside the box. There was almost an infinite variety of contraptions but even the simplest managed to entrap the willing.

Mail was the lifeline from home and mail call was looked forward to with great anticipation. With only a few days at sea under our belts no mail had arrived. We would eventually get some by way of the COD, or Carrier Onboard Delivery aircraft, but before then a classic prank had to be pulled. And a very special victim had to be selected.

One of the aircrewmen on loan from HS-8 was a friendly and slightly naive Texan who didn't want to be called "Tex." "Call me Mistrot." Fair enough, that was his name after all. Mistrot was selected by a handful of chiefs for a very special mission, this being his first deployment. The perfect instigator was Master Chief Romney. He had stood his own mail buoy watch during WWII some thirty years before.

"Mistrot, front and center. You know who I am, Master Chief Romney. You can call me by my first name—Master. Now, I have a very important job for you; you were hand-selected by us chiefs for this mission because we believe you are the best man for the job. Mail as you know is the lifeblood of a ship's crew, and we are entrusting you with looking for the next mail buoy. This will be the first such buoy of the cruise and believe me, son, you'll take pride in spotting it first. Hell, you might even have a letter from your girlfriend back home on it! There will be another watch on the port side from one of the fighter squadrons, don't let that bastard see it before you do; you'll be the pride of HS-4 if you sound off first. We'll set you up with a sound-powered phone so you can report to the bridge, and here is a special vest so the whole ship will know that you're on this crucial watch."

"But Chief..."

"'Master Chief' goddammit, it's 'Master' Chief."

"Oops, sorry Master Chief, but, is there really such a thing as a mail buoy? I mean, couldn't a plane bring on mail?"

"Oh sure, that will happen someday, but see, the mail ships leave the bags of mail on the buoy; that's how it's worked since I was a striker under Bull Halsey. When you see it, and I know you will, sound off 'mail buoy ahoy.' So, go do your duty son, and do us proud."

AWAN Mistrot took up his position on the starboard bow catwalk, donned his vibrantly colored vest, plugged in his sound-powered phone and scanned the horizon for the elusive object. Hourly he reported to the bridge, as did his counterpart on the port side. The clear bright day grew dark as he paced the catwalk. Veterans of the seven seas walking by gave him a thumb's up; attaboy they'd say, keep up the good work.

Master Chief Romney finally let him off watch at twenty-hundred hours. When it was all said and done he had reported twelve dolphins, two freighters and a hundred flying fish. No mail buoy was to be found. As he was enlightened by the master chief, there was no such thing. He took it all in stride as they knew he would; that was why they picked him.

It didn't hurt that he was from Texas, either.

Before we got to Pearl Harbor Chief Hatch pulled a flight gear inspection. We laid out all our specialized equipment: custom wetsuit, steel-toed flight boots, two Nomex fire-retardant flight suits and gloves, survival vest with flotation device. The survival gear was eclectic; it included a small handheld radio, two types of flares, a signal mirror, a holster for the gun we didn't have, dye marker and shark repellent. It was rumored the dye marker, a dayglow green meant to color the water around you should you end up there, could attract sharks. It was rumored the shark repellent acted as more of a soup stock for the human using it, an added delight for a shark's meal.

The chief looked over everything and noticed my flight jacket by its absence. After it had been stolen I didn't ask for a new one or report it taken. That was stupid. He was not happy. "Where's your flight jacket, Manthos? It's what? It's gone? You stupid ass, why didn't you report it? And don't give me that 'no excuse chief' routine. I'm about to cloud up and rain all over you, son. Good luck getting another one; how do I know you don't have it stashed away stateside or gave it to your girlfriend back home, and you're trying to wrangle another one out of *my* Navy?"

He wasn't in the mood for a discussion so I filled out a request chit for a replacement jacket and crossed my fingers. The chief wasn't going to OK it but the aircrew division officer, Lt. Nelms, took my side and I managed a replacement from paraloft. That's where we didn't get parachutes. But I did get my jacket, that time with sleeves that weren't sewn closed. I guarded it like a hawk.

The transit to Pearl Harbor was quiet with few flights, giving me time to explore the ship. It was honeycombed with 2,400 compartments. 1,500 of those compartments—steel boxes within a steel shell—were for berthing. The *Hawk* had eight decks and eleven levels, from the bilges to the uppermost reaches of the island, the superstructure that stood on the flight deck. The air wing was concentrated on the 0-3 level, just above the hangar deck and right under the flight deck. Our squadron was scattered around the 0-3 level, with the ready room the hub of activity. It was where crews briefed, lectures were given, where the coffee pot stood its duty and movies were watched on closed-circuit TV. Chief Hatch always had his observations. "When I was a lad like you on my first cruise we had ten movies, all of them 'Sgt. York.'"

The squadron's enlisted berthing compartment was forward on the 0-3 level and sat just behind the anchor chain tubes, which led down into the chain locker. Above were the two bow catapults, right over our heads. Both would add their own special resonances to the sleeping area.

The berthing compartment had rows of beds called "racks" three high and two deep, row upon row. There was barely enough room to walk between them without brushing shoulders against thin mattresses. Sailors had a habit of dangling dittybags of dirty laundry from their racks adding to the claustrophobic closeness. My rack was on the lowest tier, almost sitting on the deck. There was a class structure to it all; higher ranking guys could claim a top rack, the penthouse, so moving up in rank was more than symbolic. Guys on the bottom two racks commonly had dirty feet stepping on their sheets or worse, their heads. With lights out for twelve hour shifts, getting into and out of a small confined box in a narrow corridor shared by eleven other sailors in the dark was challenging. We had less personal space than federal prisoners. The racks and rows all looked the same. Being on a flight crew meant I was off any set schedule and would be coming and going at all hours. In the dark it was easy to get out of rhythm with where your rack was. One late night after a long flight I tiredly tried to crawl into my bottom rack only to find someone already in it.

"Hey man," I whispered. "You're in my rack, you're in the wrong one. C'mon, get out, I need to sleep."

"Fuck off dude, get lost, this is my rack, go find your own."

"No, no this is mine, see...uh, oh wait, sorry..." I made a hasty retreat before the groggy sailor could figure out who I was.

The compartment, home to 100 men, was spare on air circulation and smelled like sleep and sweat. We were only a few days out to sea.

I made my first transoceanic sea voyage at the age of six, when my father was sent to Turkey as an instructor pilot to their Air Force. Pulling away from the great steel and concrete finger of a pier in Brooklyn, we were eased away from the Continental United States by stout-nosed tugs. The water—covered with oil slicks in rainbow colors—was a two way avenue which led only to the future.

East for the next week we traveled. The sea became the bluest blue I had ever seen. Cerulean blue, cobalt blue, it was a blue by which I would judge all other blues. The Atlantic was colored by warm subtropical currents churning along the eastern seaboard bringing blue water and hurricanes.

Down on the decks the steward would cruise up and down the passageways, a ship unto himself, and sing out in a resonant baritone: "Four bells and all's well, four bells and all's well..." I didn't understand the nautical cycle of bells and I didn't care; his grand voice was all I needed to feel secure in the wake of his call.

Great swells would rise and fall in a giant rhythm, the ocean alive and breathing. As wind increased, the tops of swells would erupt in frothy whitecaps. The ship responded with motion. As the hull dipped port to starboard, fore and aft, the swaying caused my little body to absorb the nausea kicked up by the waves.

I got gut-wrenchingly seasick, huddling on the exposed weather deck for transcendently fresh air and some semblance of a horizon. It was called a weather deck because that is what you got—good or bad—the weather. A waiter took pity and brought me seltzer and soda crackers, the only food I could keep down until we were somewhere near the Azores. My seasickness calmed by the time we saw the Rock of Gibraltar. I never dreamed I would have the opportunity to get seasick again.

Three days out of San Diego I was 170 pounds of quivering, vomiting nausea. Nerves, I told myself, just nerves.

Hawaii and Pearl Harbor was a quick visit. We docked within sight of the *Arizona* Memorial, a stark reminder of where we were. I had one day and evening to see the island. "Cinderella Liberty" it was called, I had to be back aboard before midnight.

The ship's crew and air wing was broken down into four watch sections so there would be a manned ship at all times, even in port. Another AW named Chuck Fields and I took to the town after being closely scrutinized by the afterbrow duty chief, who checked for suitable liberty clothes and haircuts. I could be denied liberty if either did not meet his standards.

We walked Waikiki, snacked on mangos and ogled women on the beach. Later we parked ourselves in a bar and paid extortion prices for cheap beer while watching tired strippers go through their routine. It was a break from the ship but being back aboard before midnight had us in working uniforms and standing watches the next day, while other watch sections got their turn at occupying the town.

Refueled and with fresh food and recent mail aboard, we pulled out of Pearl bound for Subic Bay, the Philippines.

Crossing 180 degrees longitude placed us in the "Domain of the Golden Dragon, ruler of the 180th meridian." It also meant we went from a Monday night to a Wednesday morning. We crossed on the fifth of December at latitude 18.5 degrees north, and were issued a wallet-sized card commemorating the event. We had entered the Far East. I wondered what the chaplains did when a ship crossed from a Saturday to a Monday.

The squadron was put on alert and started staging crews for missions. We had entered the observation range of Soviet Tu-95 Bear bombers, multi-propellered behemoths sleek like a silver cigar and menacing in their capabilities. They had been in development from the time I was born and were geared toward high altitude bombing. They had also been modified many times for alternate missions, one of which being long range maritime patrol. We could expect an overflight anytime. We could also expect Soviet submarines to probe our perimeter manned by destroyers and frigates. And by our ASW helicopters. It was one of the first WestPacs to incorporate the attack carrier configuration with ASW capability. Before, older Essex class attack carriers had been converted to ASW carriers, but this concept was new and a real mix of missions, neither mindset being terribly comfortable with the other. This additional mission capability changed the carrier's designation from CVA, an attack carrier, to simply CV, a multi-mission carrier.

The *Hawk* also had two S-2F squadrons aboard to complete the ASW capability. Between them and us we scoured the seas for Soviet subs—the biggest threat not only to carriers but to the Continental United States. When we weren't actively looking we were on alert, ready to launch a sub hunt within minutes. Hours would be spent in the squadron ready room in full flight gear, waiting. It was a good time to get caught up on letters home.

———◆———

STEAM HISSED OUT OF the waist catapults like a fissure in an iron planet's crust. Two F-4 Phantoms sat at alert five, hooked to the two cats. They were right behind us, also at alert five. The outboard cat ran directly under us. The inboard cat sat just under our rotor blades. It was a busy place. And we would have to be out of the way in a hurry should the F-4s launch.

The two cats ran on intersecting lines; a simultaneous launch would cause a collision before the planes were ever airborne. It wouldn't be a mid-air; it would be a mid-deck. It was delicate timing and the air boss, the officer in charge of the flight deck up in his glass-enclosed pulpit, was calling the shots. The Phantom pilots weren't going anywhere until we were in the air and clear of the deck. Their cockpits were open; one pilot was reading a paperback, his back seat radar intercept officer napping in the sun, strapped tightly in his Martin Baker ejection seat. I was sitting in back of my helo doing some reading too. I was making progress with Solzhenitsyn's book but was struggling with pronouncing "Akhangorodsky." As I mouthed the syllables one at a time—"ak-hang ..." trying to link them together into a pronounceable name—the air boss electrified the radio waves: "Launch the Bear alert five! Now! I want those Phantoms up and out in under five, all flight deck personnel expedite the launch!"

I tossed the novel into my helmet bag as the engines wound up to flight RPMs, the five big rotor blades shaking the helo side to side as they gained momentum. The ground crews manned the tiedown chains and wheel chocks while the pilots brought up thousands of horsepower from the twin turbines. I looked back at the Phantoms from the cargo door and saw that their canopies were already closed, the ordnancemen readying the missiles for action. Red-tagged pins were pulled from every aircraft making them fully mission capable. Within two minutes we were given the signal to launch as the deck crew pulled chains and chocks. The pilots pulled pitch as we lifted off spot three and made a tight left turn to clear the deck as the Phantoms were launched seconds after our takeoff. I felt the force of their dual J-79 engines as they were catapulted into the clear Pacific sky.

"Black Knight 720, assume starboard delta for duration of Bear overflight," came the orders. As we leveled off at 100 feet and 50 knots, the two F-4s streaked at over a thousand miles per hour on afterburners towards the Soviet reconnaissance bomber. We waited. The closure rate for the Bear/Phantom intercept would make it a short one.

"*Kitty Hawk*, this is Phantom flight Alpha Six, tallyho Bear overflight, taking up position now-now-now." The F-4s slid onto the wingtips of the huge Soviet machine and flew escort all the way in. Listening to the radio chatter was a reality check; jets from my ship had intercepted a Soviet long range bomber flying directly towards us. We assumed it was a routine fly-over by the Russians; they would take pictures of our ship and deck load so their intelligence agency could determine our capabilities. We would take pictures of them, for the same reasons. And yet I also had to assume if *Kitty Hawk* Phantoms were fully armed and prepared to shoot the bomber down, the Soviet aircraft held weapons in its bomb bay, to sink us, if the order came. The "Cold War" suddenly turned very real. It was no longer a headline, it was flying directly towards us.

As we held our starboard delta position I sat in the aft station of the Sea King in full rescue swim gear. I strained my eyes looking out the cargo door Plexiglas window, searching for the trio of aircraft heading our way. Within minutes I saw, and sensed, the might of those three planes. I knew the Bear had huge turbine engines driving counter rotating propellers, but I *felt* the power of that plane as it made its run by the *Hawk*. The two Phantoms, in perfect harmony with the flight path of the Bear, trailed in steadfast certainty.

The Bear was beautiful, a testament to Russian aeronautical engineering. It was graceful for a bomber, any aircraft for that matter. Its wings were swept back at an elegant 35 degree angle, each wing supporting two sleek engine nacelles, each engine powering two propellers turning in opposite directions. The fuselage was metallic silver polished to a mirror shine, the big star on the tail painted Bolshevik red. Stark tropical sun was radiant in its reflection off the plane's metal skin. It was marvelous to see. It was also the enemy.

Within minutes it was over. After a low altitude counterclockwise circling of the *Hawk*, the Bear headed back to its base in Siberia. The

Phantoms trailed it beyond the horizon. The Cold War stayed cold one more day.

With the flight deck relatively quiet after the overflight lots of work was done on our squadron compartments. Chipping off rust and painting was a staple of lower rank tasks. It entailed wielding a metal bar with a bit of an edge to scrape off the ever-present rust ever-encroaching from the briny environment. A generous application of red-lead primer would be followed by a choice of psychologist approved but horrifically institutional colors. Adding weak sixty-cycle overhead light to the pale greens and very off whites in small, steel walled spaces lent an air of claustrophobic lockdown. Aircrew laid new tile on our compartment deck, a light absorbing russet red adding to the gloomy ambiance. I placed one green tile in a corner, a faint act of rebellion.

With twenty-six aircrewmen we had a full division. Rogers, Kopp, Cherry, MacClanahan and mail buoy veteran Mistrot were from HS-8. With several crewmen TAD to the mess decks or other duties we could field a dozen crews. A handful of AWs, led by Jose Guzman and Little Green Sprout, decided to shave their heads. Who cared? Nobody. It was a statement about a huge shift in perspective. We had left a whole world behind.

One of the new guys who got to HS-4 a bit after me was Malcolm Bryning. He started calling me "Thos," rhymed with "close" and after a few other nicknames that didn't stick "Thos" was close enough and did. Even the pilots started calling me that.

Navy pilots were officers with college degrees. There were a few old chiefs who had pilot's wings flying the last of the PBYs, holdovers from WWII. But all our pilots were college boys, from the CO on down to the newest ensign. And like the enlisted ranks, there were officers who were on the fast track to higher positions and those that weren't. There were also those too early in their commission to know what lay ahead. Pilots came in all shapes and sizes. Lt. Rolek was stout, angular and thick boned. Lt. Thompson was lean like a decathlete, crewing sculls in college. He had that wholesome, all American look. I joked about how his wife must have been a cheerleader.

"She *was* a cheerleader, Thos." He said with slight agitation. I never seemed to learn when to keep my mouth shut.

The *Kitty Hawk* had its own officers of the ship's company, headed by the ship's captain. Kirksey was his name, and as with other carrier captains he was an aviator. Kirksey was a trim and fit attack pilot willing to dive down into the enlisted mess decks and chat with his crew. Our paths didn't cross much, and I stayed away from the lofty decks of the island where the high ranking officers circulated.

As we transited to Subic Bay, the Philippines, I practiced my jump-roping skills. Jumping rope on a ship moving in three dimensions was a challenge and at times downright ridiculous. The nonskid chewed up the rope where it hit the flight deck as I danced with the ship's motion.

I expanded my small library to include Kurt Vonnegut's *Welcome to the Monkey House*, a fitting counterpart to Solzhenitsyn's book. I would become an avid fan of both authors.

———— •> ————

"FIRE." THAT'S ALL HE said at first, just that one word—"Fire." There was strict protocol for calling out a fire over the 1MC; it was "fire, fire" and then the compartment designation. Firefighting teams had territory assigned covering the whole ship, and if mustered, even on a drill, they had priority in moving about; everyone got out of their way, even the captain. But I just heard that one word, "Fire." It was finally followed by the proper procedure after a dead-calm silence during which it felt like the entire ship's crew took in a long breath and held it. He, whoever "he" was, quickly gathered his composure and barked out the fire's location: the main machinery room. That was several decks down and aft from where I was in the ready room, so I didn't need to call on what I had learned in bootcamp firefighting school. For the young men on the firefighting teams that was likely the only experience they had.

Tension filled the ready room as aircrews instinctively prepared themselves for flight; there was a chance helos would be needed even though we were still 700 miles from Subic Bay. Not long after the fire call went out general quarters was sounded. "This is not a drill." He concluded instinctively. He felt we all needed to know, to be absolutely sure. General quarters meant a lockdown of the ship; all hatches were secured and movement was restricted. Just like I had seen in the *Victory at Sea* movies at bootcamp, men scrambled to their assigned sectors and closed heavy steel doors and lowered hatches, dogging them down tight against whatever may come. Two of the four ancient Greek elements—fire and water—were a ship's worst enemies; special hatches could help control both.

We were locked into our own little orbit within the galaxy of other locked-down spaces. Somewhere deep in the guts of the ship a battle was being waged against an unthinking, uncaring enemy with no objective but to consume everything it could before its own certain death—something it could not even fear.

We communicated within the ship through intercom systems including sound-powered phones and the squawk box. More calls went out to add firefighting crews to the machinery room confla- gration. We were unable to do anything as minutes slowly ticked off on the twenty-four hour clock. Some of the Black Knight spaces manned at general quarters were told to evacuate: get out, get clear, go to the flight deck.

It was a dark Pacific night, and hundreds of miles of deep ocean held us away from any land. Smoke began to pour out from the hangar bay doors; we could smell it up on the 0-3 level. It smelled like someone trying to arc-weld tractor tires, it smelled like a cutting torch slicing through a manhole cover, it smelled like sailors were in a fight for their lives.

The young men battling the blaze were fighting for all of our lives, for the life of the ship, fighting to keep the fire—burning at 1,000 degrees—from turning the machinery room into a blistering mausoleum.

The order was given to evacuate the 4,600 square foot compart- ment, to surrender red hot steel to the fire and regroup, to forge a new line of defense, perhaps to outflank its encroachment upon other compartments. It was a fuel oil fire, a burning semi-liquid connected to two million gallons of itself. It had to be cut off, isolated, the almost endless supply of fuel for the fire had to be contained.

There was nothing I could do. Rumors quickly spread via the sound-powered phones that the fire was a deck away from the bomb locker, where untold amounts of weaponry was stored. Before the cruise started a Navy spokesman said the *Kitty Hawk* was taking to sea "the most potent weapons system ever on a surface warship." We were carrying the most devastating weapons ever on a carrier and the fire might have been playing tag with them. I didn't know. The guy manning the 1MC wasn't saying.

Chief Hatch spoke to no one in particular as he stood in the ready room. "We're DIW, dead in the water. The only difference between a destroyer sinking and an aircraft carrier sinking is that a carrier makes a bigger hole in the water. Let's hope this thing stays afloat." 80,000 tons listed heavily to port. Smoke continued to snake its way throughout the entire ship. All we could do was wait until we were needed. Firefighters, following the order, evacuated the burning space save for six young men who, for reasons never fully known except unto themselves, stayed behind.

Both Mom and Dad sent newspaper clippings of the event, each from their local paper. Dad's was from the Austin American Statesman, dated December 12. The headline, in bold type, read: "Blaze aboard *Kitty Hawk* kills six men, injures 38." Mom's article from the December 16 Denver Post: "*Kitty* sailors died in 'wall of flame.'" They were young men. One kid was just seventeen. He should have stayed in high school. I didn't know any of them, I hardly knew my own squadronmates at that point. But they were shipmates: perhaps the guys in front of me in the chow line at lunch, joking and keeping to themselves just like aircrew did. Maybe they had snuck up to the flight deck that day to catch some fresh air, a place likely as foreign to them as the lower decks were to me. But they were dead and we were over a thousand miles from Vietnam. It was one hell of a way to start a cruise.

Thirty-eight men had smoke inhalation and burns and were

treated in the ship's hospital, which was geared toward catastrophic injuries of a grand magnitude—it was a warship after all. We couldn't fly the casualties to medical help; we were too far out for the helos to do any good.

We finally secured from general quarters and hastily opened up everything we could to get the smoke to dissipate. Hatches leading to the flight deck catwalk were opened and some sea air worked its way into the 0-3 level.

Captain Kirksey came over the 1MC and spoke of the bravery of the young men below decks. He also said we had other functioning machinery rooms and were still a mission capable, combat-ready ship of war. The *Kitty Hawk* still listed hard to port, so we leaned to starboard as we went about our business.

We would make it to Subic Bay on schedule.

THE PHILIPPINE ISLANDS LIE south of the Tropic of Cancer, between 6 and 18 degrees north latitude, and 118 and 126 degrees east longitude. We navigated through the archipelago of over seven thousand islands to the west coast of Luzon, passing such historic places as Leyte and Corregidor.

Subic Bay was a natural anchorage northwest of Manila, the Bataan Peninsula separating the harbors. My head was swirling with stories told by my godfather who served in the area during WWII. He had not been on the Death March across Bataan but hated with a passion those who made the march happen. Thirty years later, he still refused to buy anything made in Japan.

I asked Lt. Gray, our intel officer, why we had a base in the Philippines. He had a history background in college and was always adding his perspective. "It's like this Thos, we simply bought the Philippines. And call it 'the PI,' that sounds like you know what you're talking about. A war with Spain and 20 million dollars later we had ourselves a bunch of islands that were in the midst of a rebellion against Spanish colonial power. We inherited that rebellion, which my history teacher always called a war, and ended up fighting a lot of folks including the Moros, who really wanted us out of there. My grandpa, who fought them on Mindanao, said even his Colt .45, his 'young cannon,' wouldn't stop them. He had nightmares for years about having his throat slit at night by a Moro. My father was Navy, he served on the USS *Fremont* in World War Two. They spent time near Leyte Island, dodging Kamikazes. So, a couple of wars and three generations later, here I am."

"My dad was in Europe, but stationed in the PI after the war. He told me to be careful about the 'benny boys.' What's a 'benny boy' anyway, Mr. Gray?"

"Thos, go ask your chief."

I flew off the carrier into Subic with Ghost Chief from 100 miles out. I was still apprenticing as a crewman and went through the whole briefing and preflight with meticulous precision, not wanting to give him any reason to write a bad flight report. He looked bemused as I followed the checklist to the letter. I noticed he wasn't wearing his required steel-toed flight boots; instead he sported spit-shined brown leather Wellingtons. He was ready to go party. His mission was to have some fun, maybe get reacquainted with some gal, maybe find a barstool in his favorite portside joint and drink semi-cold San Miguels. All he said was, "Look out for those LBFMs." I had to ask, just in case. "Little Brown Fucking Machines, the hookers, they'll fuck you silly. But don't pay too much, a few bucks should cover it."

"So chief, what's a 'benny boy'?"

"Go ask Chief Hatch."

I wondered if I would ever find out what a benny boy was. And I readjusted my attitude for that flight. Ghost Chief didn't care if I found a Soviet sub; he just made sure I knew where to buy condoms.

A gaggle of helo crews hit the beach well before the *Hawk* pulled in. Once changed into the civvies we had crammed into our helmet bags Clyde Dog, Mistrot and I headed out Subic's main gate and across Shit River. I smelled it before I got near it. It was a brown, thick watered channel—drainage ditch to be precise—and its nickname was an understatement. Young kids were diving in it for Pisos, the national coinage. A few kids held up baskets to catch coins tossed off the bridge. The begging had started before we were on sovereign Filipino territory.

Entering Olongapo, the town appended to the naval base, was like falling down a rabbit hole into an otherworldly plane; it was like an Old West town inhabited by a disparate culture. Bars and clubs lined Magsaysay Street, the main drag, for miles. Side streets were crammed with wooden buildings, leading to more side streets crowded with shanties and pieced together shacks. But my focus was immediately drawn to the street kids who mobbed me and asked for money or tried to sell me something, anything. They followed me and hung onto my belt like hungry lampreys. I had to fight them off, be rude, be persistent; it was like wading through waist-high boney flesh draped in dirty T-shirts and ragged shorts.

The three of us found refuge in a bar. A big sign out front said: "Welcome *Kitty Hawk* sailors." San Miguel was the national beer. It came in squat, dark brown bottles which was a good thing; clear glass wouldn't have been a good marketing strategy. It had a strong chemical aftertaste, but after five or eight it didn't much matter. And it was cheap. So was sex if you wanted it. The bar girls were as aggressive as the street kids; they just grabbed at something different in your pocket. Some would even stick their thin arms down into your skivvies and grope. Most had a command of basic English: "You want short time?" "You want sensation?" "You buy me air conditioned Honda?" "You take me America?" Lt. Nelms said we would need the CO's permission to marry a Filipino national. The thought hadn't crossed my mind.

The three of us drank beer and joked with the girls in broken English until 11:30. Then it was time to make a decision. Lt. Gray had told aircrew why a few days before. "Listen up men. You can have a lot of fun in the PI but it isn't like wherever it is you're from. There is martial law. President Ferdinand Marcos imposed it to gain control, maybe too much, over all the groups that want to fight him or each other or both, for any number of reasons. You have communists, Muslim nationalists, separatists of all stripes and a bunch of other unhappy folks plus his own party, all teetering on the brink of chaos. So, martial law means you get off the streets by midnight. And stay off. If you get caught between twenty-four-hundred and zero-eight-hundred by the national police or worse, insurgents, no one can guarantee what will happen, except that it won't be pretty. If it's the police that get you, don't fight with them, cooperate and play dumb; maybe they won't beat you to within an inch of your life. Don't give them the chance; they like it, it's sport to them. If it's Huks that get you, well, you do have that insurance policy for your family. We can't help you if you get nabbed after midnight. If you want to keep your balls, your tongue, your eyes, your head or anything else precious to you, stay clear of the streets during that eight hours; either get back on base or hole up with some LBFM until the next morning. OK then, have fun fellas."

We decided to head back to the ship. We had duty the next day and there would be plenty of time to shack up overnight with a local girl and go "long time."

Dad had been stationed in the Philippines at Clark Field in '49 and '50. He didn't talk about it much. He had a few things from his time there, including some arrows from a hill tribe. They were menacing looking weapons, barbed and formed from steel traded to them for perhaps a shrunken head. Rumors spread about helos taking occasional small arms fire from Huks and other antigovernment forces out in the countryside. A story circulated about an Air Force Sea King coming back to Clark with arrows stuck in its metallic skin. We were told the perimeter of Subic was patrolled by local mercenaries to fight off any attacks on the base. Severed heads hung on the fence were the warning sign, so the story went.

Since the *Kitty Hawk* was going to be in port for a while for fire repairs and funeral services, aircrew was scheduled for JEST: Jungle Environmental Survival Training. We were going to be tutored by the fellows who patrolled that fence.

On the south side of the bay was the Cubi Point Naval Air Station—airdale country. It was where the helo beach detachment would be, a shore based section from the squadron that tended to have people in transit and perhaps a helicopter or two that needed extensive maintenance.

Whenever I could I would secure from the squadron aboard ship and sneak over to the big chow hall at Cubi. The food was good and plentiful, and a swim in the base pool afterwards topped off the day. There was also a library I investigated. My eye caught a book with a spinning wheel embossed on the spine. It was in the biography section and my curiosity caused me to pull it down and take a look. It was a biography of Mahatma Gandhi. I had heard of him but didn't know much beyond seeing pictures of his thin frame and round glasses. I had no idea what a spinning wheel had to do with the man. I decided to check it out.

For two weeks the ship sat moored to the Alava pier, needing major work done to the fire-stricken areas. JP fuel for the helos was in short supply so we weren't flying much. I was working on my typing skills doing aircrew division paperwork. Chief Hatch stopped giving me grief over it. The flight schedule took just a scant few minutes to type and print out on the mimeograph. Long slow days aboard were punctuated by long slow waits in the chow line. At least the food was fresh off the docks.

The ready room acey deucey board got a workout. It was a variant of backgammon and games moved quickly. The perfect time killer for flight crews, it was in almost constant use while we sat tied to Subic Bay. Nobody kept a tally; so many games were played it became an exercise of being in the moment. Even the junior pilots and aircrew would wage mock warfare on the board, rolling dice and hoping for double sixes.

Allen found a chess board and I routinely got my ass kicked playing him, but it was perfect for longer periods of the mental doldrums.

"Manthos, you really should, you know, by some means learn a methodology of this ancient and revered game. You don't have to be Boris Spassky you understand, just learning a few simple strategies would be helpful in your endeavors here. I hate to see you struggle so." He slid the big glasses back up the ridge of his aquiline nose.

"Allen, I don't give a rat's ass, I just want to kill some time."

Killing time was an exercise in patience, creativity and cunning, all skills that needed acquiring on my part. I would have ample time to learn.

It didn't take long to shift my focus to the wonderland of the PX. It sat atop Cubi Point near the library and chow hall. There was a sizable Marine contingent at Cubi and the area was awash in olive drab utilities and starched covers. The PX was common ground for Navy "squids," Marine "jar heads" and officers of all persuasions. We mingled and gawked at the electronics, cameras, watches, trinkets, baubles and just plain junk. I needed to replace the stereo that I had given to my friend Mark. It was old and not great quality, but I sure didn't want to leave it at our, then Marsha's, apartment.

I decided to pass some in-port time with some SCUBA diving, which was excellent in the area. The waters around Subic and Grande Island were clear, but it wasn't always that way. The area had seen combat in World War II, the waters murky with leaking fuel oil and blood. Skeletal remains of landing craft lay beached in the bay. Grande had a collection of jungle covered gun batteries once defending Subic, a small version of its big brother guarding Manila Bay, Corregidor. Grande Island had been turned into a recreation spot, complete with a downscaled golf course. I wondered what the combat vets who once manned those weapons would think of their tiny fortress island being made into a recreation paradise. Maybe that every fortress should be made into a recreation paradise. Maybe Chief Romney knew. He knew a lot, so I asked him what a benny boy was. He said go ask anybody but him.

I spent Christmas Eve in an Olongapo bar drinking lukewarm San Miguels and staring at a sparse tree branch stuck in a beer bottle sporting a few pieces of ribbon and a P-38 can opener as decorations.

JEST: JUNGLE ENVIRONMENTAL SURVIVAL TRAINING. The PI was covered with jungle and it made for good training should aircrews find themselves in the Vietnamese version. SERE prepared me for the will to survive under severe conditions. JEST would teach me the tools specific to that part of the world. The likelihood of landing or worse, crashing, in Vietnam—north or south—had grown remote. But the war was still being fought and we would inevitably end up in the coastal waters, perhaps being called upon for some sort of "feet dry" mission. "Feet dry" meant over land, and Navy helo rescue squadrons had spent plenty of time over North Vietnam. I had no idea what lay ahead, but taking JEST would be invaluable regardless of what effect war or congress would have on my future.

After a short bus ride from the Subic side of the bay and up the steep hill through patches of jungle we arrived at the JEST compound. It sat atop Cubi Point not far from the enlisted men's Sky Club. We were greeted by a tall, lean, dark haired E-7 in olive drab fatigues. Next to him stood a stocky fireplug of a man wearing shorts and flip-flops. "My name is Chief Petty Officer Partz, and there will be no jokes about whether or not I have any 'spare parts.' I don't. Welcome to JEST. This is not SERE, which all of you have completed or you wouldn't be here today enjoying our hospitality. We won't torture you or cram you into a little box, but we will show you how to survive in the jungle. It may look hostile to you but it holds a banquet of delicacies and is a haven if you know how to work with it. If you work against it, it will let you die without a second thought. The jungle is neutral, keep that in mind. You are in the food chain here, insects alone can turn you into a skeleton in less time than it takes to get a good night's sleep.

"The backbone of JEST is the Negrito. It is Spanish for 'little Negro' and if you show any disrespect towards them I'll let them take you into their jungle and they will give you a private lesson in survival. This man here is called 'Sarge.' His ancestry goes back perhaps 70,000 years on these islands; he comes from the most ancient race in Asia. Sarge is from the Atis tribe, so if you call him a 'Negrito' he'll just think you're stupid and don't know anything about his tribe. He would be right. Call him 'Sarge' and he'll know that you mean him."

Sarge was well under five feet. Marsha would have seemed tall next to him. His skin was the color of ebony and his eyes looked right through me. Dressed in a brown T-shirt and camouflage cut-offs with a belt holding a huge machete that almost dragged on the ground, he squatted down on his heels next to the chief. He looked like a little obsidian boulder. He gestured for us to sit the same way. As we struggled with our long legs and inflexible tendons he pointed and laughed.

We settled for sitting cross-legged as the chief gave us one last pointer. "Sarge's dad fought the Japanese in World War II. His grandfather fought the Americans during the insurrection after we took control of the PI. He has tales of great ancestors fighting the Spanish over a hundred years ago. He has no great love of big ugly westerners but he takes pity on you and we pay him well. Plus, he can have all the fruitbats he can eat from off the trees around here. And if you find a snake on your jungle orientation, don't touch it, just let him know, it could be his dinner."

Sarge had his work cut out for him for the day-long course. He first showed us the wonders of bamboo. Making a cup from a section, he drank from it. Then he made a cup for us, complete with a cutout for our "big noses." He seemed to never tire of making that point. We learned how to make fire, boil rice, make weapons, utensils, just about anything a person might need, from bamboo. He wielded his machete like a surgeon's scalpel. I had no idea how his ancestors got by without steel for the big knives but they had survived for sixty-nine thousand six hundred years without western metallurgy, so it didn't seem critical. Jungle vines could be made into temporary canteens, and one type could be used for soap.

The afternoon was taken up with a game of hide and seek. First round was the big-nosed Americans. stumbling around in Sarge's paradise. I hid between two huge supporting roots of a towering top-level triple canopy tree, a giant sentinel guarding its influence. I piled dry leaves up around me and waited. It was a short wait. Sarge came sauntering by and looked right at me through the dead leaves. "I see you, sailuh boy. You hidey-job numbah 10." He scoffed. "If you Huk you be dead already big OK."

He found all of us in short order. Then it was his turn. Chief Partz gave Sarge the nod and off he sped into the verdant arms of his beloved jungle. Moments later I spotted a huge greenish-black lizard bolt off into the distance. I wondered if Sarge was chasing down his clan's next meal. We followed a few minutes later and I felt futility set in immediately. It felt like my first try at the swim test back at Memphis; I was clearly out of my element. I strained my eyes into canopy, I peered around tree trunks, I listened for human noise in the din of jungle sounds. I came up empty handed. Everyone else in the class did too. Chief Partz let the sun filter down into dusk before he called a halt to our fruitless dragnet. With a blast of Partz's boatswain's whistle Sarge materialized phantom-like out of thick jungle air.

We held a final muster as the jungle sounds dimmed and switched to a nocturnal timbre. I received yet another Department of the Navy, FASOTRAGRUPAC certificate dated December 27, 1973.

As any good leader does, the chief asked if there were any final questions. I took a chance. "So Chief, what's a 'benny boy'?"

"Son, this must be your first time in the PI. If you have to ask you don't want to know." He chuckled. "Just be careful close to twenty-four-hundred hours who makes you an offer that sounds too good to be true while you're stumbling back down Magsaysay to the main gate."

"Roger that, Chief." I had no idea what he was talking about.

As we boarded the gray bus to take us back to the *Kitty Hawk* I saw Sarge eyeballing a clutch of bats readying to search the night. My bets were on Sarge sleeping on a full belly.

Ships get rusty at sea but aviators get rusty in port. After the lengthy transit and two week port period recovering from the fire's devastation and huge amounts of San Miguel beer, Air Wing 11 was in need of a serious tune-up. The flight deck was no place to lose the sharp edge honed on white caps and the dark of night.

The *Kitty Hawk* and Air Wing 11 began patrolling the South China Sea within days.

———◦———

WE HAD OUR FIRST man-overboard not long after putting to sea—a sailor from our own squadron. But Aviation Ordnance Airman Bill Clemens didn't just fall six stories from the flight deck. He was lifted up and violently thrown over the side by the jet exhaust of an A-6 Intruder. He got tossed over the catwalk and into the South China Sea like a cigarette butt being flicked into oblivion. Fighting for air as momentum plunged him deep into the water, he struggled to the surface after what seemed a lifetime wrapped in an aquamarine shroud.

I was on the plane guard helo that picked him up. His entire episode—from flight deck to sea back to flight deck—took a total of seven minutes. It seemed like seconds to me. I was in my rescue gear ready to jump but Chief Hatch got me to put my helmet back on, lose my fins and take over the verbal commands to the pilots, the CO and Lt. Rolek. As the chief ran the hoist I helped position the helo over Clemens with directions to the pilots since neither could see where he was.

I wanted to jump badly. After my struggle with swimming going back to Memphis I was pumped and ready to prove I could do it. I felt like a thoroughbred in the gate waiting for a big race; sitting on the helo deck, feet hanging out, mask, fins, rescue harness and UDT vest all positioned as I had been trained, I scanned the water looking for Bill somewhere in the nine foot swells. The chief had me in a firm grip by my harness and I waited for his three taps on my head to abandon the helicopter and plunge into the water. I was off the Internal Communications System—the ICS—and had only his touch connecting me to the rest of the crew. He pulled me back in. I didn't jump, someone had made that decision. We had found Bill and he looked not only alert but ready to climb up the rescue cable hand over hand with or without my help. After dropping off Bill we resumed the plane guard position. It would not be the last time Bill Clemens had an impact on a commanding officer.

The *Kitty Hawk* Flyer for December 31 had a short article on our rescue on page 1, plus a few other headlines culled from wherever they got their news. Venezuela was almost doubling its price of oil to $14.08 a barrel. Air Mail was going up to 13¢ but was postponed for a few months. Congress sent its budget to Nixon, containing $24 billion for the Department of the Navy. Keeping the *Kitty Hawk* afloat would take a small chunk of that.

During the previous Christmas the US was bombing North Vietnam. A year later we were patrolling the South China Sea with no specific orders to attack, support, defend or otherwise involve ourselves with the segmented country called Vietnam. Yet there we were.

Task Force 77 remained on station.

PART THREE
1974

7: CROSSING THE SOUTH CHINA SEA

Lands bordering the South China Sea included the Philippine archipelago spreading down the eastern edge and stretching a finger of jungle-covered island called Palawan towards Borneo. The equator ran along the southern edge. Sumatra, Malaysia, the two Vietnams and China formed the southern and western boundary. Taiwan stood to the north. Gaps between the islands allowed for exit and entry: the Balabac, Malacca, Taiwan and Luzon Straights stood as seaways and national boundaries. Some were contested heavily. The Java Sea and Gulfs of Thailand and Tonkin were smaller bodies of water orbiting the greater South China Sea. The Vietnam war, for America at least, found its birthplace in the Tonkin Gulf. Every sailor on a WestPac knew the basic story, but the series of events that led to the congressional act by that name—The Tonkin Gulf Resolution—would be debated for decades. All I knew was that the Tonkin Gulf, circled by North Vietnam and China, could very well be where we would end up.

Getting there meant traversing the South China Sea. To the south lay the Spratleys, a mix of islands, shoals, atolls and reefs marked "dangerous ground" on maps. Names like Mischief Reef, North Danger Reef and Fancy Wreck Shoal left little doubt. The Paracel Islands occupied a more northern point, almost as if guarding the entry to the Gulf of Tonkin. The South Vietnamese claimed the islands but China wanted control.

Most of the time I had no idea where we were. One morning it became very clear. I walked into the squadron ready room and came face to face with the map of Vietnam. Pulled down from the rack of maps at the front of the room it hung in silence, a quiet witness to the gravity of the situation.

Aircrews had assembled in the early hours of the morning for Lt. Gray's intelligence brief. "You all know this outline, with its thread of land between the Annamite Cordillera and the sea. The rice bowl is to the south in ARVN control, sort of, and the North, with its love-hate relationship with China, holds the power center of the Vietnamese communist party. XO, I believe you've paid your respects to that neighborhood in an F-8, as I read in your file." The new XO, Cdr. Rich, just smiled. He was the only person in the squadron rated to ride the brakes of a Crusader taking up hangar space back at Cubi.

"Many of you have been here before like the XO, many have not. Things have changed a bit. The U.S. is no longer actively supporting the South Vietnamese government through military assistance. We are in a state of ambivalence christened 'The decent interval' by Mr. Kissinger. Perhaps only he really knows what that means. South Vietnamese President Thieu has stated recently that the war has started up again. I don't know what the White House or the Pentagon has in store for us but we are nonetheless here and Vietnam is, as you can see, right over the horizon. Now, I've been instructed to tell you not to go sightseeing on your own if you have a few hours of fuel left at the end of a mission. The coastline from here to here is stacked with AAA sites and they would love to use you as target practice." Lt. Gray swept his pointer from Hai Phong to the 17th parallel. "And if you do go take a look, I don't know if or when we could come get what would be left of your Sea King or crew. So please, don't go looking for trouble. Remember, we want to go home. The NVA antiaircraft gunners already are."

Lt. Gray's brief included how to deal with the annoying Soviet

AGIs that trailed us from the moment we got on station. There was a definite protocol involved, we could not intimidate, harass, impede or otherwise mess with the little rustbuckets. And they were barely more than old fishing vessels fitted with a hefty amount of the best electronics gear the Soviet Union could patch together. They would trail the *Hawk* everywhere we went monitoring every take-off, landing, radio transmission not scrambled and every turn of the ship or bag of garbage tossed over the side. I felt sorry for their crews; the small boats looked barely seaworthy and their job must have been mind-numbingly monotonous. But their radios were likely linked to Hanoi via Moscow, or perhaps the other way, but regardless, our every move was watched. It would have been easy to blow them out of the water, sink them with ease with one of our homing torpedoes, but it was the Cold War. We weren't supposed to make obscene or even benign gestures towards them, lest that become propaganda for front page pictures in newspapers. I thought about SERE school and how they had twisted my words around to make me look like a vicious killer; I sure didn't want the real thing to happen caused by some spur of the moment reaction to flying by one of those AGIs. I behaved myself when we flew by the rusty craft, they taking pictures of me taking theirs, our cameras pointed at each other like short-barreled, soundless weapons of politics.

———— • ————

"DAMN SEA SNAKES, ONE bite and you're dead." Ghost Chief was leaning over the flight deck catwalk, staring down at turquoise-colored water. Tiny starbursts of light reflected back up at our unshielded eyes from small ripples reflecting harsh tropical sun. "Goddamn sea snakes will kill ya' in no time flat, so quick you don't have time to drown. Ya' wanna die from a sea snake bite? Go for a swim in the afternoon, that's all ya' have to do."

"So Chief, what do they look like? And I mean, c'mon, sea snakes? Isn't that like a 'sea bat,' just some old salt's con of a seaman recruit?"

I had come upon Ghost Chief on my way up to the flight deck

for a mission. The chief and I had flown together a few times but he never really seemed to be in the present moment or remember me. Maybe retirement was so close for him he lived in the future. He seemed distant, wistful, reflective, elsewhere. He just looked at me like I was some stranger in a portside bar.

"Goddamn sea snakes, kill ya' in a second." He turned to go below into the chief's compartment, their refuge from the likes of me. Left not knowing if sea snakes were real or the figment of delirious sailors' imaginations, I walked the few steps up to the flight deck of a massive ship sailing a sea licking at the shores of Singapore and Hai Phong.

Aircraft were crammed together: fighters, bombers, sub trackers, reconnaissance, early warning, tankers and our helos all cluttered the flight deck. During air operations there would be constant jet intake and jet blast ready to suck you in and shred you or blow you over the side like so much chaff, as Bill Clemens had found out. The S-2 Trackers were powered by two radial piston engines turning three-bladed propellers in a hum of invisible death. The flight deck was no place to take a stroll during business hours, which could run twenty-four hours straight.

Death—it was never very far away up there. I was amazed more sailors weren't maimed or killed. Aside from the planes there were the catapults and arresting gear; either one could remove a limb before you knew what happened. When you add aircraft to either the cats or cables, you get a deadly combination of incredible power and lethal potential.

HS-4 had a man named Keller who once encountered a propeller before it was finished with its day. He carried a dent in his head where the prop had slammed into his skull to prove it. He lived to tell his story perhaps only because the engine driving the prop he thought had stopped kicked over one more revolution before coughing and sputtering to a halt. His skull carried embedded yellow paint for years. He thought he was a badass dude and after that episode who could argue that.

Flight deck operations were driven at a precision madhouse of a pace. As always, one of our helos was first to launch, and the tension started well before we took to the air. Multiple missions had to be planned and coordinated: A-6 tankers for refueling and E-2 Hawkeyes for early warning needed to be pre-positioned and combat air patrol was crucial, as was the full mission schedule. It took almost 6,000 men to make it all happen. The pressure to be on schedule, to launch on time, to refuel on time, to arrive back on time, to complete the mission, was nerve-wracking. The air boss, the main man in charge of the whole air show, was not to be one of indecision. More than once I caught his booming voice on the radios commanding us to launch immediately—until we were airborne the catapult our helo straddled could not be used.

I saw my other future—my *Hancock* orders—on the flight deck: sailors wearing blue shirts, purple shirts, yellow shirts, white, red, green—every color held meaning. Had I not been offered AW A school I could see the work I would have been doing aboard the *Hancock*. Blue or purple: that would have been my fate. Carrying chains, pushing airplanes, dragging heavy fuel hoses, inhaling raw fuel fumes and jet exhaust for twelve hours a day: that would have been my job. Not exciting, save for dodging a propeller or a jet intake. Menial labor, dirty and exposed to the elements all day long, was hardly the work I envisioned back when I gazed at Navy brochures at the post office. The *Hancock* had been tied up at Subic across the bay from us in December. And while I was flying as the rescue swimmer on plane guard flights off the coast of Vietnam, the *Hancock* was on her way back to the States. That could have been me on CVA-19, but it wasn't. My first deployment would have been all but over but it was just starting. I had no regrets about the decision I had made to go for the AW rate, but I missed home and we had barely started the real cruise.

Vietnam had been unstable since the Japanese Army surrendered control in 1945 and it was no more stable when the *Hawk* cruised the South China Sea January of 1974. All was not quiet on the South East Asian front. Vietnam bled from the DMZ to the Mekong Delta. History was not finished writing the story of Indochina.

I had no idea what was going on back in Washington or the Pentagon, save for a scant few headlines from time to time in the *Kitty Hawk Flyer* or the *Stars and Stripes*. I didn't know if we would be called into action in some capacity should things turn ugly, or uglier. Just over the horizon Vietnamese were dying by the tens of thousands. Political, religious and geographic alliances and influences—plus a hefty dose of chance—determined the dead, while we sailed in our racetrack to nowhere pattern, waiting.

Gandhi's nonviolent resistance seemed a world away. His book gained dog-eared pages as I read about his struggle against the British Empire in India as catapults right over my head slung fighters into the tar-black night with a bulkhead rattling thud. French colonialists had left a mess in Vietnam, and non-violent resistance was not employed by the North Vietnamese Army or the Viet Cong.

———— • ————

As ONE OF THE junior crewmen in the squadron I drew the most flights since even aircrew adhered to the most basic of military rules: shit rolls downhill. I accepted it, it was only fair that I pulled extra flights to fill in. Multiple missions in a twenty-four hour period could leave me drained. One early morning I managed to catch some sleep before my next flight by stretching out on a metal cruise box. Still in my sweaty flight gear, I was so tired I fell fast asleep on the steel crate, my long legs hanging off the end.

At least I had escaped TAD—Temporary Additional Duty. Every sailor E-3 and below was obligated to serve ninety days as part of the ship's workforce. That could mean working in the scullery, laundry, or where menial but necessary tasks were performed. Workers were culled from every section of the ship's manifest, from aviation squadrons to the forecastle division. Chief Hatch helped determine who went TAD, and since I was on his crew I was thus far insulated from going. But time was catching up to me; as other aircrew went my number was advancing toward the inevitability of smelly skivvies or dirty food trays for three months.

In the hard heat of the tropics I longed for the sharp cold of a Colorado winter, the kind of dry cold that freezes your nostrils together, that dries out surface snow to a crisp crust, that hardens ice to an impenetrable layer. The winter sky on the Front Range could be so bright and blue you'd need sunglasses just to walk out and find the morning paper.

But the tropics were an altogether different story in January. My feet developed fungal growths and felt wrapped in a heat pad saturated with poison oak and turned on high. The small green cylindrical cans of foot powder were at a premium, and a ritual of dumping a quarter of a can into flight boots took root. In the confined space of the ship the air smelled like a boxing club workout ring. The ship claimed air conditioning but it was clear where the cold air went: into sensitive electrical equipment spaces. The rest of the ship sweltered in a humid atmosphere permeating every deck. My body felt oily, like I had secreted a second skin, a skin that morphed me into an amphibian of sorts, where I could coexist in the ship's environment and outside of it.

One sweltering night I dreamt about speeding across a shiny, snow covered mountain meadow on my motorcycle, wearing my flight suit and survival vest, chasing a giant sea snake.

Sailors seemed to be falling off the ship left and right, or rather, port and starboard. There were sailors posted on man-overboard watch near the fantail, so as to see any bobbing heads or bodies as the *Hawk* steamed by. Sometimes sailors didn't just fall.

The ship held a brig for sailors violating the UCMJ, the Uniform Code of Military Justice. Violence was rare, it was mostly full of kids caught with drugs, going AWOL, disobeying direct orders or petty crimes like theft. The shipmates in the brig were marched to chow by their guards, culled from the Marine Detachment aboard. The brig detainees had to wear the Navy white hat, dyed pink and pulled down, as an added embarrassment. One afternoon as the inmates were marched across the hangar deck, one decided to go for a swim, bolting from the group and launching himself off the starboard elevator and into the sea.

Clyde Dog was the swimmer on the plane guard helo. We waited in the ready room for his side of the story. Dripping wet from his jump, he couldn't keep his wide toothy grin from betraying a tale he would never forget.

"He was fuckin' nuts! There's this guy thrashing around, trying to swim *away* from me! He didn't want me to get near him! I said 'Do you know where the hell you are?' and he said 'I don't care, I'm swimming home.' So I told him 'Look, you're just shark-bait out here, we're a hundred miles from the closest land and that's Vietnam, you're coming with me.' He was getting ready to fight with me so I pulled back my fist and said, 'This is over with, we're getting out of here right now, you will cooperate or I'll kick your ass and drag you out of the water.' He got this sad look and just mumbled 'OK' and I got him in the horse collar and gave the thumbs up for the hoist. I hope we have a shrink on board, that guy's going to need one."

A pink-dyed white hat floated somewhere along the swells of the South China Sea.

————◦————

TIME COULD BEND AND warp into a seamless ribbon of light and dark; weeks at sea could feel like one endless day, one endless breath, one endless heartbeat. I began to learn on some primal level how to accomplish an incomplete, subcutaneous, superficial sleep, but sleeplike enough that I could drift off into a dreamless state of sedation to the sounds of Phantoms and Intruders being flung off the flight deck a few feet above my head.

The catapults ran within the skin of the flight deck like steel arteries pumping lifeblood. Using water more pure than we drank, steam blasted a catapult piston along its track, slamming it into a water brake before it self-destructed having reached 150 miles per hour in 2.5 seconds in 263 feet of travel. During night operations the slamming could go on in cycles until dawn. Between launch cycles I could sink deeper into sleep and maybe start to dream before the next cycle kicked in, stirring disturbing sleep images of mountains crashing into the sea. Enclosed in my tiny bottom rack, my orange canvass curtain drawn to ward off intruders of other kinds, I felt as alone as a bee larva in a honeycomb of thousands.

Aircrew had no regular schedule; I could fly two or three times a day off any set period, so sleep was essential but not in tune with the shift-imposed rhythms of the day and night crews. That meant, when the compartment lights were on between shifts, I might be trying to get much needed sleep as sailors skylarked and played cards on the corner table. Eleven other guys sharing my cubicle might be trying to get past each other, climb up or down from the top rack two levels above me, might be trying to put clothes away that had been returned from the ship's laundry, while I tried to sleep inches away from the commotion.

And then there were the watches; every sailor—captain or seaman recruit—stood some kind of watch, and the different watch sections rotated the duty. After a long tiring mission and a couple of hours of flight operations disturbed sleep I could be rousted out to go wander some space that needed watching for four hours. We all knew the need for fire watches; no one who was there for the December fire needed to be reminded of that. The Navy depended on our youthful resilience to pull off the demands on our bodies and minds.

But the Navy also knew we needed periodic liberty on dry land to pull it back together before we unraveled into a horde of dysfunctional bodies wandering the flight deck in a stupor, or maybe even jumping off the ship and trying to swim home.

The *Hawk* pulled back into port after weeks of bombing fish and other national security threats.

China invaded the Paracel Islands on the nineteenth of January, fighting off the South Vietnamese Navy and laying claim to the small archipelago. The 7th Fleet had been asked for help by our allies and refused. The *Hawk* stayed moored to the pier as the South Vietnamese engaged in a naval battle, struggling against the superior Chinese fleet to retain their claim to the islands. North Vietnam stood idly by, claiming neither the islands for Vietnam nor indignity at China's military occupation of sovereign Vietnamese soil.

———— ●◄ ————

MAIL CALL WAS FREQUENT while we were in Subic. Mom wrote saying she was considering filing for divorce. The news came as no surprise; I was amazed I had been conceived at all. My parents never expressed tenderness or love towards each other; it had always been antagonistic as far back as my memory could see. They slept in different bedrooms and I had no idea how I came to be but I was too much like both of them to be the result of an affair.

I was relieved that the tension in the house might evaporate with the separation. I was guessing Dad would stay in Texas and Mom would keep the house. I wasn't sure where "home" might be when I got back and I was too far away to do much about it.

I hadn't heard anything from Dad about it but he didn't write much, never was one for letters. Years before, if he was sober he would tell me to keep my head on a swivel as I drove, good advice for a fighter pilot over France and probably not bad advice for a kid driving his first car. If he was drunk he might say he'd killed better men than me, perhaps confusing me with one of his flight cadets from 1942, or maybe just angry and taking it out on me. Either way, drunk or between bottles, he was pretty predictable.

Mom was much harder to forecast; I never knew when I was doing OK or when I was in her sights, like the day she kicked me out of the house when I was seventeen—that came as a total surprise. But I was long gone from having to worry about family dynamics, plus I had missions to fly, flight schedules to type and sea snakes to see for myself.

After a brief period in Subic we steamed south to Manila Bay. Once ashore we saw signs everywhere welcoming us. Most of the signs were posted by bars and massage parlors. The PR folks knew their market.

I parked myself in a decent looking joint and proceeded to swill

San Miguels and ward off the swarming bar girls. I couldn't do both for very long and succumbed to a tall, lovely woman's offer to go "long time." That meant I would "buy" her time away from the bar so the establishment wouldn't lose cash flow by her absence, and stay at her place through the martial law curfew. She entertained me by showing me pictures of her Merchant Marine boyfriend. He may have been going long time with a bar girl in Macao for all I knew, and it was just business anyway. Still, she treated me nicely and took care of all my pent-up needs.

The next morning after the curfew was lifted I headed back to the quay to catch a liberty boat. As I strolled along a wide, palm tree lined boulevard a man ran from behind a building straight towards me, yelling at the top of his lungs. When he got close I could make out the word "Hitler" as he glared at me, screaming, his face flush with anger. I ignored him as best I could and thought how lucky I was that he didn't find me on the street after dark. I was sure he had a butterfly knife tucked away and could make quick work of slicing off a few precious body parts, if nothing but my ears.

Back aboard the relative safety of a carrier at anchor, I camped out on the flight deck for the next few days, reading about Gandhi and catching some tropical sun. At times like that, when the flight deck was awash in sailors relaxing, jogging, tossing a football or just daydreaming, the deck became "Steel Beach." It wasn't uncommon to see aluminum folding chairs and beach blankets set on the unyielding "sand" of the flight deck. It was all we had and it would have to do. The feel of skillet-hot flight deck nonskid on tender skin would not be easily forgotten.

Everyone was getting restless; too much idle time was making us complacent, languid, lethargic. When the order came to weigh anchor and the mighty ship came to life, the open sea beckoned with a westerly wind. All hands found purpose and Steel Beach, cleared of lawn chairs and beach towels and with aircraft fueled, armed and positioned, once again looked like a compact flight deck crammed with lethal combat-ready aircraft.

On station in the Tonkin Gulf, we resumed plane guard and

ASW missions in a rhythm all its own. Once pilots got to know and trust me, they started letting me into their world, the cockpit. Actually flying the Sea King was a whole new experience. Lt. Middleton, who was with the squadron when I arrived, enjoyed getting a crewman at the flight controls. Sitting in the cockpit, feeling that machine respond to every input, every touch, watching the instruments change as if they could read my mind, was exhilarating. I was truly flying the helicopter. I could get used to that.

Back from another plane guard hop and letting me fly for a bit, Lt. Middleton wrestled the big Sea King right into the center of spot 3 as daylight began to fade. Five big white rings painted on the portside deck marked the helo landing spots, and number 3 was forward-most on the angle deck. Once Lt. Middleton lowered the collective all the way, 18,000 lbs of helo relaxed onto its landing gear struts with assertive weightiness claiming, at least temporarily, that small patch of steel.

A strictly choreographed dance of tired kids in different colored jerseys working long hours handling multimillion dollar aircraft was at work. The brown shirts did much of the preparation and launching of their squadron's planes. Removing safety pins from ordnance and landing gear, pulling chocks and a quick once over of the planes were some of their grindingly routine but important jobs.

Airman Roger Feek was pulling just such duty. He was called "Feek the freak," a Huntington Beach surfer dude known for his fondness of weed grown on the Hawaiian Islands. He was working towards getting his plane captain certificate and was trying hard not to miss any details as he helped get us chained and chocked.

It was sweltering on the flight deck. The sunset was again glorious but almost everybody was too tired to notice the rays of pumpkin-orange light streaking across tropical clouds readying to spawn a cyclone.

It was a "hot refuel"; we were staying inside the helo as it took on hundreds of pounds of fuel to feed the twin turbine engines. The combination of fuel fumes and turbine exhaust made everyone's eyes water. I opened the wide cargo door to monitor the refuel. Squatting on the helo deck, I checked the quart-sized bottle of jp-4 fuel sample, looking for contamination. After a cursory glance I gave the purple shirt re-fuelers the thumbs-up to pump 4,000 pounds worth. Feek noticed something dripping from beneath the helo and I watched as he, as a good plane captain trainee should, investigated. The SH-3D was notorious for leaking fluids worse than an English motorcycle with blown gaskets. Several overflow points were on the centerline of the boat-shaped hull of the sea worthy Sea King, and he crawled underneath to see what was dribbling from the bottom of the helo.

A certain amount of fluid loss was expected, but with night approaching he wanted to be sure the helo was going to be air worthy for at least the next six hours. He bent down, extended his hand out and tasted the liquid dribbling from the small tube.

Seconds before this, Lt. Middleton had un-strapped from his quad harness and carefully backed out of the cockpit. During the boring but vigilant starboard delta flight, he let a new copilot, Mr. Voucatich, do some of the flying while he drank hot coffee out of his thermos. By the time we had set down on the deck Middleton was feeling the pressure of several cups of famous Navy coffee.

Hydraulic fluid—purple and machineblood like—had its own taste, as did oil. This dribble tasted like neither to Feek. Puzzlement overcame him. Behind the safety goggles his eyes looked baffled, troubled, confused.

From the left seat Mr. Voucatich held the aircraft to the flight deck and monitored the fueling while Middleton leaned against the control rod compartment, unzipped his green Nomex flight suit from the bottom up, and deposited his member into the little black funnel which was the relief tube. At that very moment, Middleton and Feek were united in a singular event that neither was aware of. Until poor Feek realized just what he was tasting. I could just make out his words over the din of the engines as he put two and two together. "Unfuckingbelievable." He always said it as one long word. Matter of fact it was his favorite word, for good or bad.

I doubted Feek's plane captain training covered that kind of "leak."

I WAS MISSING HOME. wondering when we would be back in the US was a constant fixation, even with more than six months to go. The world's political dynamic caused our schedule to be flexed like a rapier, we at the sharp tip not knowing what was behind the motion; all we knew was that the future was uncertain and unpredictable. Grumbling about it was elevated to an art form by some. "Stand by for a gagglefuck," commented Master Chief Romney whenever our schedule changed. "Those shitbirds at TF 77 couldn't find their dicks with both hands."

But mail call was a connection to home, it could be like water to a man in a desert. Some letters were worth untold contentment. Some were like a knife to the aorta. Plenty of sailors got "Dear John" letters, I could almost smell it on them—the rejection, the sadness, the despair. I would see guys leaning heavily over the railing, looking deep into the sea, thinking about how their young lives were meaningless after having their girlfriends or wives tell them they no longer mattered. And there was no alcohol, there were no bar girls, nothing aboard ship to help distract or drown sorrow.

I longed for a letter from Marsha saying she had thought it all over and changed her mind, that she wanted me back and would be waiting for me when the *Kitty Hawk* pulled in to San Diego later that year. At least I wasn't going to get one of those Dear Johns. I had already drowned my sorrow, already distracted myself from Marsha's rejection. But that didn't stop me from letting my mind wander to the world of ridiculous possibility in matters of the heart. I did get letters from female friends but that was different; it was almost like extended family news, not sweet romantic pillow talk from a warm body back home. The few letters of Marsha's I saved had shed their perfume and lipstick. I finally tossed them off the flight deck, forwarding them to eternity in the South China Sea.

I consoled myself with reading of Solzhenitsyn's horrors of WWI and of Gandhi's vision that all men are brothers. Trying to get a grip on those two commentaries on human nature left me baffled. Solzhenitsyn had been recently banished from the Soviet Union for his book *The Gulag Archipelago*. I would have to put that on my reading list.

I was an ASW aircrewman and had two degrees of advancement to the senior position. ASW 2nd and ASW 1st crewman were the stations one must pass through to be journeyman and master, of sorts. And before I could be eligible for ASW 2nd I had to pass a few hurdles. One was plane captain training. Plane captains and line crew, the aircraft handlers, wore brown jerseys on the flight deck. They were squadron assigned airdales, and younger brown shirts were in training to become plane captains, ones who were not only tasked with servicing their respective aircraft, but must be able to launch and recover them in any weather condition, day or night. Millions of dollars of machine and four lives depended on the SH-3 plane captain. The work was not over after recovery; he must be able to get the helo into storage condition which meant getting the rotor blades folded, the tail rotor nested against the pylon and then ride the brakes—sitting in the cockpit—down the massive elevators into the dark hold of the hangar deck. One of the reasons for riding the brakes was that if the helo fell over the side, the plane captain was to ride it into the ocean, then calmly activate the flotation bags on each landing gear sponson, deploy the sea anchor, keep the helo afloat and wait. It sounded like quite the ride. The responsibility of being a plane captain fell on a kid around eighteen years old. I had that bested by two and was approaching my twenty-first.

When I was assigned to the line shack for plane captain training I was feeling older than most of the gang who hung out in the small, cramped and noisy space near the catwalk for fast access topside. I had gotten my new brown cotton jersey from paraloft, I had to look the part. "It ain't the 'flight deck,' it's the 'fright deck,'" quipped Clyde Dog. "You keep a good lookout while you're up there; it's one thing to fly off the deck, it's another to hang out there for twelve or fourteen hours. And don't worry, the mimeograph machine will be waiting for you when you get back."

I took Solzhenitsyn and Gandhi with me to the line shack which amused the young gang. Endless games of cards, played on a table with a stenciled on checkerboard, filled in between launch and recovery cycles, but I passed on being dealt a hand. Mom had banished me from the living room for her weekly bridge games for years when I was a kid and I never wanted to hear a deck of cards shuffled ever again, so I just tried to read in the dim light when I had the chance. I also brought my NATOPS so I could study for my next checkride. Flunking a flight check was akin to falling flat on your face in front of your girlfriend at the prom night dance. After my struggle with SAR swims I never wanted to feel that kind of disappointment again.

Starting from the bottom rung of line work, I carried heavy tiedown chains to secure the helo and big chocks for the landing gear. Helos were chained to the deck until right before take-off to prevent accidental loss over the side. The chocks resembled big clamps—two blocks on a metal rod that would block the wheels from moving. Those items helped hold on to the government's investment. I also had to remove and insert safety pins in the landing gear struts and other equipment. All this meant working around the landing gear and main and tail rotor blades. It could be done safely but carelessness cost lives. A young brown shirt in a sister squadron lost his life because he forced out a landing gear strut safety pin. I was taught from day one that if the pin didn't slide out it meant the knuckle of the gear was compressed, meaning hydraulic failure. This young kid forced it out, causing the gear and thousands of pounds of aircraft to collapse on his head. In spite of superior skills shown by the pilot in pulling the helo up while still chained to the flight deck, it was too late. It was a grim reminder to listen to what I was being told, if even by a kid younger than me.

<hr />

AIRCREW HAD THREE NEW AWs: along with Malcolm Bryning there were Pete Cassidy and George Wine. All got to meet Chief Hatch in their own special time. We were losing Papa Gire soon and a couple of other guys were getting short, so we needed new replacements even though we would be losing experience. I had flown a little with all of the older guys and would miss their know-how and perspective on the madness that seemed to rule. One of them left a copy of Heller's *Catch 22* in the aircrew space, a parting message.

Personnel rotated at a constant rate. A new pilot arrived named Lt. Sandin. He came with his nickname already, "Zipper," so skinny if he stood sideways and stuck his tongue out he looked like one. He had been with the Navy's in-country Huey outfit flying the Delta. The Sea King must have seemed cavernous compared to the Hueys he had been piloting. I had no idea how the flight deck would look to someone used to putting skids in rice paddies, but it was going to be a new world for him. That he survived his Huey tour was testament enough for me that he knew how to fly helicopters. I trusted him in the cockpit from the very start.

Pete Cassidy got sent TAD to the mess-decks almost immediately. I got passed over once again after I became a certified plane captain. I was flying a lot but Chief Hatch was saving me from TAD. I didn't know why he was taking care of me but it demanded some loyalty to him on my part—not easy with a stern, sharp-tongued old salt. He was retiring soon, not long after Ghost Chief was headed stateside, so I figured I could deal with it.

Night sonar missions were tense. It stressed everyone's nerves, especially in bad weather. AJ Kopp and I had ridden out a night electrical storm which developed so fast the pilots couldn't fly around it much less complete the mission. Our ten tons of helo got tossed around like a pinball. Lightning bolts streaked across the sky sounding like colliding freight trains. For split-seconds the sky would be illuminated enough by the lightning to see the horizon and the *Hawk*'s bulk rolling in the heavy sea state.

AJ looked at me as we waited in starboard delta for all the fixed wing aircraft to get back aboard. "You look scared."

I was. I pushed my fear down deep to where the helplessness already was, since there was little I could do but hold on and watch the storm-ravaged waves pound away at themselves in the electrical lightshow and hope that all our rotor blades stayed where they were.

After multiple attempts at landings on the pitching, rolling deck illuminated by flashes of electrical bolts splitting the night sky apart, all the fixed-wingers eventually got aboard. Then, finally, it was our turn. All we accomplished that night was surviving the storm, but it was enough.

Back in the ready room Allen saw the residue of fear in my eyes—as much as I tried to hide it—and said quietly, "The sea can reach up with a liquid hand and pluck you from the sky like a curiosity, dragging you down into her womb like a child to be reborn into the dark quiet eternity of the deep." He pushed his glasses back up his nose and added as an afterthought, "Looks like you have another flight in the morning, better get some rack time."

I was ready for some in-port time, if nothing else it meant sailors would empty out into Olongapo and the berthing compartment would be relatively quiet. It was a good time to do some reading and I wanted to finish Gandhi's biography. I was fascinated that such a frail man swathed in hand-spun cloth defied the British Empire and brought it to its knees.

We pulled back into Subic in February after racking up flight hours and getting the air wing current on launches and landings, or "traps." HS-4 did plenty of searching for Soviet submarines in the South China Sea, the cat and mouse game played out with lethal seriousness.

———— • ————

THE SPANISH HAD SOLD the Philippines to the US. Before that, Subic Bay had been a Spanish naval center, the original fortress gate still standing on the American base. The gate didn't look like much but times had changed. The Japanese had taken control of the natural harbor during WWII and left their legacy on Bataan, which lay just to the south.

Turmoil had a grip on the islands. My Filipino roommate back in

Memphis told me life was cheap: "Up north a bullet is too valuable to waste on killing a man," he volunteered. That was where western-ers weren't often seen and were rarely welcomed. But Marcos had a firm grip on the populated areas and suppressed dissent. Dissent in some part against the US. My guess was the fellow in Manila was not happy to see American military in his city. Americans had liber-ated the PI during WWII at great cost in lives, but in part because we considered it ours. The Japanese during WWII held the locals in moderate contempt, but Western attitudes were typical at the turn of the century, during the insurgency. At the Cubi library I came across a picture of some Filipinos in a book written in 1899. The caption read: "These people represent the lower orders and mixed races. Their squatting positions, similar to the monkey's favorite atti-tude, indicate no distant removal from the 'connecting link.'"

To be sure, they could squat on their haunches and I couldn't, but I knew Sarge back at JEST felt sorry for me that I was unable to, as if I had been crippled at birth. I was to find out the Filipinos, while squatting on their haunches, were shrewd chess players, mas-ter tacticians of the game. I could have blamed the San Miguel, but I never won a game of chess in the Philippines. I knew few who had. Even Allen met his match in a Magsaysay Street bar.

The Navy scheduled maintenance for its ships in Subic and we were no exception. Labor was cheap and there were plenty of locals willing to toil in the ship's harsh environment. By the thousands, workers would assault the ship and weld, chip, scrape, wire, just about anything that needed to be done outside the confines of clas-sified areas. These men looked frail by American standards. Protein was sparse in their diet. The workers were mostly dressed in second-hand clothes. One of these laborers got nicknamed "Ernie."

Donated clothing from the U.S. showed up on those men. It got donated from San Francisco to Boston, Minneapolis to Houston. A hard working man in Tulsa finally wrangled a new shirt from his boss at the service station and he had a new name tag sewn on. His old shirt was dropped down a metal chute at the collection center, cleaned, mended, folded, boxed and sent to the Philippines. There, at some pick-up point for the needy, it was taken out and placed on a table. Soon along came another hard working man who had no shirt. He saw it, it almost fit, and he came to work at the docks in it. The guy's name in Tulsa was Ernie. Now his name, in the stitched cursive script of the name-tag maker, marked this new owner of the shirt.

Another forgettable meal done I headed to the scullery window to dump the remains of my food in a big galvanized trash can, slide the tray under the window—knife, fork and spoon into the once soapy water, glass in the green plastic tray—and head back up to the O-3 level. There, waiting by the ever-filling galvanized garbage cans, was a line of workers: thin, barely clothed and hungry. They would look for their mark—a sympathetic eye, a distracted glance, an unwary new guy to this ritual. Faster than an F-4 on a catapult launch they would shoot out a hand and grab anything left on the tray, anything: bread, cottage cheese, scrambled eggs, lima beans, beans and franks, boiled cabbage, anything.

And there at the head of the line was "Ernie" of the Tulsa gas station attendant's resurrected shirt. Ernie smiled as best he could. Ernie had a cleft palate that looked like a hatchet had cleaved his upper lip and maxillary bone clear to his nose. Ernie grabbed a handful of cottage cheese off my tray and stuffed it into his mouth, smiling the uneven smile of the deformed. Cottage cheese came spilling back out through the cleft gap, dribbling down his chin. Ernie ate that way every day, when he ate.

I didn't know what to do. I was partly taken aback, partly moved by compassion, partly wanting to push him away. It was the look in his eyes, impossible to describe because it contained at once a thousand expressions and none at all. I didn't know what he was thinking. I didn't want to.

Some days food lost its taste.

———◆———

THERE WERE IN-PORT DAYS when I didn't have the duty, when I

would wander from the Spanish Gate Cafeteria to the movie theater to the PX, finally settling down at Cubi Point's Sky Club.

The PX was a wonderland. The camera selection was enormous; I decided on a Canon 35mm single lens reflex. It had a nice heft and fit my E-3 pay, about a month's worth. Saving up at sea was paying off.

Guerrero Cab Company charged 35¢ for a ride around the bay from the Alava Pier to the enlisted men's Sky Club. Beer was cheap and the bands did their best to mimic the Beatles or Santana or Three Dog Night. Two Go-Go dancers flanked the stage, gyrating on huge pedestals made up to look like drums. The place was cavernous and catered to young sailors and Marines. It was a volatile mix: sailors in from line periods and Marines back from the field. Marines could spend their share of time at sea too, often in a holding pattern, waiting. We all did a lot of waiting.

When I wasn't wandering the sprawling base I stayed shipboard and tended to my NATOPS studies. Sleep was also stockpiled—I knew once we were back at sea it would be in short supply.

I finished reading the biography of India's Gandhi. He had encouraged countrymen to weave their own cloth and make their own salt from the sea, each act weaning the country from British dependency. Each act also defiantly stood up against the Empire, and each act was a nonviolent victory. Gandhi paid for his rebellion with his life, not at the hands of the British but by one of his own. The book left me filled with hope for mankind and yet a deep sorrow for mankind's insanity.

Within months India would share with the world the news of its successful detonation of an atomic bomb.

I had completed plane captain training and received the usual Navy certificate, but it was vital. It was a step towards 2nd crewman and having already taken my E-4 exams, I was working my way upwards. We were still short of 1st crewman so a lot of 2nds were flying as 1st, in the left seat. That meant they were no longer the designated rescue swimmer, but rather the hoist operator/communications crewman. If I made E-4 I would be exempt from going

TAD. As other E-3s in aircrew went my name crept up the list, even as much as Chief Hatch could make it slide back down a notch. I had pretty much resigned myself to going within a few weeks, it was just a matter of time.

———◆———

RUNNING ON THE SHIP was never a good idea, even in port. I hit the small hatch at full speed. Not all were the same size and as I gathered momentum I noticed it looked a bit different. Up close it looked real different but I had no time to do anything but hear the flesh on my skull being ripped by the sharp steel edge of the frame. My full six feet and 170 pounds was rocked back on my heels as the already dim shipboard lighting shrunk into a black tunnel. I didn't hear my body hit the steel deck but Brady did; he was about five paces ahead of me and trying hard to keep that distance. When I came to I had forgotten why I was running after him and he didn't remind me; he just took my arm and draped it over his shoulder, guiding me down several decks to sick bay. My head throbbed and the stitches kept me off the non-existent flight schedule.

Brady said he knew just the cure. "You need a Mojo," he declared, talking me into heading over to the Sky Club that evening. The club sold the local Mojo concoction, coming in its own pitcher and looking innocent, like a fruit punch. The punch was in there alright: it was rum, cherry brandy and San Miguel beer mixed with various juices and sodas in a semi-lethal dose. Machismo, according to Brady, demanded downing at least one Mojo, crossing that bridge to quasi-hallucinations and a days-long, brain hammering hangover.

"Chief Hatch told me you've never really been to the PI unless you've had one," Brady claimed. And he was buying, since it was partly his fault that I was running after him in the first place.

A short cab ride later we were deposited at the club's front door and found an empty table. He got the Mojo ordered and sat back as I contemplated the massive drink.

"C'mon Manthos, go ahead and drink it, it won't be that bad!"

Brady was replaying his strategy from Iwo Jima Eddie's tattoo parlor almost a year before.

"How do you know; how many of these have you had?" I asked, knowing full well he hadn't had a single one. And a single one could change your life.

The first glass tasted great. After the second my stitches no longer hurt. Once the whole drink—two pints of hard liquor and beer to blend it together—was downed I felt pretty damn good. I laughed, told jokes, watched the slender dancing girls do their thing. Soon I was recalling how wonderful and sexy Marsha was, how we had set up house in our little apartment. Then I fixated on how she dumped me for an older guy. My mood swung 180 degrees. I started leaning on my elbows, which kept slipping off the table. I downed another Mojo to really hammer home my new found melancholy. I wanted a third but we were pulling out in the morning.

As I stood up to leave the entire universe seemed to pivot on a sharp spike driven through the top of my skull. Had I eaten anything for dinner it wouldn't have stayed down. I swayed and tottered out to the curb and we caught a cab back to the *Hawk*. That was the easy part. I still had the afterbrow to climb, a hangar deck full of aircraft to navigate and three steep ladders to scale before I could even think of crawling into my deck-level rack and hope for death in my sleep. I couldn't recall how I made it back to my rack but I did. I had proof. At 0600 the bosun's mates hoisted the anchors, snaking hundreds of feet of iron anchor chain—360 pounds per link—down through steel tubes and into the storage locker, all of a dozen feet from my head. Our berthing compartment stood just one frame aft of the chain locker feed tubes. It sounded like the earth was ending in a collision with massive iron asteroids.

As I awoke with a startle to the din I thrashed about in the confines of my enclosed rack, not knowing for sure at first if I was in my grave or just wanted to be. My head felt halved by a splitting maul, the hangover layered over the stitches conspiring to make me swear I would never drink again.

It wasn't going to happen again anytime soon anyway; we were pulling out of Subic, bound for the Indian Ocean. I was on the flight schedule for that afternoon.

——◆——

IT TOOK TIME TO get a ship the size of the *Kitty Hawk* out to sea. I took advantage of the Special Sea and Anchor Detail's work to grab some chow, hoping to keep it down. Scoops of scrambled eggs and toast helped my recovery. It was hard to tell from the mess decks if the big ship was even moving. My head still felt like it had been run over by a freight train but the chow was helping me gain some footing.

Back at the ready room I longed for some thick, heavy Navy coffee, but I had to make it first. Aircrew was tasked with keeping the large coffee urn going and the chiefs in particular expected it to be ready to go at all times. "And don't forget the two salt tablets," Chief Hatch reminded me. I got the pot going and waited patiently for my turn—rank held strong at the spigot. Heavy ceramic mugs were the only way to drink the stuff. I had an official Black Knights mug emblazoned with my name and aircrew wings. It was pretty much standard equipment for flight crews but mine was new and had yet to garner the burnt-umber colored stain in the cup, the proud mark of a never washed and heavily seasoned mug.

Master Chief Romney made that very clear. "Never my boy, never wash my coffee cup, ever. If I catch you doing that I'll kick your head so far up your ass you'll need a window in your belly button to see where you're going." I always knew where I stood with the master chief.

The Navy blend seemed the perfect antidote for the Mojos; after a few cups my head stopped hurting and my vision cleared up. I saw I was on 30 minute alert on the flight schedule so I donned my flight suit, a "zoombag" according to Ghost Chief, and stationed myself in the ready room. I was crewed up with short-timer Jim Helms since Chief Hatch didn't stand alerts. We had a couple of new pilots so we all briefed procedures extensively. Then we waited. Air operations began almost as soon as we cleared Grande Island in the bay. We had a long transit to somewhere—we had no idea where other than the IO, the Indian Ocean—so getting the air wing back up to speed was essential. We had a plane guard helo airborne already, and the launch and recovery of aircraft commenced.

We could watch landings on the closed circuit TV, cross hairs on the camera lens designating the point for a perfect trap. It didn't matter much to helo crews but it passed some time as the coffee worked its magic. All of a sudden there seemed to be a mad scramble on the flight deck, and just then the order came to ready the alert helo. Air Wing 11 had just started flight ops and already something had gone terribly wrong.

"Let's go Thos, the alert helo is still on the hangar deck, let's get down there and ride it up so we have everything ready." Helms was already hurrying out the ready room door. I immediately thought I'd need to get my rescue swim gear on but Chief Hatch, watching the whole event said no, it was a flight back to Subic. I caught up with Helms and ran down the ladders to the helo and started getting it flight-ready. A few moments later the pilots arrived and after a quick preflight they claimed the cockpit as theirs and were ready to get airborne as soon as we were lifted up to the flight deck by the big starboard elevator.

As soon as the elevator hit the flight deck yellow shirts swarmed around us getting us spotted for a take-off. I was still trying to figure out what had happened. I spotted Feek in his brown shirt and motioned for him to come over. "What the fuck is going on?" I asked pointedly.

"An arresting cable broke. This Phantom came in and wham, the cable snapped in two. It whipped around and caught the flight deck safety officer right at the knees. Knocked him over like a bowling pin. Man, there is blood everywhere. They got him down to sick bay; you're taking him back to Subic where they can operate on him. He's done with his career, if he lives. The flight deck safety officer—unfuckingbelievable."

We waited a few minutes after getting the rotor blades turning before the corpsmen brought the injured man out to us. Finally he arrived, a man looking to be in his mid-thirties, wrapped in a Stokes Litter like a newborn baby and carried by four white-shirted medics. Pumped full of morphine he seemed calm, a distant glassy look in his eyes. It took me a minute to take it in. He was short. Shorter than he should be. The Stokes Litter was a wire cradle for the human body— a place for the head, torso, arms, legs—but there were no legs, just empty space. He left his legs wrapped around a steel arresting cable the thickness of a shovel handle traveling 150 miles per hour pulled along by fifty thousand pounds of fighter landing on 300 feet of moving runway. And he was the flight deck safety officer, the person responsible for hundreds of men working in the unforgiving environment of the flight deck, where death was as close as your shadow. The irony stunned me. If he wasn't safe nobody was.

We redlined the helo at 144 knots all the way back to Subic. His bandages were starting to change color. As we left the ship I could see a new cable being fitted to the deck. Flight operations would be back to normal within minutes.

The dangers of flight deck duty were driven home when the officer lost his legs. "Is this a regular thing out here?" Lt. Zipper Sandin asked as he sipped coffee in the ready room the next day. "Regular enough," noted Keller, rubbing the dent in his head.

About three days out the sick-call line ran the length of the *Hawk*. Seventy-two hours was the usual incubation period for gonorrhea and Subic was a massive, sprawling vortex for the disease. Some guys took pride in how many times they got infected. I was glad I had avoided that line but it was pure luck that kept me out of it. The corpsmen would warn sailors: "The third time you get it I make you back into the needle, and it's a big square one." I don't think that scared away many young men; biology was stronger than a threat.

"Better not get the Black Syph," Master Chief Romney had advised us new guys. "You'd be shipped out to an island where they just dump you to rot and be eaten by vultures. The Navy's been sending sailors there since nineteen-and-forty-four. It's fatal, my boy, fatal, no cure, no hope, no going home. You'll never be heard from again. So, hope you just get the drip if you get anything. Me, I sip my Mojo and watch the sun set over the bay. From the Chief's Club, I don't want to look at you shitbirds anymore than I have to."

8: INTO THE IO

We were headed into the Indian Ocean for a big operation but nobody who knew was saying exactly what it was going to be. The rumor mill was working at top speed with 5,800 theories, one for each sailor aboard. Since we sailed right past Vietnam I figured it was something secret, maybe even a classified NASA space mission recovery. HS-4 had made five Apollo astronaut pick-ups, all five in the same helo which we still flew, side number 740. It was painted with number 66 for the NASA missions but the Navy Bureau Number never changed: 152711. The helo had five little Apollo space capsules painted on its airframe, right under the cockpit windows. That was one famous helicopter. Rumors abounded about it too—that it was destined for the Smithsonian Museum when it was retired from flight. That was a long way off; we were still flying that helo on a regular basis for every kind of mission.

We had the last mail call for some time and just one chance to get a letter out since we were getting out of range of the COD and heading into open ocean. We had no idea when more mail would get out or come in; it might be weeks or even a month. Dad sent me a check for my birthday half way around the world from Texas to South East Asia and I was sending it all the way back to Mom in Colorado so she could deposit it in my savings and loan account. That didn't seem out of the ordinary for the way my family functioned.

As I sat in the ready room writing a hasty letter home to go with the check Lt. Gray approached me. He had that "everything's going to be fine" look on his face. "Thos, we need to talk about something very important." That got my defenses up. "Now, you're an aircrewman; that carries with it a lot of responsibility. You're trained to help drop torpedoes on submarines, to kill hundreds of sailors deep under the sea and send them to a watery grave. I know you could do it if we were at war with the Soviets. And dammit, we almost are. That Russian destroyer following us is no canoe; they have us in their sights just like we do them and my guess is a November-class sub is out there too. You have a secret clearance; that means you can be detailed to handle nuclear bombs. The Sea King can carry a nuclear bomb; you knew that didn't you?"

I knew it but never in my mind thought the subject would ever come up. Deep below on the bomb deck there must have been nukes, but for our helicopter? It had been a joke in training when a nuke delivered by helicopter was discussed. Even with an underwater blast at sea the chance of a helo surviving the shock wave was, as Chief Lawson had put it, "unpredictable." No shit.

"Thos, this is the 'Nuclear Weapon Personnel Reliability Program' form. We need to know if we, that is, your country, can rely on you to deliver a nuke. Will you sign it?"

Once again I was put on the spot; would I tell the truth? Would I lie? I hesitated. I had just read about and been deeply affected by the life of Gandhi, a man of nonviolent resistance to the powers that ruled. My convictions were laid bare. If I said no way would I sign that form, no way would I participate in the delivery of a nuclear weapon, I would be done for as an aircrewman. If I signed it I wondered about the gamble; what were the chances? How close to WWIII were we? What if a Yankee-class Soviet submarine surfaced, aiming its ballistic missiles at the US—at Colorado—and was ready to fire? What would I do to prevent that? Would my nonviolent inclinations stop me or would I help drop that sucker without a second thought?

"Lieutenant, I just don't know, I mean, a torpedo is one thing, a nuke is another bag of tricks. That's heavy stuff, nukes. That really bothers me." Lt. Gray took that cue and looked at Chief Hatch, who was standing by the coffee pot.

Hatch came over and settled down next to me in a sturdy, leather-covered ready room chair. "Manthos, everyone on this ship is responsible, in some way, for the overall mission. Nothing happens if the cooks or the yeomen or the clerks don't do their job, even if it isn't handling a weapon. If you're on this ship, you're tied to those nukes stowed below. Nukes bother most people; that's a good sign. Maybe sane people will prevail, but if some nutcase decides to launch them against us, a sane man, like yourself, may have to help stop it. With a nuke."

"I'm confused, Chief."

"Son, if you're not confused, you don't understand the situation."

I signed the form. It stated that the reliability screening had been accomplished, with satisfactory results.

———◦———

I TURNED TWENTY-ONE AS we sailed west through the Malacca Straights. I had counted on, planned on, conspired to be at the Black Knight Inn in Fort Collins when I turned twenty-one, scripted in my mind to be a wild, no-holds-barred blowout party. I wanted to get rip-roaring drunk, wanted to let everyone know, especially those who remembered me as Marsha's boyfriend, that I was twenty-one, a man, and could walk in and order a drink anytime I wanted. And I would want Marsha to know I was there.

It was not to be. Not only was I not at the Black Knight Inn, I couldn't even go to a bar—any bar—and have my first legal hard liquor drink. It was a rite of passage I would never experience. I was on a passage of another sort that day, one I would remember more vividly than a night of drunken revelry.

The Malacca Straights split the island of Sumatra from the Malay

Peninsula. The straights were home to pirates finding safe-haven along the coastline between raids on the high seas. They had sense enough to leave us alone. The western end of the straights emptied into the Bay of Bengal.

We continued to head west, passing by the southern tip of India into the Indian Ocean. Lapping at the shores of Africa, India, Australia and Antarctica, that body of water straddled the Equator and held the Tropics of Cancer and Capricorn at its fringes. The night skies took on a wholly foreign look, constellations I had only read about in science class became part of the nocturnal wonder.

After a long hot mission in the middle of the night—the flight deck calm and the only sound water hissing off the bow—a look up to strange and exotic stars drove home the fact that we were very far from home. Orion stood tall but to the north; something had changed, he was upside down. The Southern Cross became visible, as did Centaurus and Carina.

"Whatcha lookin' for, Thos?" Lt. Sandin asked as we gazed at the night sky after our flight.

"I'm not really sure, Mr. Sandin," I said quietly.

"If you're not careful you just might find yourself." He took a brief moment to look skyward as well, before disappearing below decks.

I would have liked to have camped out on the flight deck that night; it was warm, the breeze felt refreshing and the night sky was magnificent. A squadron of A-6s was being readied for a night bombing exercise, their specialty. So much for sleeping on Steel Beach. I would have to find myself on some other night.

Air wing 11 was flying hundreds of sorties while we steamed west across the IO. The *Kitty Hawk* recorded its 150,000th arrested landing that March. HS-4 flew almost every day: plane guard, ASW and logistics missions filled the schedule. We continued to hone our night flying skills, and often flew when no one else could—it was expected.

An essential element of being able to keep a carrier functioning in remote places was an operation called an UNREP, an acronym for

Underway Replenishment. That entailed vessels such as oilers and supply ships to steam alongside us in a parallel course while supplies were winched over and fuels pumped through thick hoses. An added touch was the VERTREP—Vertical Replenishment. While the supply ship shuffled supplies across, two H-46 helos would fly over nets full of items from the same supply ship, increasing the speed and efficiency of the transfer. It was quite a display of teamwork and coordination, and it enabled us to be underway almost indefinitely. As an E-3 I would be called away for working parties to help stock the hold with supplies, but it helped pass the time.

The weak point of it all was us humans; we needed constant care. March 10 was declared a safety-stand-down and Steel Beach was open for business. Special Services checked out footballs and baseballs while the Rod and Gun Club held a skeet-shoot off the number four elevator. More than one football was lost over the side, and getting your pay docked was almost worth watching the ball bob in the wake as we steamed on at thirty knots. Long passes called for a keen awareness as to where the end zone was; too far and a sixty-foot drop awaited the receiver.

Food was the main attraction. Four serving lines were formed on the flight deck and big open grills were set up to cook tough but delicious steaks. They tasted like they had been frozen solid in Antarctic ice for a decade but it was a nice departure from the usual fare, and we could relax on the deck and enjoy the meal without the hazards of flight ops. Big containers of bug juice were stationed at the end of the grills; no meal went without the luminescent green or orange drink being available. I had no idea what it was made from and color had no bearing on the flavor, which seemed to be primarily an acid-like solution. If the ship had sugar it would be added, if we didn't, then it had a special bite. Sometimes sterilized milk was available. It tasted like sticking your tongue on a 9 volt battery: a bitter, sharp, edgy liquid that had all the flavor killed off, replacing it with a long shelf life. Sometimes just water, even if it was warm and slightly salty, was the best choice.

I spotted some squadronmates and fell in line behind Feek. "What do you make of all this, pretty cool, eh?"

"Bitchin'." Sometimes one word was all you could get out of him. I ate my fill and leaned over the port catwalk railing. There was no land in sight, just the vast expanse of blue-green ocean accented by the small bow wave and frothy green water churned up by four huge propellers below the stern. A watery emerald tail trailed the carrier almost to the horizon. The sun's penetrating light thrust into the water like copper spears, keeping pace with the ship as if there were some aquatic race to nowhere. "Vast" was too small of a word; there was no word to describe the enormity of the ocean. My so-called supercarrier looked pretty big tied up to the pier in San Diego. A thousand feet long, it was getting smaller by the day. Some called a carrier a floating city but mostly it was a cramped ghetto of working-class men.

The hours were days and the minutes blended into each other like drops of rain into a sea, lost among the vastness of time. Everything was endless: the horizon, the sea, the sky, all shades of blue and green and punctuated by phosphorous-white clouds that drifted through that patch of universe pressing down on our watery realm. I'd done my work for the day; the flight schedule was posted stating no flights. The crew log books were brought up to date, I managed to get some chow, and I stared into the deep.

The water curling off the bow spewed a hissing sound as if it were annoyed we were disturbing it. Row upon row of swells churned up by distant storms marched through the ocean bound for beach assaults on unseen shores, slowly rocking the big ship side to side in rhythm to some watery pulse older than mankind. It was soothing, as if the ocean was rocking an orphan. The sea breeze, partially created by thirty knots of speed, felt cleansing.

Down below, the crew compartments were said to be air conditioned. Sure, stale air circulated through miles of tubes and pipes with all the force of a yawn. It was stifling with thousands of sweating bodies in close quarters.

The sun hadn't moved. If it weren't for the bracing wind I might have thought the world stood still. My mind couldn't keep itself busy. Throwing something over the side might have given me some sense of contact with the water, and it was oddly satisfying knowing that whatever was tossed sixty feet below would be gone forever. I wanted to reach down, stretch my arm to the inviting water and sail my finger across the blue velvet surface, cutting a fine wake of tiny ripples that cascade away, scattering thousands of pinpoint reflections in a blinding array of pure hypnotic light.

Porpoise raced from a mile away to play in the bow wave of the massive ship. They grinned that evolutionary grin in an almost mocking way, as if to say "we have the key to sanity." They were calling like a siren's chorus; "jump, jump, join us!" I wanted to grow gills; I wanted to de-evolve, to dive sixty feet to the water below in an impact of refreshing coolness and weightless exhilaration and join them in their world.

Nothing was on the horizon. Nothing to look at to give some sense of dimension, distance, human life beyond our own little floating galaxy. We were churning toward a destination so far away that even at thirty knots I didn't know how we would ever get there. It would have been madness to jump, but a madness that could be right and true and sane.

It seemed like I'd been staring at the sea and daydreaming for hours. I went below into the labyrinth of steel passageways to see what my buddy Pete Cassidy was up to. All he said was, "What, back so soon?"

———◆———

THE FOLLOWING DAY AIR operations were back to normal. As aircrews congregated in the smoke-filled ready room for their respective briefings, Malcolm Bryning was nowhere to be seen. Being late for a brief was a major screw-up. I had only seen it once before, and that was Chief Hatch who calmly stated, "Well, nine times out of ten I'm always on time." But it was Malcolm who was late and as a lowly E-3 he was moments away from some serious shit. Lt. Zipper Sandin, the mission briefing officer, wasn't too pleased.

"Thos, where the hell is Bryning? I better see his skinny butt in the next five minutes or he's going to be bailing out the bilges with a shot glass."

"Well Mr. Sandin, I'm pretty sure I saw him down at paraloft drawing a new flight suit. The last one he had got a big tear in it when he snagged the leg on the cargo door."

Zipper saw through my shallow attempt to cover for my buddy and was setting to skin him alive when Malcolm burst through the ready room door, out of breath and looking guilty as hell, his flight suit zipped up to his chin. We were near the equator, it was over ninety-five degrees in the confined space of the ship's compartment, and with hazy-gray cigar and cigarette smoke blanketing the stale air, I failed to grasp why he would subject himself to that discomfort. Malcolm sat down in a heavy metal briefing chair, pulled up the arm rest writing board and tried to blend in. It wasn't working.

Zipper gave him a look and admonished, "Bryning, I don't know what you've been up to and I don't want to hear about it. Next time, no slack, I have a little talk with Chief Hatch. He'll make sure you're here on time."

"Yes Sir, Mr. Sandin, it won't happen again," came his humbled reply.

After the formal brief, the pilots splitting off to discuss the mission, Malcolm and I had a moment to talk. "So where the hell have you been? You're on an aircraft carrier for fuck's sake, how far could you be from here? And why is your zoombag zipped up all the way, you skinny bastard, trying to sweat off a few pounds? It's hotter than the hinges of hell's door in here."

"Thos, you won't believe what just happened."

I could tell a tale was about to be spun. Unzipping his Nomex flight suit to cool off a bit, he revealed a bony, pale and hairless chest. Now I was really confused. There wasn't much that's more uncomfortable than a fuel, oil and hydraulic fluid stained flight suit soaked in sweat and left in a locker to baste in its own juices. They itched, scratched, annoyed, rubbed and chafed. Chief Hatch used to say he wouldn't wash his, just change the oil every few months.

Pulling a pack of smokes and his Zippo from the sleeve pocket of his flightsuit and lighting up, Malcolm began his tale. His right arm, broken by a horse in his youth and bent at an obtuse angle from his body, gave his story an exclusively Malcolmesque flair. The ever-present Marlboro dangling from his fingers drew random smoke trails in the stale air as he gestured.

"You remember those T-shirts I got at ship's stores, the size 52 longs?"

"Yeah, sure I do. They came down to your knees like a goddamn dress. Guess that's one of the bennies of being scrawny and out to sea for weeks at a time—no chance finding something that fits."

"No shit. And speaking of, well, I've been plugged up for days. Those recycled leftovers were cemented to my innards."

I was amazed at the creativity of the cooks to recombine what was left into new and interesting colors and textures. Dehydrated peas mixed with dehydrated cottage cheese was my favorite. How often could already reconstituted anything be continually reconstituted? On top of box lunches smelling and tasting like jet fuel, digestive tracts had their work cut out for them. Being plugged up for days was a way of life at sea.

"So what happened?" I mumbled, knowing full well I'd get the whole story.

"So I had to crap like an elephant. That ain't easy when you sit two feet across from some fat ugly first class who's still farting out the last of the San Miguel from Olongapo liberty weeks ago. So I was just sitting there squeezin', it was feeling like a python was slithering out of my ass. But something was missing. The sound was missing. You know, the 'plop,' the signal that ground zero is in range, that all bombs are on target."

True, even with the ship's salt water flush in a stainless steel toilet, the sounds remained the same. "What are you trying to tell me?"

"Thos, I'm trying to tell you that those goddamn T-shirts are so long on me that when I sat down, it stayed around my ass and thighs like a skirt. I never even thought to check, hell, why should I? But there it was, the size 52 long wrapped around my legs as I sat. Don't you get it, Thos? I shit into my damn T-shirt! I never imagined I'd have to hike up my undershirt just to crap. Never did it before, but then shirts never came down to my knees before. All this happening while I got this brief coming up in a few minutes. I sat there for what seemed like forever, thinkin' about my next move. Finally I was alone in the row of stalls. No doors, no privacy, just a chance to get the hell out of there."

"Please, fill me in on your evasion and escape technique."

"Well, it sure wasn't SERE but I knew I had to get out of that shit-filled shirt; my survival knife was, uh, inaccessible, and I was late. I carefully took the edge of the shirt by my knees and stretched it up as far as it would go, bending down to try and get my head back through the opening in the top."

I was beginning to conjure up a scene in a contortionist's ballet: a skinny kid entangled in a massive T-shirt filled with a week's worth of crap. It required a degree of flexibility unbeknownst to Malcolm before and perhaps since. All this while his flight suit, basically a big overall, entangled his legs.

"I leaned way over, pulled the front edge of the shirt over my head and was in the process of extricating myself when I noticed a pair of boondockers briefly pause in the passageway between the commodes. They weren't there very long, guess he couldn't handle what he saw. Anyway, I managed to get out of the goddamn thing."

"What did you do with the, uh, bundle?"

"What do you think? I left it there!"

"You bastard! You're going to make some other poor sonofabitch clean it up? I have a feeling this story will live on in that unfortunate sailor's WestPac tales."

"What else could I do? I'm just glad I got out of there without being seen."

"What about your name? Did you stencil your name and squadron on the shirt so you'd get it back from the laundry?"

"Uh, yeah, guess I forgot about that," came a rather humbled response, a glimmer of guilt in his eyes.

"Malcolm, for the remainder of the WestPac I would keep an eye over your shoulder; there may be somebody looking to return something you left behind!"

9: SHELLBACKS AND TUSKER LAGER

After not knowing what was going on for weeks we were finally told where we were headed next. Kenya. East Africa. That meant we would be crossing the equator. That also meant any sailor not previously initiated from lowly pollywog to noble Shellback would be so in a centuries-old rite.

We reached the equator on March 18. Master Chief Romney tried to talk Mistrot into standing an equator watch, where he would look for the big line in the water, like the way maps were marked. "Lookie here Mistrot, right here is the line on this map, see? So, all you have to do is look for the equator line in the water; you should see it, it's just under the surface, about fifty yards wide too, hard to miss."

"Oh, I'll miss it alright, Master Chief. You fooled me once but you won't get me twice. I'm not that dumb!"

"OK my boy, but remember, you're a pollywog, so don't let me catch you topside, lad. Oh, and before you secure for the day get me a quart of relative bearing grease!"

I was a pollywog too, but somehow the master chief didn't have me in his sights. I had the duty that day, and the plan was for the whole ship's duty section to go through the initiation first, so we could get cleaned up and resume our watches. It didn't take long for things to get started.

"All foul pollywogs on the morning watch muster on the number one aircraft elevator immediately!" The booming voice of Davey Jones, King Neptune's scribe, belted over the ship's 1MC intercom. My time had come. We were crossing the line. Longitude: 046 degrees, 18 minutes, 8 seconds, Latitude: 00000. The line, not often crossed by Europeans or Americans, was a rare event heralded by the ancient tradition of initiating sailors into the realm of the Shellback. Hundreds of years old, the ceremony had changed little except wooden hulls had been replaced with steel, grog was outlawed and flogging was an historical blemish. The equator was spoken of reverently, and those not yet crossed would never forget the day they did.

Events leading up to the initiation had been building for days. For a week prior, leftover food was collected in big galvanized steel garbage cans. Mingling rainbow colored Jell-O with meat scraps and gristle, pancakes with lima beans, apple sauce with eggs, stale cake with ketchup and mustard, breakfast with dinner, leftovers were abandoned to rot in a compost-like heap soon the color and texture of moldy oatmeal. The cockroaches wouldn't even get close. The cans were left in conspicuous places at the end of the chow line both as a collection point and as a reminder of things to come.

Other preparations were also underway. Shellbacks—those previously initiated—would make threatening noises in passageways. Rank meant nothing. No one was exempt from the ceremony, only those who opted not to participate were left alone.

A beauty contest was staged and there was no shortage of ugly seamen donning palm-frond skirts, coconut-shell breasts and mop-head wigs. A big gap tooth grin and hula girl tattoos were a bonus.

The watch section assembled as ordered by King Neptune, on hands and knees on a big aircraft elevator. The gray/black non-skid surface felt like hot 40 grit sandpaper. We bowed our pathetic heads in respect for our superiors. As the big elevator rose from the hangar deck to the flight deck, a scene unfolded before our stolen glances that stepped out from a high school play from hell. Contraptions of torture of all kinds, jury-rigged together by semiskilled hands, dotted the huge flight deck. A maze of stations manned by pirates of all colors and sizes awaited us. The Skull and Crossbones flew from the mast, waving like the mocking hand of fate.

It was an endlessly sunny equatorial day—hot, humid, and daunting. All pollywogs were decked out in the designated uniform: trousers and shirt both inside-out. One by one we were brought forth before the arbiter of our fate, the man himself, the judge, jury and executioner, Neptunus Rex! The trials were swift; there were many pollywogs to be transformed into worthy seamen. Charges were read: failure to be seaworthy; guilty! Foul and wretched pollywog; guilty! And so on, each charge trumped up, a kangaroo, or rather, Shellback court so slanted truth slipped off. I knew I was worthy, but I had to prove it. Still on hands and knees, I crawled to the first station of my pilgrimage.

There sat the Royal Baby. The fattest, grossest sailor found among the Shellback crew, he was naked above the waist. His belly button, at eye level, peered out from a layer of shiny black grease like a bubble on an oil slick. "Kiss the Royal Baby's belly," boomed the order from a minion of his regalness. The fat son-of-a-bitch then grabbed my ears and rubbed my face into his belly, smearing thick grease into every pore.

"Quickly now," came the directive, "go see the Royal Dentist!" Still on all fours, still crawling across skillet-hot nonskid, I scurried through a gantlet of pirate-uniformed Shellbacks wielding yard-long lengths of old fire hose. These snapped at my stern, lapped at my beam, and danced on my main deck, hurrying me along to the Royal Dentist in short order.

Once there a sinister looking pirate, complete with black headband, cardboard cutlass and a syringe the size of my forearm, spewed instructions. "Open wide, I have to examine your pathetic teeth, pollywog. Great shark shit! I see cavities numerous as barnacles on a sunken hull! I must administer medication." And with that proclamation he proceeded to squirt a concoction resembling vinegar, rotten peanut butter, pepper, Tabasco and sardine juice into my reluctantly open mouth. "Swallow, you worthless piece of whale dung!" I tried, I failed, I drooled the cocktail from hell's happy hour all over my chin and chest. "Get thee away, unworthy creature, away!"

On I crawled to a trough hastily made of plywood lined with black plastic bags, forming a tube. Plywood, on an aircraft carrier? What the hell for, to fix a leak in the thick steel hull? But that was not the time to ponder such mysteries; it was the time to low-crawl through the black plastic tube. It was filled with the rotten food so earnestly saved that past week. Crawl I must, or forever remain a lowly pollywog. It was small enough that I had to slither on my belly. Slithering was easy, the slimy contents facilitated rapid movement. I felt a bit like the contents of a dysentery attack. The Shellbacks astride the tube, however, made sure travel was slow. I was sat upon several times, so as to make sure I paid my dues.

After transiting the tube I emerged, only to be confronted by a big tub of salt water. What lay ahead I didn't know, but in I plunged, as ordered by yet another sailor dressed as a buccaneer. Up I came for some air, and much to my delight, was welcomed to the realm.

"Avast matey, ye are now a Shellback!" proclaimed the seadog. And so I followed the line of newly-christened Shellbacks to the stern of the ship where I peeled off my inside-out uniform, now right-side-out, and hurled it into the briny equatorial water. The trail of floating dungarees signaled our course for miles.

After going below and showering, trying but failing to remove some of the smell, I returned to the flight deck to witness my squadron going through the routine. Chief Rice, who was replacing Chief Hatch in aircrew, had never crossed in all his years of active duty. He caught a little extra for that.

As for me, there was a lingering odor I couldn't get rid of for days. After some deep thinking I realized that my thick, Greek heritage mustache, the sign of virility I clung to so dearly, harbored odors un-removable. It being so close to my nose and the smell impossible to ignore, I broke down and shaved it off, ridding myself of the stench and feeling the sea breeze on my upper lip for the first time.

Less than a week after the Shellback ceremony we dropped anchor off the coast of Mombasa, Kenya. The *Hawk* was far larger than anything the harbor could handle and the water too shallow for us to get very close. We were some distance out which meant riding liberty boats ashore, but we had fewer available than in Manila. The powers-that-be made the decision to reverse the watch and liberty schedule so that each watch section only had one day of liberty for the enlisted men, resulting in one day out of six at anchor for me to get on dry land for the first time in a month, with a long wait in lines to get ashore and return. The hope was that the city wouldn't be overwhelmed with sailors. We were lectured to behave well, to act as ambassadors and not cause any trouble. We were also warned about street drugs; street heroin was uncut, potent and cheap. I had no desire to do drugs but a cold beer was sure sounding good. The local brew was called Tusker Lager.

As I waited several days for my watch section to have liberty I caught up on my sleep and finished Solzhenitsyn's *August 1914*. The last line read: "Untruth did not begin with us; nor shall it end with us."

Finally my day came. I suited up in my best liberty clothes as per Navy regs and took my place in a line stretching the length of the hangar bay. That was one of the few times I envied the black shoe Navy sailors and their "tin cans." The smaller ships in our battle group were able to pull right up to the pier.

Feek was in front of me and hadn't paid any attention to the regulations about what we could wear, which were more strict there than back in the PI. He had on a tie-dyed Grateful Dead shirt and frayed cuffs on his bellbottoms and got turned away to change his attire. That meant losing his place and having to start all over again waiting in line once he switched clothes. He turned and sauntered back up to the berthing compartment, muttering obscenities under his breath.

"So long Feek, see ya' in another six hours."

The forty-five minute boat ride took us up the mouth of a small river into Kilindini Harbor and the old port section of town. It looked like a scene out of a Lowell Thomas documentary. I was in equatorial Africa. The very sound of it conjured up images of rusting freighters, pirates, spices and trade winds. And I was standing in the epicenter. Arab dhows filled the harbor. Merchant ships flying a multitude of national flags were moored. Laborers toiled under the harsh sun carrying bundles of ivory and fabric and ebony and crates holding mysteries. Slaves had been sold and traded out of that place, one of the few commodities no longer available.

As I walked into town I saw shops with tiger hides, mosaic patterned snake skins, dagger scabbards of Rhino horn. Apothecaries full of ancient potions, elixirs, extracts and remedies based on folklore and tradition dotted narrow back-alleys, the air around them heavy with fragrant wonder. There was a timelessness that penetrated my senses to a degree unknown before. A cornucopia of languages filled my ears: English, Swahili, Arabic, German, Indian; it all swirled around my head mixing into a cocktail of unintelligible puzzlement. Beggars were everywhere and seemed even more destitute than the kids back in Olongapo. One man, his legs twisted into a pretzel, hobbled on his arms after me for a block.

I sought refuge from the beggars and street hawkers in a bar where I dared to get a bite to eat and have my first Tusker Lager. The beer was frothy, just one shade past warm, and tasted wonderful. I noticed a painting on the wall across from my table. It was of a reclining nude black woman, her hair in an Afro, her skin the color of sable. She looked beautiful and familiar. I stared and stared but couldn't for the life of me remember where I had seen that painting.

After leaving the bar to wander the streets, where I had seen the picture came to me. But the first time I had seen it, the woman was a Nordic-looking blonde. Her picture had been a men's magazine foldout, where blondes predominated. The local artist had taken her form and transformed it into something more relevant.

Finally settling down in a spot Hemingway would have approved of, I enjoyed more Tusker Lagers. Big, slow-turning ceiling fans circulated the dense air as musky odors mixed with the ether. A small group of musicians ensconced in a corner strummed ouds and beat tablas to an exotic rhythm. An elephant foot umbrella stand stood by the door. Wildebeest heads dotted the walls. A small monkey hung from the exposed rafters. I could hardly take it all in.

Many Tuskers later it was time to hit the beach in reverse, and wait my turn to ride back out to the ship before my liberty expired at 12 p.m. While piled up in a gaggle of sleepy, drunk and irritable sailors, a group of officers in starched dress whites, gold braided caps and swaggers waltzed down the pier past hundreds of us and proceeded to board the admiral's launch. I, as one of the drunk and irritable sailors, muttered words which captured the sentiment of the entire collection of enlisted men. "Fuckin' officers." Much to my surprise, from out of the sweltering African night came a very familiar voice.

"Careful, Manthos." It was Cdr. Rich, my squadron executive officer. And he was my judge, jury and executioner, all rolled into one. As blood drained from my body, as a vision of hanging from the yard arm passed before my eyes, I managed to yelp a pathetic "Sorry, XO." He boarded the admiral's launch without another word aimed at my heart. I could only guess what his companions had to say about one of his own sailors mouthing off.

When I encountered him the next day nothing was said, implied or hinted at—by him or by me. I wasn't about to bring it up. I was a very well-behaved little sailor for a long long time. And I learned a couple of lessons that night. Lesson one: keep my mouth shut. Lesson two: good leadership sometimes only requires a few words. He had my undying loyalty for the remainder of his command.

We were in port for a few more days after my ten-hour liberty break from the ship. One night Captain Kirksey came up on the 1MC and made an announcement while I was sitting in the ready room reading Kurt Vonnegut. "This is the captain speaking, listen up. Turn on the closed circuit TV and watch what comes on. It is videotape of one of your shipmates. He isn't looking too good, is he?"

The ready room TV was switched to the right channel. The sailor wasn't looking good at all. He was being hoisted aboard in a Stokes Litter, while convulsing and shaking violently.

"His name was Willie. I passed the word that drugs in Mombasa were lethal but Willie didn't listen. You think doing drugs is cool? Well, Willie's cool. Willie's in the meat locker." Willie's overdosed body was kept in cold storage until he could be shipped back to the States, which wouldn't be for some time. It didn't take long for ghost stories about Willie haunting the food storage freezer to start circulating.

The U.S. Ambassador to Kenya sent his congratulations to the *Kitty Hawk* on our exemplary behavior while on liberty in Mombasa.

While we were at anchor George Foreman TKO'd Ken Norton in the second round of their heavyweight bout. Foreman was unstoppable. Brady didn't take a bet.

I had several days to sleep off my Tusker Lager hangover before the special detail hoisted the two thirty-ton anchors from African waters. It still made a racket but I was prepared for it; I was topside watching the forecastle crew hose off Indian Ocean mud from the port anchor as 60,000 pounds of steel neared the hawsepipe.

We were on our way to Iran.

10: THE PERSIAN GULF

The main reason for pulling us off the line in the South China Sea and sending us out into the IO was now clear. We were headed to Iran and were going to play host to the Chairman of the Joint Chiefs of Staff, Admiral Thomas Moorer, the highest-ranking military man in the United States Armed Forces. And he had invited someone to lunch. The Shah of Iran, better known as His Imperial Majesty Shahanshah Aryamehr, was to join Adm. Moorer for a visit to the *Hawk*. Tagging along would be Richard Helms, the Ambassador to Iran and former head of the CIA. I had no idea why the ex-director of the CIA was where he was, but it all seemed a bit convenient, given the oil and Middle East situation. I wondered if he was still working for the agency while masquerading as an ambassador. The *Hawk* was going to put on an air show for the heavy-hitting guests, and we as a squadron would be flying the Shah out to the carrier.

That meant a little housekeeping. The whole squadron pitched in to hand-wash and then hand-wax all ten of our helicopters. The soot from the twin turbines was caked on and the salt air had taken its toll on the airframes. The interior of helo number 740, the one tasked with flying the Shah out to the ship, got fresh paint in classic Navy gray.

The CO briefed us on the mission as we departed African waters heading north. He was going to fly the Shah along with Lt. Rolek and Chief Hatch so I was included since I was Hatch's crewman. We put together three H-3 crews alongside four H-46 crews from other battle group ships for a major beach assault. But it wasn't combat; it was politics. We would be flying to Bandar Abbas, Iran.

Chief Hatch had kept me off the mess decks since December but it was getting harder for him to do. There were still plenty of menial jobs: field day the aircrew space and ready room, chip off old paint, paint on new red lead primer, polish the knee knocker step, polish the brass that dotted the bulkheads, go on working parties, garbage detail, it was a long list. I was due to make 3rd class petty officer soon, that would exempt me from the work details and TAD duty. I was counting the days until I heard the news.

Clyde Dog and AJ Kopp managed to scrounge-up a big floor fan to stave off the equatorial heat. It was magnificent. It stood almost five feet tall with a blade span of several feet. It kicked up its own little monsoon wind, bringing welcome relief from the stifling air. They got a bargain on it since the blade guard was missing on one side. No big deal, just stay clear of it.

AJ was spinning a tale of his last WestPac as we headed north. One to talk with his hands, he gestured widely about a close call and managed to slam his arm into the unprotected blades. They shredded his arm in a flash. The fan splattered fresh blood all over the small compartment. It was over so fast AJ didn't even cry out, but muttered, "I guess I should get down to sick bay." He turned pale and started to wobble so Clyde Dog braced him up and got him down to sickbay. When he got back he was still pretty shaken, his arm wrapped tightly in bandages. "Goddamn fan. I'm tossing that fucking thing over the side."

"Can ya' hold off until we're past Hawaii headin' home?" asked Clyde Dog."

DURING OUR TRANSIT TO the Persian Gulf a Soviet "recovery" ship trailed us like a lost puppy. It was larger and cleaner than the AGIs off Vietnam; it even had a small swimming pool on the aft deck. And it carried a small helicopter. Their helo buzzed us one day like a big cicada. Russian aircraft designers seemed to like the counter-rotating blade concept; the helo had the same opposite spinning dual rotorblade setup as the Bear bomber had dual propellers. With counter-rotating rotor blades the helo, called a "Hormone," didn't need a tail rotor since the dual blade-sets offset the torque. The fixed quad landing gear looked like the legs of a flying wasp, dangling down and impeding forward motion. An odd looking contraption, it wasn't very fast or sleek, but this time it was their crewman taking our pictures from the back of the aircraft. The big red stars on its tail rudders were another reminder that the Cold War was following us. Unless we had chased it into the Indian Ocean. My turn would come to fly past that helo's mother ship and take my own pictures.

As we neared Iran the air wing worked on its "airpower demonstration." After all, that was what we were all about: air power. HS-4 was going to put on a sub tracking demonstration with three helos dipping sonar and running MAD gear, while the jets were displaying their capabilities. It was tight airspace for that much activity but it was being well rehearsed. After an A-7 did a strafing run with its multi-barreled gun sounding like thick denim fabric being ripped, A-6s did precision bombing runs. I could feel the concussions pass through me and slam into my spine. As the Intruders cleared out, two F-4 Phantoms came at each other at deck level, on a collision course. At the last second they rolled 45 degrees in opposite directions, almost rubbing bellies as they passed each other. They then leveled out, pulled up into a vertical climb and spun on their axis, letting flares fly off their wings and leaving spirals of light behind them as they punctured the clouds. The final demonstration was an RA-5C Vigilante inbound at supersonic speed, right at deck level. As it soundlessly passed portside of the flight deck the pilot dumped raw fuel which was ignited by the after-burners. The fuel became a huge ball of flame following the A-5. It was awesome.

An overflight of twenty jets all in perfect V formation finished the show. A picture taken from above the overflight just as it passed the bow of the *Hawk* was snapped by the Vigilante from high altitude. The big carrier really did look like a coffin from the air.

We were issued new gear for the important flight; it seemed no expense was spared in making a good impression on the Shah and his entourage. I replaced my SERE damaged flight boots and polished the new ones to a bootcamp inspection shine.

"Crews, listen up." Cdr. Pearigen was doing the brief. "Today we're going to fly into Bandar Abbas; it's a dry run. Tomorrow we will carry the Shah and anybody else he wants in helo 740 and bring them back to the *Kitty Hawk*. If you have to speak to him, address him as 'Your Royal Majesty,' try not to look into his eyes, and for God's sake don't screw up. Now, he is a certified helo pilot and will sit left seat, so he may want to do some flying. Lt. Rolek, you sit in the jump seat and back me up on the throttles and instruments. Chief, you and Thos take care of the guys in back."

We did the dry run into Bandar Abbas, avoiding a rugged mountainous island off-shore. We were told that insurgents were on that island and they wanted the Shah dead, which meant they would do their best to shoot us down. We stayed clear.

Once on the tarmac we had a few hours to kill. It was a desolate place: desert as far as my eyes could see. The other crewmen and I strolled into the terminal. As a handful of western military in strange uniforms we got a lot of stares. Bedouins were gathered around a central seating area, men smoking big water-pipes, women covered head to toe. We were also watched closely by Iranian security, and were told in no uncertain terms, no pictures. I managed a cloudy picture of the terminal through the cargo door window of my helo on the way in.

As I took in the sights around the terminal I noticed a P-3 Orion parked not far from our helos. I strolled over, chatted with a few of its crew and took up their offer to enjoy the shade provided by the big wings. Within a few minutes a jeep drove up with the rest of the crew. I immediately recognized one of the guys in back. It was Mike

Johnson, from my boot camp company and Memphis. There we were, standing at 27 degrees North Latitude and 56 degrees East Longitude, and we ran into each other. The Navy could make the world a very small place. After Mike and I got caught up on our lives it was time to head back to the *Hawk* and prepare for the big event.

The next day was the real thing. Shiny waxed helos converged on the small airstrip in crisp formation. Once on the ground we were lined up beside our respective birds and waited. After a short bit a Leer jet made a spot-on landing and taxied up to a very red carpet. Out came the Shah himself. He walked down a reception line of Iranian military and every one of the high-ranking Iranian generals, admirals and diplomats bent down, genuflected and kissed his ring. I doubted anyone wanted to stand out as a dissenter. Next was the line of international dignitaries. Richard Helms, Adm. Moorer and a host of lesser generals and admirals from the U.S. rounded out the brass.

Finally the Shah did a slow inspection of us as he approached our helo. I stood as tall as I could, which was a couple of inches over his head. I gave a snappy salute and kept my eyes looking straight ahead.

Once he was in the left seat of the H-3 we piled in. Three burly, mean looking SAVAK secret police followed me. They seemed well-fed but with a hungry look in their eyes. They refused any helmets or flotation gear—they were both ultra-alert and expendable. Their bulging jackets hid a compact but lethal arsenal.

The Shah flew the Sea King and did a decent job. As we transited out to the *Hawk* across the Straights of Hormuz he looked over towards the United Arab Emirates and said in perfect English, "It looks so desolate over there." I couldn't for the life of me see a difference between his desert and theirs.

Once at the *Kitty Hawk* the Shah and all the rest were treated to the world-class air show we had previewed the day before. It was an unforgettable show of flying skill that would have impressed anyone.

The Shah and his cadre returned via the COD. My encounter with a powerful and notorious world leader was done.

Oil embargoes, unrest in the Middle East, listening posts on the Soviet frontier and shiny new F-14 Tomcats all laid the base for our little party. Once again I had no idea how any of it was stitched together; I was a bit-player in a power game of worldly proportions. All I could do was stand tall, look proud, do my job and be professional.

The April 8 *Kitty Hawk* Flyer had a long write-up on the visit. There was a smaller article saying how Libya's Colonel Khadafy had fallen from power and was relegated to a figurehead position.

───── • ─────

THE PERSIAN GULF WAS saturated with sea life and activity. I saw pods of gigantic manta rays slowly flying underwater. We sailed through a school of hundreds of Hammerhead sharks, eyes wide-apart and looking more menacing than any sea creature I had yet seen. Porpoise were everywhere. As we steamed out of the region and into the Arabian Sea, dhows dotted the water's surface. A small wooden trader ship, its design remained unchanged for centuries. They sailed the trade-winds between the Indian subcontinent and East Africa. Ivory, exotic hides and horn exchanged for carpets, spices and jewels kept the small ships sailing. They were a vision right out of a Joseph Conrad novel.

The *Kitty Hawk* was striking a different kind of vision on the transit to Singapore for a few day's liberty. The pace had slowed a bit after the Iran visit. Sailors checked out fishing rods from Special Services and trolled off the lowered aircraft elevators. Laundry services were stretched thin after almost two months at sea and uniforms, held in nylon net bags and closed with a huge safety pin, were tossed over the side, secured by ropes. Along with mops tied off the same way, bags of smelly laundry were dragged alongside the massive ship, a thirty knot wash-job in salt water. Mops and bags of skivvies dangling off the side of a modern supercarrier and bouncing along the waves must have made for interesting pictures for the Soviet photo-recon folks. I passed on doing my laundry that way; the only thing I could imagine being more uncomfortable than my dirty clothes were clothes "washed" in salt water. My flight suit was getting pretty ripe but I stopped noticing the odor. I figured Chief Hatch was right, maybe I should just change the oil.

We were at the far end of supply lines and had to refuel from a commercial tanker off India. It was an amazing sight to see: a ship as long as the *Hawk* but slung close to the water, like a low-rider vessel, with just a few old Merchant Marine deck hands getting the hoses connected and pumping fuel oil into our hold. The tanker's deck-hands were stripped down to cutoff jeans and tennis shoes, their skin copper-colored by the brazen Indian Ocean sun. In a way I admired their apparent independence: they seemed free in their world, a world of timelessness and leagues of open sea. I wondered what books they read. I wondered if maybe one of them was the steady boyfriend of the woman I spent the night with in Manila.

One thing that helped with the hot, humid days was going topside when there were no flight ops and sitting on the bow. I could raise up the cuffs of my bellbottom dungarees and let fresh air circulate. It felt great. Showers were rare—fresh water was at a premium and the Navy shower under water hours was in effect. Just a touch of water to get wet, water off, lather up, scrub, maybe even wash a pair of socks, then rinse off. When fresh water was scarce a 1st Class would be stationed in the heads timing water use. I couldn't wait to get back to Subic and take a real long, hot shower, letting it run as long as I wanted. Chief Hatch called that a "hotel shower."

When it was quiet up on the flight deck I could hear the big search radar antenna crackling the air as if it were frying oxygen. Rumors abounded about how the radar would sterilize you, mutate you, kill you slowly with an invisible invader so you died from a mysterious cancer in middle age. But it was positioned high enough that only the foolish would be caught in its path. Still, the power of that radar sent a small jolt throughout the exposed deck. It rotated and scanned the horizon for 300 miles in every direction, seeking enemies foolish enough to approach our floating arsenal.

As always, an F-4 was positioned to launch and intercept in a matter of minutes if the radar picked up something, and a Sea King was positioned to launch before the Phantom. Even at the most relaxed of times the *Hawk* had the hammer cocked, a round in the chamber, and was aiming at anything in sight. We were loaded and ready to fire, even just sailing east through calm seas. The tension was a palpable current that continuously ran throughout the ship. General Quarters could be called at any second, for any reason. A few moments sitting on the bow, feeling fresh air on my clammy skin, my mind wandering to thoughts of a Colorado spring, was heaven.

We steamed into Singapore Harbor on April 28 after 58 days at sea. A port-of-call there meant mooring out in the channel but there were plenty of local water taxis; most big ships there had to set anchor away from the docks. I booked a tour along with Mistrot; it was an easy way to see the sights and we didn't have to worry about getting lost or mugged.

One stop was the Tiger Balm Gardens, built on the fortune the balm company had accumulated. The topical analgesic, developed by a Chinese herbalist from Rangoon, had been made in Singapore since the '20s. There the family business opened the gardens. It was a fantastical place, a surreal world captured in miniature forms. Some were human, some grotesque, some looking to be born of opium dreams and heroin hallucinations. By the time we left there I felt like I had dropped LSD.

Visits to an alligator farm and Buddhist Temple plus a trip around the island filled in the day. And we saw a prison. I had been reading James Clavell's *King Rat* and I wondered if it was Changi Prison, the WWII POW hellhole Clavell placed his novel in. The Japanese had conquered Singapore, the island jewel at the southern tip of the Malay Peninsula, and interred troops of the British Empire who had been defending it. Their treatment differed little from other POWs of the Imperial Japanese Army; it was brutal.

Chief Hatch was history. He retired after twenty-three years,

10,000 flight hours in seventeen different aircraft and a legacy of hard-nosed mentoring. Chief Rice took his place and the cycle of personnel rotation continued. Jim Helms was getting real short too, and eager to start college back in Colorado. I envied him but was not even halfway through my enlistment. All I seemed to think about was when we were going to return to the States and when I could take some leave.

11: Subic and the South China Sea

W e pulled back into Subic May 2. The Indian Ocean jaunt was a success and killed sixty days off the WestPac schedule. That was two months we didn't have to spend in the Gulf of Tonkin, but we were headed back there soon.

We got word when we returned that three naval construction battalion officers had been ambushed and murdered on a remote part of the base. No one knew if it was Huks or some other nationalist group, but it drove home the fact that we were not welcomed by all Filipinos. I wondered if Sarge, the Negrito JEST instructor, knew anything about it. If paid enough he might go headhunting for the culprits, even if Western heads were prized the most.

After a brief in-port period the *Hawk* headed back into the South China Sea rejoining Task Force 77, the Tonkin Gulf Yacht Club. That name was forged from the decks of destroyers and air wing missions over Hanoi. The Navy had been patrolling those waters for a decade, many sailors and airmen returning multiple times. Short of another Gulf of Tonkin incident—real or perceived—the *Hawk*'s bombs would not fall on Vietnamese soil, nor were the Black Knights likely to be called to go feet-dry and rescue a downed pilot north of the DMZ. But we were there, prepared, regardless. There was the "Uncola." Now we had the "unwar."

We pulled in close to South Vietnam and the COD went ashore, picking up some ARVN officers. The ship got close enough that you could see the coastline. Had they sent helos I might have set foot on Vietnamese soil, but as it was I leaned over the catwalk rail looking for sea snakes. And I finally saw them. They were for real. Elongated and leathery-black against the green water, they slithered across the surface in a big S shape. They seemed totally at ease in the aquatic environment, and I hoped I never had to jump into a brood of the menacing looking reptiles to make a rescue. Once we entered the ocean all our cunning and evolutionary superiority sank to the bottom and we took our place at the low rung of the food chain. All you had to do was ask one of the guys who fell overboard—ask them how they felt. Except perhaps for the brig inmate who wanted to swim home; I wasn't sure if he could make a sane judgment about anything.

We sailed north under radio silence, the massive ship slipping along the coastline in an ominous quiet, save for the sea being parted temporarily by the hull. We could be seen—we were hard to miss—but we could not be heard. The little rusty AGI tagging along had nothing to listen to on its radio interceptors.

Passing stone columns rising out of the sea like the spires of Poseidon's underwater temple, where aquatic spirits worshiped in the cold dark of the deep, the *Hawk* lumbered its way towards the 17th parallel and points beyond.

We were back to the serious business of not waging war against the North Vietnamese. They seemed to be withholding from major offensives against the South even as tens of thousands of soldiers on both sides died. I asked Lt. Sandin what was going on as we hung around the ready room, drinking strong coffee and looking over the maps pulled down at the front of the room.

"So Zipper, er, Lt. Sandin, are we going to be doing anything while we're off the coast? I mean, is the *Hawk* going to launch air strikes or something?"

"We couldn't attack North Vietnam unless Nixon declared war against them, or they attacked us, and neither is likely to happen.

We couldn't even likely do support air strikes for the ARVN if they asked; it would take something really major to get us involved again. Congress just passed the War Powers Act, didn't you read up on that?"

"No Sir, I guess I've been busy with other stuff, anyway I don't pay much attention to that sort of thing."

"Besides Thos, our main mission is ASW, don't forget that. Just because this gagglefuck of a war is fizzling out that doesn't mean there aren't Soviet subs out there doing their best to find us. Let's keep their periscopes down, shall we?"

Zipper was right; even if the war had been dragging along HS-4 wouldn't have been deeply involved. Aside from plane guard our mission was keeping track of and harassing Soviet subs.

————•————

IT WAS AS DARK as a month of midnights. I had an ASW mission scheduled and needed some grub to pull me through the late hours of the flight. Once the sun broke the horizon I could wake up a bit, but those carbon-black hours between midnight and dawn seemed a time better surrendered to astronomy students, instead of sitting in a hover drenched in sweat listening for a sonar return from Soviet steel.

I made my way down to the speed-line mess, open off-hours to feed unmoored and adrift sailors roaming the decks. Some sailors were vagabonds with nowhere to go. Bombs littered the decks and blocked my way. I had to step over and around 1,000 pound bombs, their yellow nose stripes contrasting with the wrinkly olive drab paint, just to make my way to the chow line. Food, bombs: they both fed a hunger.

As I ate, jets above were thrown into the horizonless night as regular as clockwork. I knew when I had to be topside—between the launch and recovery cycle, when the flight deck was calm and preparations made to land aircraft returning from far flung and varied missions. As the last plane left the deck on that cycle I polished off my beans and franks, gulped down the last of the green-tinted bug juice and headed up.

On my way up to the 0-3 level I rode the escalator. It looked just like one from a department store except it could go either direction, determined by a switch at each end. And it was populated not by shoppers but by green-Nomex clad aviators: pilots, radar intercept officers, navigator/bombardiers and the occasional aircrewman. Once I had donned all my flight gear I could pass for a young pilot if my name-tag wasn't checked out. Many times as I walked the passageways to my helicopter enlisted men would yield the right-of-way, thinking I was commissioned and a pilot. I usually said, "I'm one of you," but it was interesting being treated as an officer and not a simple E-3, low on the scale by any test. I could be decked-out in my flight gear look-ing all the more like a young ensign on the way to his Phantom and within hours be assigned to field day the ready room.

Once topside I joined my first crewman in the preflight ritual. It could seem redundant but our lives depended on it being done, and done correctly. I tossed my SAR gear in the back and took my place in the right seat, in front of the sonar gear.

Once the whole crew was strapped in the small powerful T58 turbines were fired up and the big rotor blades began to spin. With power on, the sonar gear as well as the instrument panel came to life, red lights illuminating a myriad of critical gauges, dials and instruments.

Lt. Mack was the pilot: a decent, affable man who had been in the Black Knights for a few years. The copilot, Lt.j.g. Gross, was new like me, we both on our first WestPac.

"Another routine sub hunt, Mr. Gross?" I said as we all checked our ICS, the helo internal communication system.

"No flight is routine Thos, you should know that. Remember, anything can happen."

We were living up to our reputation as Black Knights on a black night. Little Green Sprout would have said, "I told ya' so." I couldn't see a thing beyond the lit surface of the flight deck, the nonskid holding onto the first of the early hour's dew. We had scant moments before returning planes would be circling above, waiting their turn to trap a wire and be done with their black night.

"Launch the helo," came the order from the air boss. Lt. Mack pulled collective and eased the cyclic over, bringing us around to clear the deck as jets lined up to land behind us. It was a dance of seconds between success and catastrophic failure.

"*Hawk*, this is Black Knight seven-four-one standing by for vector to operating area, over." Lt. Mack made the standard call to the *Hawk*'s air controllers. No answer.

"*Hawk*, this is Black Knight seven-four-one, do you read, over?" No answer.

"Sonar, pilot, do you read?"

"Roger, Mr. Mack, loud and clear." We could talk to each other; at least the ICS was working.

"Guys, I think we lost our radios. Gross, try some different frequencies and see if you can raise anybody."

"Mack, will do, let's stick to starboard delta for now until we can get this figured out."

Great, no radios, that should make for a short and uneventful flight. I figured we'd land as soon as possible and "down" the helo, relegating it to the maintenance guys.

Gross had no luck—we had lost all exterior communications. No big deal, we were only 50 yards from the ship. Phantoms and Intruders and the occasional Skywarrior made their landings; I could see them through the port hatch window as we made our pass by starboard.

There wasn't much I could do. With no mission and no way to talk to anybody on the ship, all I could do was sit tight. We had a full load of fuel so we could stay airborne for at least four hours.

Hours ticked by on the eight-day clock on my console. Lt. Mack slowly but surely began to lose his control of the situation. I could hear the tension in his voice. I couldn't see a thing out of my crew window except a solid curtain of darkness. At least I could catch a glimpse of the ship out the port side when we made our pass. The ship's island had rows of special lights, each with a specific meaning.

A certain combination meant the helo in starboard delta was cleared to land.

I had a whole set of procedures if some things went wrong, things I could do something about. If the sonar dome wouldn't raise, if it wouldn't lower, if the rescue hoist fouled or shredded or any number of scenarios occurred over which I could affect the outcome, I could do something. But that night I couldn't do anything but look at my small starboard-side crew window and wonder if I could fit through it.

"Guys, I see the light clearance for us, I'm bringing us in." Mack seemed certain. I trusted him. I had no choice.

"I'm not sure, Mack, let's take another look," responded Gross.

"No, I'm sure; let's get this puppy back on the deck and shut her down." Mack swung us in a wide arc and lined up on the visual approach lights. We couldn't talk to the controllers; he just had to fly the light system into a landing and hope he had it right.

Within seconds the helo shuddered and shook with the force of a typhoon. The already thin skin seemed to twist and pull at its rivets. The red equipment lights danced in front of my eyes as if another world existed behind the sonar panel. We were caught in a whirlpool of violent air. As I looked out the cockpit I saw the unmistakable dual exhaust of an F-4 Phantom, from behind. The F-4 had missed us by what felt like less than my arm span. We had flown right in front of the Phantom on its approach to the flight deck.

Gross manhandled the controls away from Mack and swung us out of the way of other fighters approaching the deck. It became very quiet on the ICS. We waited. We had a bit of fuel left but would need to land soon if we were going to avoid putting the helo into the deep briny.

Finally it was apparent that we were the last Air Wing 11 aircraft airborne in the South China Sea. Brown shirts, yellow shirts, just about everyone on the deck was waving to us to land. "OK guys, we're about done, this night is almost over," said Mack. He lined us up with the center-line of the deck and proceeded to lower the collective. Too much.

Gross asserted himself and said, "We're too low, we're too low," and pulled up on the controls.

Mack disagreed, in a self-deluded way. "No way, Gross, we're too high, I know we're too high," and he pushed down on the collective. A push-and-shove match ensued in the cramped quarters of the Sea King cockpit, two men fighting over the fate of the helicopter as we approached the deck. I was still helpless. I instinctively placed my feet up on the sonar gear to cushion the impact I sensed was just seconds away. I really didn't think it would help, but it was all I could do.

The spud locker. That's what we called it. The fantail of the carrier often stored food like potatoes, so if you came in too low you'd fly into the rear of the ship right about where the spuds were stored. And die. We were headed for the spud locker.

Gross was in the fight of his life with a superior officer over control of 20,000 pounds of helicopter. I doubted he was thinking of his career—self preservation was the motivation that night. The fight went on in a timeless void.

"We're too low."

"No, we're too high."

The helo tried to respond to both pilots' inputs, tried to do what it was designed to do, keep people alive, not kill them in a mangled fireball. We approached the rounddown of the deck, a make-it-or-break-it point of every landing of every aircraft.

Gross won the tug of war. Not long after, Lt. Mack gave up his right to fly, his right to wear coveted naval aviator wings. He didn't want to repeat a night like that, especially if he would win the next tug of war—it would mean certain death for the whole crew. That took character, to admit his flying days were over. I was just glad Gross had the stronger pull.

In the ready room after the flight Gross and I locked eyes and his seemed to say, see, I told you no flight was routine. I would never forget those two pilots and what transpired between them, and what it meant to me. I would never remember who the other crewman was.

As I shed my sweat-soaked flight gear Clyde Dog said, "Thos, what happened? You look like you've been shot at and missed and shit at and hit."

I had no words to speak. I just dumped my gear in the aircrew space, walked the dimly-lit passageway back to my rack, crawled in and tried to sleep to the thump of catapults launching jets into the early dawn. That was my third flight of the day, and I was beat. I awoke to the sound of eight bells but had no idea which of the three times in twenty-four hours it was.

I HAD BEEN ASSIGNED to a weapons team, which meant loading the MK 46 homing torpedo. It was everything a torpedo should be: long, finned, propellered, and heavy. And menacing. It was all business: no frills or extras, just a sleek tube filled with propellant, search sonar and high explosives. Designed to seek out its prey, it could not be outrun or outmaneuvered. The SH-3D could carry two of the lethal underwater weapons, enough to issue any sub a death sentence. I got a red flight deck jersey for being on the weapons team. I added it to my brown jersey for being a plane captain and green for operating electronics. My collection was growing.

If I helped drop a torpedo on a submarine it would have meant World War III was underway. We practiced for it daily. The Soviet destroyer we came across drove home the Cold War standoff. It was belching smoke and obviously having serious problems. Maybe they had a fire in their main machine room. The *Hawk* steamed alongside to within a mile. In an odd but time-tested brotherhood, the *Hawk* offered its assistance, help for fellow sailors in trouble. I looked over the secret messageboard's entries, and they read like a cordial exchange between members of a gentlemen's club: May we be of assistance to you, Captain, Sir. No, thank you, we are able to cope with the situation at hand, thank you very much, Sir. Well then, fellow travelers of the open seas, please feel free to call on us if we may be of any assistance in the future. We most certainly will, if at such time it is deemed necessary, good and kind Sir. And on it went, back and forth, they making it very clear they didn't want our help, we almost insisting on it. My mind considered the wild possibility of them needing some helo medevacs and me being on the crew to fly over and pick up their casualties—what a story that would make. But it didn't happen. Instead, a ship that I had been taught was my enemy limped along under its own power as we disengaged. That Soviet destroyer held enough ordnance to blow us out of the water several times.

As in all wars fought on the high seas, the water won't take sides—it drowns one and all alike regardless of uniform or politics or anything else. In an odd way that was what bonded us to the crew of the Soviet warship; even as enemies we shared in the ultimate fate should war happen. A sailor is a sailor, brothers in the hardships and risks of blue water operations.

I was promoted to E-4 on May 16. Making 3rd Class was fantastic. I was up next to go mess cooking; every other E-3 in aircrew had gone. I was ready to go, it was only fair, but now I was ineligible. I was glad to accept the added responsibilities of being a petty officer in trade for not working long miserable hours below decks. If I could pass my checkrides coming up I would have accomplished as much as possible in as short of time as possible. Being designated a 0000 seemed a lifetime ago. My flight jacket was even accumulating WestPac patches.

IT WAS A CALM night in the Tonkin Gulf. Phosphorescent-green bursts of micro sea life glowed beside the ship like underwater flashbulbs, punctuating the veil of darkness that enveloped the ship.

The *Hawk* was engaged in an UNREP, a supply ship transferring tons of oil, aviation fuel, bombs, and most importantly, reasonably fresh food for the weary crew. The baked beans we had been eating, canned before I was born, would not be missed.

Jim Helms and I, along with pilots Lt. Grupe and Lt.j.g. Gross, were standing an alert five on the dark flight deck, waiting for something to go wrong.

The deck had been quiet until the "launch the alert helo" call came down from the air boss high up in his green glass cage. We scrambled to put on flight helmets and get the helo powered up. Helms and I didn't bother to strap in; it would take precious time away from being ready for whatever awaited us.

Something had happened on the supply ship and we were ordered to simply fly the fifty yards to the ship's small deck, land, pick somebody up, and return. No sweat, except flying into the tangled mass of cranes, cables, ropes, fuel hoses and assorted gear on a pitching deck that was moving at twenty knots at night—with little room to spare except for a perfect landing—would tax everyone on our helicopter. And to make it even more challenging, we would have no way out if the attempted landing got dicey, since we would be flying directly towards a wall of steel that was the very ship we were on.

Lt. Grupe was the first to speak up on the ICS. "I don't like this at all, it's too damn dangerous. I'll need both of you crewmen back there to be extra-alert when we go in; there won't be room to sneeze and make it back out in one piece. This will have to be perfect, no other options."

Off the flight deck in well under five minutes, we punched into the black horizonless night in the controlled chaos that is a helicopter in flight, torque and gravity fighting for possession of the Sea King. With quick action on the flight controls Grupe swung us around behind the carrier and lined up on the moving parade of ships locked together by hoses and lines. At a snail's pace we approached the supply ship. I lay on my belly in the back, half out of the aft station of the helo watching the rotor blades and tail wheel for clearance. Flying sideways, keeping pace with the ships, inching forward closer to the deck, the scene was surreal. The supply ship was slowly swaying side to side, deck lights of red and yellow and blue punctuated the blackness, while sailors scurried in and out of the shadows moving pallets of bombs and food around with chess-game-like precision.

All four of us were riveted to the scene, watching the cranes sway in unison like a row of boat masts riding a swell. Grupe picked our way through the tangled mess and slowly lowered down to the small landing platform. I cleared the tail wheel over the pad while Gross attended to the rotor blade clearance in front as Grupe set the big helo down, lowering the collective control as far as it would go as though that would somehow glue us to the deck. It wouldn't, but it made us feel better.

I stood up, slid open the cargo door the rest of the way and breathed in the cool night air. Helms turned the interior lights to the red lens setting, enabling us to see without ruining our night vision. A blast of white light can ruin the ability to see at night, and it can prove fatal.

Four sailors hunched over to stay clear of the turning rotor blades approached us carrying a Stokes Litter. So this was serious, somebody was hurt bad. Helms and I pulled in the injured sailor.

"What happened?" yelled Helms over the din of the twin turbines.

"Bombs, a pallet of bombs. A thousand-pounds worth got away and slammed him up against the bulkhead. Squashed him bigtime. You guys hurry, he's my buddy," said a voice from the darkness.

I kneeled down by the injured man's right side, looking into a face younger than my own. In the eerie red light it was difficult to tell what was pouring out of his mouth, but something was flowing like intestinal lava. I hoped it wasn't blood since it didn't look red in a world the same color. As I leaned closer to his pale youthful face, lost in pain and agony, I smelled sickly-sweet vomit. Good, at least it wasn't blood. I quickly cleared out as much as I could from his mouth with my fingers so he wouldn't suffocate on his own fluid.

As we carefully backed out of our predicament—flying sideways, backwards, and up—the side of our own ship looming ghostlike in the darkness in front of us was a reminder that this, too, had to be perfect. There would be no second chance.

Finally away from the maze of obstructions offered up by the supply ship, we headed back to the big flight deck. Helms was shouting something to me over the turbine noise. I couldn't hear. "What? He's what? He's dead?" I asked.

"No, no, his head, get a helmet on his head." The crushed man was so motionless in the litter I thought we had lost him. Cradling his head in my hands and slipping the helmet on I noticed his eyes: glassy, half closed and with a distant, otherworldly look. I wasn't sure he would live long enough to make it to the carrier's hospital just moments away. His arm had slipped from the litter and I set it back into place, taking just a moment to hold his cold limp hand to let him know someone was there. To my amazement, he squeezed back. Using what little strength he had left he let me know he was still struggling to hold on to life.

Within minutes he was pulled from our helicopter and rushed to the *Hawk*'s hospital. As I watched him be carried away I sensed that spark of life within him would grow stronger.

We resumed the remainder of our alert five status on the flight deck, on spot three, until dawn.

———◆———

THE *KITTY HAWK* BATTLE group went about its business in the South China Sea. "Power projection mode" was being tested as a new concept, which integrated the attack carrier configuration—the CVA—with ASW squadrons. Those two worlds collided on almost every level, from air traffic control to flight deck arrangements. Even the fixed wing S-2 Trackers were slow and lumbering ASW planes, the antithesis of a Phantom fighter. Someone somewhere in the bowels of the Pentagon had decided to graft the two concepts together, and we were doing our best to make it work. At times it was as if the fixed wing squadrons wanted one or two helos on board as plane guard, but more than that were just in the way. We called the jets "go fast do nothings."

The *Hawk* would set up a position and steam in a huge racetrack pattern: into the wind to launch and recover aircraft, downwind to be roughly in the same place to start the cycle all over again. Normal ship's activities went on regardless, including tossing bags of trash over the fantail. As we stayed on station we would sail back through our own garbage, which attracted sharks and anything else hungry enough to eat what we tossed overboard.

While on-station Lt. Gray had some important news to update us on. It didn't sound good. "Gentlemen, we have strong evidence that the North Vietnamese are slowly but surely massing troops and materiel below the 17th parallel. They've been doing this for some time now, while methodically attacking ARVN positions. An all-out thrust south to take Saigon could happen, but I don't see it occurring until the '76 dry season. They've improved the Ho Chi Minh Trail so much I expect to see a Howard Johnson's along there soon. What does this all mean to us, you ask? I haven't a clue. As usual, there is China, the Soviets and us, all involved with Laos, Cambodia and the two Vietnams, and I'm sensing it will all implode within a few years. How that will affect us, I don't know. What will affect us is this: the Soviets have slipped a Charlie-class sub into the South China Sea. It's packing missiles and we're its prey. The P-3 boys are on its trail but you can rest assured it's going to be trying to sneak up on us."

After the briefing aircrew gathered to go over the specifics of the Charlie-class sub. It was a nuke, it was armed with missiles designed to take out a carrier, and it was looking for us. The Orions would be passing along their data to the air wing, and we would be deploying search strategies to protect the carrier. I wondered if the jet jockeys—the fighter pilots—might have appreciated us more if they were aware a Soviet nuclear submarine was looking for the *Hawk*.

As we screened the waters surrounding the carrier battle group, the Cold War continued to be played out in the warm waters of the South China Sea.

We got bits and pieces of news from home: sports scores, recent movie reviews, unusual weather. And news of the impeachment hearings against Nixon. It was looking like there was a whole lot the public didn't know, and it was about to hit the fan. Nixon had his defenders and detractors aboard but I steered clear of those debates; I was busy preparing for my 1st crew checkrides. If I passed I would fly left seat over a year before I could officially be designated a 1st Crewman. That meant lots of NATOPS study. And believing in myself: that I could do it, be ready, assume the added responsibility of being the senior enlisted aircrew on a flight, of having a rescue swimmer under my direction.

And I was getting real sonar contact with Soviet subs. Not much, they were good at what they did, but I would be flying my checkrides on the real thing, not some imaginary adversary off Imperial Beach. It made me think about what Chief Lawson had told me; about how there was nothing to compare to experiencing a deployment, living the mission, being a part of the fleet in action. My thinking about how I once envied that instructor who never left IB seemed short sighted.

The Vietnam war had given both the U.S. and Soviet navies reason to be deployed in the area, and it was a chance to rehearse for World War III. Both sides knew it could happen, and both knew events could spiral out of control: a bluff called, national honor at stake, a rogue general or admiral taking things into his own hands— the potential for unleashing the nuclear arsenal ensconced within the hulls of our collective ships was held at bay by a thread. And HS-4 played its part. That Charlie-class SSGN was out there. It was all very real.

Weeks passed, driven by routine and mission. The uneasy alliance between jets and helicopters was being molded into a new definition for the modern carrier. The fixed wing aircraft continued to be armed with bombs, rockets and missiles. HS-4 continued to keep a rescue helo airborne almost continually while at the same time searching for Soviet subs, hovering over destroyer and frigate decks medevacing injured sailors, delivering precious bags of mail to ecstatic crews of far flung ships, and a myriad of other tasks that only an all-weather and night-time capable helicopter could accomplish. It wasn't glamorous, but it was essential to Task Force 77.

———◆———

AS MAY ENDED WITHOUT WWIII erupting, we steamed northeast

a scant 7 degrees East and 2 degrees North into the British Crown Colony of Hong Kong. The *Hawk* moored in Victoria Harbor, the channel running between Hong Kong Island and the mainland. Kowloon and the New Territories—also run by the British—lay to the north, separated from mainland communist China by the Pearl River estuary.

It was liberty time. Hong Kong had been a seaport for centuries and was well-equipped to handle a crew the size of the *Hawk*'s. Water taxis ran continually, the fare cheap and the ride short. Dumped off at Fenwick Pier, *Kitty Hawk* sailors fanned out into the huge vibrant city in search of dreams and visions. Armed with my "Serviceman's Guide to Hong Kong" a handful of aircrew and I took to the town. Hong Kong was beyond belief; everything imagined—for a price— was available. Watches, stereos, TVs, cameras, precious gems, ivory carvings, porcelain, cinnabar, cloisonné, gold: if man or woman or vanity desired it, it was for sale. You could even buy oranges from Florida. Most prominent were the tailor shops. The mark of a sea- soned China Seas sailor was a pair of Hong Kong-tailored gabar- dine dress blues, complete with silk dragon patches sewn into the inner cuff of the jumper. When cuffs were turned back the elaborate mythical beast showed its splendid colors, proclaiming the wearer had been to the Orient.

Mistrot, Clyde Dog, Chuck Fields and I made our way through the narrow busy streets to the Diamond Horse-Shoe restaurant. In the heart of exotic and sensual food I gorged on a T-bone steak. And cold beer. The steak was tough but it reminded me of steaks back at the Black Knight Inn.

The city held endless fascinations. I took the steepest funicu- lar tram in the world to the top of Victoria Peak. I watched school children practice martial arts with the older, more serious kids up front, the younger ones in back goofing off, like kids everywhere. I walked the halls of the China Fleet Club, where a sailor could get everything from a beer to an elephant tusk carved into an ivory village. It seemed like Rolls Royces outnumbered taxis. Rickshaws still provided man-powered travel in the shadows of skyscrapers. A whole cross-section of Chinese lived their entire lives aboard small boats, while modern hydrofoils crisscrossed the bay. Poverty and wealth walked side-by-side in Hong Kong, where the destitute and the affluent shared only air.

The *Hawk* was at anchor for several days so I had another turn at liberty. I ran into Feek at the afterbrow as I was heading into town and we decided to hit the beach together. He made plane captain about the same time I had and we developed a good rapport on the flight deck, both before and after missions. We had a whole evening to get drunk before we had to be back aboard. Shitty Kitty goodbye, at least until midnight, a time better known as Cinderella Liberty.

We headed to Kowloon on rumor that a British bar, The Yellow Submarine, was a cool place to hang out. After a little tourist shopping we took the crowded Star Ferry across the channel and made a beeline for the bar. It was below street level by eight or ten steps. It sat—submarine like—partly submerged. There were a few British women hanging out in the bar. "Bitchin'," Feek muttered under his breath, staring at the women while stashing the poster he had bought earlier next to our bar stools. We proceeded to order the main course by the bucketful. Five pitchers of beer later we were duly shitfaced. Nearing the time we needed to head back in order to make the midnight deadline, we mustered our strength to get off our drunk butts. We staggered up the now seemingly endless steep steps and onto the quiet street, looking for a cab. Suddenly Feek yelled out, "Twins! Look, Thos, twins, right there!"

Twins? I didn't see anybody much less a matched pair. "What the hell are you talking about? There isn't anyone here; I don't see jack-shit."

"Right here, twins, see?" Feek commenced to hang his arms around a dual parking meter. It was going to be a long night.

"Feek, let's forget the twins for now and get a cab back to the ferry; we don't have any spare time to sweet-talk parking meters, our own meter is running ya' know."

Prying Feek's heavy arms off the meters I hailed a Toyota cab passing by. "You go ferry, go big ship?" asked the driver. Guess we sort of stood out. Two drunk sailors in Hong Kong on liberty, bet that was something the cab driver hadn't seen before.

"Yes, please," I responded and off we went into the tropical night. Since Feek hopped in front he felt compelled for some reason to get the driver's attention. This he accomplished quite nicely by taking his rolled-up poster and wielding it like a trumpet, sticking it in the cab driver's ear. Then, to my amazement, he began yelling into the tube with all his energy. "You fucking communist! You want to take over the whole fucking world, you fucking commie bastard!"

"Feek, take it easy, will ya? Pipe down, this guy could slice us up with a butterfly knife and dump us in the channel and nobody would find us for a week."

The driver probably *was* a communist, but that was no time to bring up a political debate. I could see the driver was becoming extremely annoyed, so I made a big deal out of getting my wallet and shoving a handful of Hong Kong dollars his way. He glanced at me through the rear view mirror, shaking his head as we pulled into the ferry landing.

After the cab ejected its drunken contents and before Feek could say his special goodbyes I clamped my hand over his mouth. "Jee-zuz, are you trying to get us killed? What the fuck were you thinking back there? Now let's get on the ferry and back to the ship before you get us in any trouble."

Feek managed to calm down a bit on the ferry ride back. Perhaps it was from the Technicolor yodel he heaved over the side, most of which blew back in his face from the wind. Finally at the ship's ladder leading to the hangar deck, I figured we made it. I was wrong. Once on the cavernous hangar deck he started yelling, "Fuck the Navy, fuck the goddamn Navy," and launched himself at an A-7 Corsair II attack jet. He kicked wildly at it, bruising his foot and not making a scratch or dent in the armor-plated jet.

"Hey you two, get over here, now!" came the command from the Quarter Deck. Great, a newly-minted ensign who had to prove his authority. He looked at Feek and pronounced, "You are hereby charged with attempting to destroy government property. I am putting you on report."

"Unfuc—"

"Shut up Feek," I piped in. "Sir, I almost have him to his rack, we're almost there, Sir. And plus, how could he hurt an A-7 with a tennis shoe? That plane has been over North Vietnam a hundred times, and Feek ain't no SAM missile."

"Another word from you sailor, and I'll write you up along with your buddy here."

"Uh, roger that. Sir. See ya' Feek, just try to not fall down a ladder on the way back to your rack, OK?"

I left him swaying in front of the young Officer of the Watch and tumbled into my tiny rack. It was small, but it was mine. At least I managed to find the right one in my drunken fog.

Bright and early the next morning the anchor chains once again banged and scraped their way down the steel tubes and into the chain locker, once again just a few feet away from my pounding head. That Feek's rack was even closer than mine was small consolation. Groans could be heard from half of the ninety-nine racks in the berthing space as the steel-on-steel cacophony accompanied the ritual of weighing anchor.

Feek made it to muster with a slight limp and a pounding headache. I didn't know which hurt him more, his head or his foot.

I never did find out what that damn poster had on it.

◄●►

THE *HAWK* HAD ONE last at-sea period before heading back to the States. We sailed back down to Subic Bay from Hong Kong and made some personnel changes. Along with Lt. Gray, I was sent to the Cubi Point beach det for a week. The WestPac was all but over for me. The *Hawk* steamed back into the South China Sea as I unpacked my gear, stowing it in a big gray metal floor locker. The extra room was almost sinful.

We were billeted in a Quonset hut butting up against the lush jungle. All the earthly colors and smells were a welcome relief from the ubiquitous steel of the carrier. Even the odors of rotting vegetation and animal excrement added their own unique element to the jungle aroma. At night I could feel the eyes of Sarge peering at my vulnerability from within his verdant cover of darkness.

I wrote my last letter of the deployment home. I had access to a telephone through base services, and even with long lines it was a happy time to spend waiting as the operators attempted to make the connection. I never could make contact with Dad. I wasn't sure when I would see him again.

The beach det was a piece of cake. The squadron helos and operations office were just past the east end of the runway and were close to things Cubi Point had to offer, like the great chow hall, the swimming pool and the Sky Club, which was stumbling distance from my Quonset. Just across the tarmac from our helos was a detachment of Marine helicopters. Just beyond them was a row of F-5 fighter jets. Painted in camouflage greens and browns, the small agile planes were bound for the South Vietnamese Air Force.

Lt. Gray watched me checking them out. "Too little too late for those guys," he informed me as I walked back into the ops office. "It's all but over for the South Vietnamese. I can't see them surviving very long without our air power. My best guess, communists will be flying those planes by late 1976."

It was feeling like the war was taking in one last deep breath before it exhaled South Vietnam into oblivion.

By late 1976 I would be a civilian again.

———◆———

LITTLE GREEN SPROUT WAS packing his seabag and getting ready to fly home for good. He had been on the beach det the whole time and was well acquainted with the ways of Olongapo. With over two years to go on my enlistment he had some passing words for me. "Thos, steer clear of those benny boys and you'll do OK."

"Goddammit Sprout, what the fuck is a 'benny boy'? Nobody will tell me!"

"Haven't you found out yet? Didn't Master Chief Romney fill

you in? No? Well, OK, I'm going to do this as a personal favor, not because I like you, but because I pity you. Have you ever looked at a bar girl in one of these joints in town and thought to yourself, something looks wrong? Maybe the shoulders are too wide, the hips too narrow, the faint mustache a bit too obvious? Maybe the stride is a bit long, the makeup applied a bit heavily, even for Shit River socialites? Maybe they're a bit too eager to perform oral sex? Think about it, son."

"So you're trying to tell me benny boys are transvestites?"

"Hell, I'm no Sigmund Freud, look, they're guys dressed like gals who want to have sex with guys. Call it what you will, just be careful as you're leaving a bar at curfew who makes you an offer you can't refuse."

I hadn't encountered any benny boys but had made some bad decisions a few times with bar girls. One night was just plain sad. I had succumbed to the advances of a young woman, really just a girl, and followed her home. She stumbled along on huge platform shoes, her delicate feet held aloft of the dirty street.

After a short walk we entered her home: mom, dad, sisters, brothers, all huddled in the small quarters, all looking at me as I towered above them. She led me into the tiny kitchen where a small corner had been curtained off. Behind it was a cot. Her bed. For earning the rent. Her father followed us in. He was wearing an old T-shirt, several sizes too big, with a picture of an F-4 Phantom printed on it captioned "Fly the friendly skies of Vietnam." He looked at me with a glance that held a thousand accusations and condemnations while smiling a smile that betrayed little of what his eyes spoke. He held out his hand. She looked up at me with weary adolescent eyes already showing the strains of her work.

"You go short time, you pay ten Pisos, OK sailuhboy?" Father stood resolute in his business offer. Daughter stood obediently nearby. I looked at the cot behind the thin fabric, just a foot from the stove and a few more from her entire family. It was getting close to midnight, with martial law lurking behind the advancing hands of the clock. The state police were gearing up for some post 12 p.m.

**Home on leave for the first time in Fort
Collins, Colorado, December 1972.**

Being congratulated by my father upon receiving my aircrew wings, September 1973. Photo courtesy US Navy.

SH-3D Sea King, with *Kitty Hawk* in background.

Front view of a Sea King on the flight deck with rotor blades folded.

Getting ready to preflight a helo on flight deck spot three.

Cockpit of a Sea King as seen from the left crewman's seat.

Taken from right behind the pilots' seats. Note
angle of horizon seen through the cockpit.

Flight deck of the *Kitty Hawk* looking aft.

**F-4 Phantom landing on the *Kitty Hawk*. Note tailhook extended
below rear of aircraft to catch the arresting cable.**

Kitty Hawk as seen from the starboard delta position.

Flight of SH-3Ds inbound to Bandar Abbas, Iran, 1974.

I'm on Steel Beach next to helo landing spot 3.

Bow of the *Kitty Hawk* at sunset.

An UNREP in progress. Supply ship USS *Ashtabula*, O 51, in center, guided missile frigate USS *Horne*, DLG 30, on starboard side of the *Ashtabula*.

The destroyer escort USS *Bradley* along side the *Kitty Hawk*.

Me (on the left) and Terry Mistrot on the *Kitty Hawk* as it departs Subic Bay for a line period in the South China Sea.

Brady Turner next to a Sea King.

Terraced rice paddies at the mouth of a valley leading into the central mountains of Luzon Island, the Philippines.

Subic Bay Naval Base seen from the *Kitty Hawk's* flight deck while moored at the Alava Pier.

Soviet intelligence ship, Persian Gulf, 1974.

Merchant dhow in the Persian Gulf, 1974.

In the aft cabin of a Sea King, on a plane guard mission.

SH-3 Sea King on a mission.

Plane guard detachment, USS *Ranger*. I'm seventh from the left in the second row. Photo courtesy US Navy.

Kitty Hawk at the Alava Pier, Subic Bay, the Philippines.

Flying into the sunset, taken from the aft cabin of a Sea King.

"sports" events. I needed to make a decision and soon. I hadn't been with a woman in a long time.

It could wait. I slapped a handful of coins in his hand to assuage my embarrassment and darted out the door, headed for a jeepney ride back to the main gate and away from the shame for something I had even remotely considered.

Olongapo was full of girls in her predicament. And full of benny boys, beggars, street urchins, hustlers, hawkers, pimps, dealers, thieves, and survivors. Beneath the city beat a heart of tarnished gold.

The acey-deucey board was getting a workout in the beach det ops office. We had just two helos and one was missing an engine, a classic hangar queen. The flight schedule was short and mostly to see if the one machine could get off the ground. I had time to finish reading *King Rat* and started Vonnegut's *Welcome to the Monkey House*.

There was a flight going up to Baguio I managed to get on. It was a trip right out of a 100 mph travelogue. We flew north past Mt. Pinatubo and across farmland until we reached the valley leading up into the mountains. There the terraced rice paddies began to dominate, their shimmering surfaces reflecting blue sky.

Baguio was a gem of a city nestled in a mountain park. I had but a few moments to breathe in the cool clean mountain air filled with forest scent before we headed back down the valley weaving back and forth, side to side, sliding down the cushion of air until we flattened out at the bottom of the hills, skimming over rice paddies and banana trees.

Beach det days were relaxed and filled with sun and San Miguel and swimming in the afternoon heat. I was on dry land and it was just helicopters at that end of the field and there were no night flights into electrical storms or hovers above a raging sea threatening to pluck me from the sky and crush my helo like a ten ton curiosity. I couldn't fall overboard, be sliced in two by an arresting cable or be sucked into a jet intake. I could still die in a crash if we lost an engine at low altitude or flew into a jungle-covered mountain but it would have been on a sunny day after a good night's sleep and that wasn't a bad way to go. And the Sky Club was just minutes away if I made it through the day, with Mojos aplenty for the foolishly brave.

———————◆————————

A WEEK LATER THE *Hawk* pulled back into Subic for nine days of last minute ship repairs and the onloading of PX trophies for the crew. The hangar bay was cleared out as much as possible to accommodate the stereos, TVs, papasan chairs and other assorted plunder gathered from the hold of the Cubi Point store. Somewhere in the pile was my coveted Marantz receiver, Dual turntable and massive Pioneer speakers. I had no idea where I was going to put them but that didn't matter one whit; I had my booty from South East Asia.

On June 21, the solstice in a land of eternal summer, the *Hawk* pointed its massive hull to the east and steamed directly for Hawaii. We were headed home at last. On the same day, The USS *Constellation* left the States heading to the South China Sea. We would cross paths in mid-ocean.

It was a three-week transit back to the States. With a hangar deck full of Exchange booty blocking aircraft below we were a ripe target for a Soviet submarine. I was sure their sub crews knew that. That thought offset my elation at going home by a scant degree. At the halfway point we passed the *Connie* heading west. The two carriers steamed close by, close enough that you could hear the crew on the *Constellation* hurl invectives at us as we returned fire with jovial taunts. Sound could carry amazingly well across water.

I had passed my 1st crew checkrides so I was able to fly as a 1st crewman even though it wasn't official. I was hoping that meant I would be on the fly-off, where all the helos capable of getting off the flight deck would form up and make a grand entry into Imperial Beach and Ream Field.

Crews went by seniority; the top ten would make the fly-off. AJ Kopp was ahead of me but still off the flight schedule because of his now scarred and still sore arm. He wouldn't fly off the *Hawk*, but he had a date with a piece of equipment. "OK Clyde Dog, I promised I wouldn't get rid of that goddamn fan until we were east of Hawaii. We just passed 130 degrees longitude. Now can I deep six that fucking thing?"

"AJ, I'll even help!" Clyde Dog hoisted the weighted bottom of the fan on his shoulder as Kopp took what was left of the blade guard in his fingers and the two of them wrestled the offending fan down to the hangar deck and back to the fantail sponson. It was AJ's moment of revenge. In a Herculean move he single-handedly hoisted the big metal floor fan over his head and with a mighty heave, tossed it into the beautiful blue Pacific. His victorious grin lasted all the way back home. The fan sank deep into the Molokai Fracture Zone.

With Sprout and Helms sent back before we departed the PI and Kopp still off the flight schedule, I made it on the last helo crew. I would be going back in style.

The day before the *Hawk* pulled into North Island the squadrons had their flyoffs. I watched jets one by one launch into American airspace. The last F-4 took a bow cat shot, stayed on afterburners and climbed straight up into the sky. I lost sight of him after a moment but my mind rode along as he gained altitude at over 40,000 feet per minute, passing 50,000 feet in less time than it would take to make a cup of tea.

The flight deck was barren except for Black Knight helos. We loaded them up with gear and squadronmates and made a beeline for Imperial Beach and runway 27.

All ten Sea Kings were airborne and we did a fly-by of the base in perfect formation, peeling off one by one to land. Once taxied up to our newly assigned area, I slid the cargo door back to be greeted by a fellow Black Knight wielding a cold beer and a simple phrase: "Welcome home, warrior."

12: "GET LOST"

Western Airlines got me to Denver and Greyhound got me to Fort Collins. I was wearing my brown leather flight jacket replete with WestPac patches and gold wing embossed name tag. I was feeling strong, seasoned, a veteran of the real Navy and carrier aviation.

I scheduled a rendezvous with Marsha, if only in my head. It had been almost two years since I left for bootcamp, and a long long time since I had seen her much less spoken to her. I wondered if she was still in "our" apartment, if she still had Rudy, our Black Lab puppy. I wondered if she still, somehow, loved me as I loved her. All the San Miguel and easy sex in the PI couldn't extinguish the heat that slow-burned for her in my heart.

I ensconced myself at my parents' house. Dad wasn't there, just his empty, cold bedroom in the basement as a reminder of his habits. Aside from his pinning on my wings, he was far away and rarely communicated. I imagined him showing off pictures I had sent of the WestPac to his buddies in Texas. I imagined him glowing with pride when I made E-4, or when I passed the rigorous checkrides. I heard him say in my imagination, "That's my son."

I made the rounds with my buddy Mark, hitting bars and parties and getting drunk on bourbon and Coke, Dad's drink of choice. I would borrow Mom's white '65 Caddy and cruise College Avenue—up and down, north and south—looking for something I had left two years before. But I was a changed man and time did not stand still. Fort Collins would never again feel as it did before September 15, 1972.

It was easy to find where Marsha was working. She was still bartending, at a new place over by the hospital. I swaggered in wearing a faded green flight deck jersey under my flight jacket. I was standing tall; I could still feel the salt air of the South China Sea on my face, still hear the roar of Phantoms launching into the dark of night. I could still hear the groans of the crushed sailor. I could still see the mangled body of the flight deck safety officer. My eyes focused in the dim tavern light on the little glass cup of maraschino cherries on the counter. The place smelled like stale cigarette smoke.

Marsha stood behind the bar, her dimpled grin flash-frozen as she recognized me standing in the harsh daylight penetrating through the open door. "What would you like?" she asked in her best customer-service voice as I settled down on a stool.

"Coors. And you don't need to check my ID; I'm old enough now ya' know. I turned twenty-one heading west through the Malacca—" I hadn't even finished the sentence before she turned away to get the beer from the cooler behind the bar, leaving me speaking to the darkness. "What do I owe you?" I asked after she returned, setting the cold beer down on a small square napkin. Frost slid down the bottle, moistening the thin paper.

"That's a good question," she mumbled, turning once again to disappear into the dark recesses of the back room. I was left alone with a beer I really didn't want and a lingering, haunting feeling I could no longer sustain. She emerged from the shadows.

"Marsha, I need to talk to you. Can we go outside?"

"OK, but I can't be gone long, I'm working you know."

We went outside into the bright mile-high sky. Horsetooth Rock jutted up to the southwest. Huge white clouds rode the high plains, building up for an afternoon thundershower. Our eyes met. I spoke first. "Look, is it over between us? Is there nothing left to try to save?"

"Save what? Don't you understand why I never wrote to you again?"

"I don't understand anything. I just know that I still love you. From that look I guess you don't still love me. I need you to say something. At the very least, tell me to get lost; I need you to say something."

"OK, get lost." Her words had sharp edges, like they had been broken off a longer thought and tossed at my feet.

Turning on my heels, I walked away in slow somber steps. Just as I had done that day so long ago as I left her to enter the enlistment center in Denver, I could not turn and look back.

I fired up the Caddy and cruised College Avenue for hours. I knew the way even if I couldn't see it clearly.

President Richard M. Nixon resigned while I was home. Gerald Ford ascended to the president's office and stated that the nightmare was over. Nixon climbed into the presidential H-3 Sea King and waved to the press one last time. His home in San Clemente, California, would be dubbed "San Clemency" after Ford pardoned him.

Some things had changed while I had been overseas. The 55 mph speed limit was in force. UPC labels were showing up on items in stores. A series of lines of varied thicknesses which could be scanned by a computer recording the price without using the little sticky pricing labels, the code seemed futuristic. Friends joked about the government making people get an individual barcode on the backs of their necks.

⸺◦⸺

BACK AT IMPERIAL BEACH things settled into a routine. Pete, Malcolm and I rented an apartment. We were all E-4s and getting extra pay to live off base. It was almost too good to be true. No more inspections of living quarters, no more barracks, no more Reveille or Taps—it was heaven. It also meant we had to learn how to cook. That proved the biggest challenge. Hamburger Helper and Rice-a-Roni, the "San

Francisco treat," provided the basic meal plans. Beer served as an appetizer. And since I was twenty-one, I could buy hard liquor. Wild Turkey bottles began to clutter the garbage can. There would be the occasional evening when we would be on ready duty, meaning we could be called out to fly a SAR mission at anytime during the night. One night a week without liquor was manageable.

The 55 mile-per-hour speed limit was a drag but my Honda 750 fired right up and I put it to work. Long rides across Southern California filled in my time off. I took it north to find my brother, who had settled near Santa Cruz. I rode east into the Anza-Borrego desert. I rode up to Warner Springs to see what it looked like from the other side of SERE. The area looked innocent enough from the road. I stopped by a log cabin café to get some gas and a bite to eat. As I sat on the wide front porch digesting a full meal I started a conversation with a man smoking a pipe and gazing into the hills.

"What brings you up this way?"

"I work for the Navy," was all he volunteered.

"Yeah? I'm an AW, up from Ream Field."

"I figured; I can see the base sticker on the front fork of your bike. An AW you say? Been to Warner Springs before?"

"Sure have, SERE school, it's just over there I think."

"Well shipmate, you're right. That's where I am, with FASO. I've been one of the good guys but soon I get to be one of the bad guys. The fun should really start then. But believe me, I got worked over pretty good before I would be considered for the interrogator role. I still have nightmares about the waterboard."

"Sounds tough. But what a lovely place to be, up here in the mountains."

"It's nice alright. I've been here a year now. I hardly hear the screams anymore."

That sent a chill down my spine. I rode my bike back down the mountain and away from the epicenter of so many unforgettable memories.

It didn't take long for my Honda 750 to be stolen. From right beside the apartment. In broad daylight. While I was home. Some welcome-home gesture. It made me wonder who my enemy really was.

Aircrewmen and pilots continued to rotate in and out of HS-4. AW1 Doc Bliven—my instructor from the year before—checked in. He had lost his humanitarian shore duty. That meant his young daughter had died. We all steered clear of mentioning it; the pain of her death was etched into his face. But it didn't stop us from giving him a hard time about finally being in a fleet squadron.

"Hey Doc, ever sleep on a door stuck inside a closet before?" asked Teddy Bear.

"I hear the next WestPac is going to be nine months. Nine long, lonely months!" added Allen, sliding his glasses back up his nose.

"Ship life sucks," was Clyde Dog's contribution.

"We're going to cross the equator to be sure, Doc, next time out. You're not a Shellback are you? Oh, of course not, sorry. Well, we'll take care of that," I assured him.

He took the ribbing well and only slightly betrayed his apprehensions about deploying on a carrier. That mystified me since he had his corpsman combat tour with the Marines. Perhaps trepidation of the unknown was more powerful than I realized. I knew I would have been scared shitless had I been in his shoes and on the way to the Republic of South Vietnam.

LIFE AT NAS IMPERIAL BEACH took on a job-like aura. I went to work. I flew. I cared for the flight logs and ran aircrew training. I went home. I cruised the streets and country roads on my Harley Davidson Superglide, a recent acquisition to replace my stolen Honda. Painted jade like the coastal waters of Vietnam, it was a monster of a bike. 1200 cubic centimeters of power propelled me across dry lake beds and over mountains. Pete Cassidy bought Feek's Sportster and we would cruise country roads in a single minded solitude, escaping the airfield's routine.

Escaping routine was as important as escaping the madness of shipboard life. Yet "routine" for helicopter crews meant anything could happen at any time.

It was a Saturday. I was home listening to Fleetwood Mac on my new stereo when the call came in. "Thos, get here as fast as you can." Doc Bliven was calling up available aircrewmen for an urgent mission.

"What's up?" I had to ask.

"A ship's on fire and they need help, that's all I know. Now get your ass down here in a hurry, speed if you have to, but get that Harley fired up."

I did. I was quickly at the squadron space along with Teddy Bear and Jose Guzman. Jose suffered from short-timer's disease. He had turned in his wings figuring he made it that far, why court fate with a few months to go. But he responded because he was needed and experienced and available. Two complete crews were assembled within minutes.

Lt. Larson, a recent addition to the pilot's roster, briefed us as I squeezed into my custom wet suit. Doc was going to fly as my 1st crewman and I took it for granted I was going in the water. A ship on fire conjured up men jumping over the side to escape killer flames. I couldn't help but think of the *Kitty Hawk* fire and the casualties it begot.

Larson kept it short. "Listen up, the USS *Enhance* is burning off the coast of Mexico. It's an old wooden-hulled mine sweeper and they're in deep trouble. Right now they're tied up alongside their sister ship but they need firefighting foam and medevacs so let's forgo the usual formalities and get out there ASAP."

We bolted out to the helos and with a cursory pre-flight got ready to fly. Doc and I loaded cans of fire-suppressing foam as Jose and Teddy Bear readied the other helo.

Soon at the scene, we began to lower the foam as smoke inhalation and burn victims gathered on the deck. There weren't any men in the water—just a lot of sharks—so I stayed aboard and helped Doc. Billowing clouds of smoke obscured our vision while towering ship's antennas swayed with the swells, both hazardous to our hover

over the stricken ship. After our load of foam had been lowered we began to hoist up sailors who needed medical attention.

Once we had the casualties aboard we raced to Balboa Hospital. The sailors looked like they had peered into hell: stained soot-black by smoke, exhausted by fighting flames in a confined space capable of being totally devoured by fire, their weary eyes peered out of faces framed by fear.

It was all over within a few hours. Back at the aircrew locker Jose had some parting comments as I peeled off my sweat-filled wet suit. "See, I told you so! Did you hear it? We had a rotorblade strike! Lucky we didn't snap a blade and crash on top of that poor little boat out there. That's why I turned in my wings, Thos; I just knew fate would catch up to me, and today it almost did. That was a close one, another foot and the rotor blade would have been ripped open, maybe even completely off. I'm done. I'm really, really fuckin' done. Here, you can have my 90 degree flashlight, I know you could use an extra one, and take my checklist too, I won't be needing it anymore. Adios, Thos. And good luck, you'll need it."

The day ended with a deep feeling of satisfaction and the dull edge of dread about my own safety in the air.

Late 1974 brought a switch of air wings for the Black Knights to Air Wing 2, which put us on the USS *Ranger*, CV-61. The "Stranger" as I christened it. We started flying plane guard for our new air wing immediately.

Muhammad Ali upset George Foreman in the "rumble in the jungle" in Zaire on October 20. I lost that bet to Brady; I thought George was unbeatable. Ali used cunning and lightning-fast speed, wearing Foreman out by feigning resignation to brutal hammerings by George's huge fists.

As 1974 came to a close the winds of change blew across the Pacific from South East Asia. "The status quo there can't hold," Lt. Gray assured me.

PART FOUR
1975

13: ON THE BEACH

The USS *Ranger* wasn't scheduled to go to Vietnamese waters in 1975 which meant the Black Knights weren't either. Commander Rich, who had become the CO, had his work cut out for him, however. Not only did he need to keep his squadron combat ready, but he was also working on further integrating helicopter ASW with fixed wing attack carrier tactics. That concept was the future of carrier operations. Some of the old Essex-class carriers, holdovers from WWII, had been converted solely to ASW but their time was running out.

The *Hancock*, my ship-that-almost-was, steamed west on March 18, heading back into the South China Sea. It was Essex class, heavily modified since its WWII combat days. Carriers continued to rotate in and out of Task Force 77, stationed off the Vietnamese coast. I didn't know anybody who knew why.

Chief Rice, who replaced Chief Hatch on the WestPac, had the set answer. "Ours is not to wonder why, ours is but to fly and fly. And Manthos, you have a NATOPS checkride coming up, best you be thinking about that and not world politics."

Flying out of Imperial Beach after having been on a WestPac was a piece of cake. Heading west, over the Oneonta Slough and across the beach, we would fly to one of several operating areas to practice antisubmarine warfare. We were increasingly using sono-buoys—devices a yard long and as big around as a fence post—to search for submarines. We would throw them out of the cargo door and watch as they spiraled down on spinning blades like a helo in an autorotation. Each buoy was on a separate frequency and a grid would be set to cover a large area. A hydrophone inside the sono-buoy would be released on impact and run to depth, listening for any sounds. The master plan was to have receiver equipment on the *Ranger* to translate the signals into visible data. Each submarine had its own unique sound signature, and if all went well it could be discerned from other sound sources, like merchant ships or simply the constant ambient noise the ocean generates.

Aircrew had much to learn about the new ASW equipment the *Ranger* would have tucked into a tiny compartment. Special schools would be attended by those of us who would be completing the next WestPac, due sometime in 1976. That was about the time Lt. Gray figured South Vietnam would fall.

Being "on the beach" gave me time to look inward. Reading Gan-dhi's biography had deeply affected me, and having been trained as a warrior quite by accident, I felt torn. I considered learning how to fly Marine Cobra attack helicopters, the most advanced killing machine on rotor blades the United States had. I enjoyed rescue and medevac flights the most. I admired Gandhi's strength through nonviolence. I wanted to avenge the harm done to my friend Tom, whose Army Loach observation helicopter had been shot down in South Vietnam. I picked up a book on yoga in a Chula Vista bookstore and started stretching my body and mind. I would go to the Westerner bar dur-ing "five for one" hour and get drunk on cheap bourbon and flirt with "WestPac widows," women whose husbands were in the South China Sea, maybe on the *Hancock*. One woman's husband was a submariner; perhaps I had played cat and mouse with his sub.

I picked up *In my Own Way* by Alan Watts and delved into his spiritual journey, which took him from Western religion to Eastern and places in between. I was drawn to Eastern philosophies and religions with the uncluttered mind of an infidel in the purest sense.

I rode my Harley Davidson across the desert floor so fast I couldn't read the speedometer.

Lt. Jankowsky sensed this restlessness in me. "Time is longer than rope," he tossed out one afternoon after we returned from a flight.

"Why do you say that, Mr. Jankowsky?" I had to know, even if I would likely not grasp his answer.

"Why Manthos, haven't you ever contemplated a proverb? Ever tackle a Zen Koan? You know, like 'what is the sound of one hand clapping?'"

"No, I haven't, I mean, isn't that a pointless question, Sir?"

"You're off to a good start, Thos, keep thinking about it." Later he let me listen to tapes of Baba Ram Dass. I tried to "be here now" even if I wasn't sure where that was.

He had been my pilot on the fly-off back in July. He got home ahead of the announced schedule and found his wife in bed with another man. I wondered what kind of Koan that might make: what is the sound of one man weeping?

——◆——

SHORE TIME WAS PUT to good use. A detachment was sent to NAS Fallon, Nevada, and I was included in the roster. We had a few new guys to the squadron who also went: AW3 Dungan, AW3 Amarine and Chief Dominguez, one of my former HS-10 instructors.

The det was for combat search and rescue training. It was probably a good thing we hadn't been called to do a feet-dry rescue in Vietnam; we would have had a very steep learning curve. When it came to dealing with the cold war we were well prepared, but pulling a pilot out from enemy territory under fire was an altogether different situation.

The flight there was long but getting over the Sierra Nevada mountains was a chance to see some beautiful scenery. Snow still covered the Sierras and as we landed in Fallon the cold mountain wind swept down into the high desert base.

It was a place for various types of flight crews to congregate. There was everything from Air Force Pararescue to Top Gun pilots. Our playground was at the end of a flight to the northeast, across a wide dry lake bed and over sand dunes before climbing a steep cliff face up to a mesa. Once there we practiced combat tactics. Close to the ground. I was used to flying close to the water, but even with its multitude of aquatic expressions it was still simply water in its varied moods. Dry land—high desert—held a different feel and fascination. And also danger. Losing an engine at fifty feet over hard ground all but guaranteed a fatal crash in an explosion of jp4 jet fuel and shards of twisted metal. But the sage and scrub oak and tufts of bunch grass zooming by at 100 knots made for exciting rides.

On one run off the mountain and into another dry lake bed in a simulated flight into enemy territory, I had a front row seat to combat rescue tactics. As I sat in the aft station looking out the starboard side I watched three A-7 Corsair IIs fly in a racetrack pattern tilted at a 45 degree angle to the horizon. They were there to protect us, the rescue helo, from any threat. Each Corsair carried a 20mm rapid fire gun and up to 15,000 pounds of ordnance, and their pilots had perfected the rhythm of one Corsair coming by our starboard side every few seconds to give almost continuous firepower. It felt good, even just as an exercise. It also felt like payback for all the hours I spent in plane guard flights sweating in a wetsuit ready to help them out. They looked like swept-winged avenging angels dropping out of the sky.

On the flight back to Fallon I was dangling my legs out of the helo, tossing soda bottles using WWI bombing tactics, trying to hit a rock or cactus. We were low to the ground over the dry lake bed, any water having evaporated a millennia before. It had been a perfect day: the weather clear, the flying fun, and nobody got hurt.

All of a sudden the Sea King reared up like a stallion spooked by a rattlesnake. The nose reaching high and the engines screaming power to the rotors, we climbed a steep hill of air. The blades bit into cold desert oxygen as the airframe pulsed under the bite of the leading blade.

I didn't see them until a split-second after the pilots did. Power lines. Dead ahead. G forces pushed me into the deck while I stared out at 50-foot tall poles with multiple wooden outstretched arms like a row of Shivas dancing across the desert holding delicate threads of fatal volts between them. We could have left tire marks on the cable sheathing we were so close. As we climbed over the trap of wires I watched fading sunlight race down the length of cable just like it would have if we hadn't almost been ensnarled and electrocuted.

That night would begin a lifelong series of nightmares involving flying into entanglements of varied dreamscape settings, each impossible to fly through. Anxiety would lead to despair before I would bolt upright in a sweat.

The power lines continued to stretch across the desert like a spider's web, waiting for errant aircrews momentarily distracted or preoccupied.

After a week of combat tactics training and losing cash at the casinos in Fallon we headed back to IB and the routine of flying out of Ream Field.

———————◆———————

EARLY APRIL. LT. GRAY brought us up to date on South Vietnam. "I give it nine months before the South falls, without our intervention. Right now we have a handful of carriers over there: the Enterprise, Coral Sea, *Hancock* and Midway. My best guess is that the NVA will back off a bit with that kind of firepower right off the coast. We still have six thousand Americans in South Vietnam. Somebody is going to have to get them out at some point."

The *Hancock*. My ship that almost was. Had things gone differently in Memphis that would have been me off the Vietnamese coast as that world collapsed. But it wasn't.

I waited for the news that we were to pack up, onload our gear and head for the *Ranger* and a fast deployment to the South China Sea. It never came. The daily news reports and Lt. Gray's briefings were nothing but ever-worsening news. The Communists were crashing south so fast they amazed even themselves at how quickly the South's defenses crumbled. It wasn't a matter of months but weeks.

The crash of a C-5 Galaxy cargo plane as it was leaving Tan Son Nhut airport in Saigon was tragic news. It was loaded with babies. Operation Baby Lift had been dealt a terrible blow in a land already ripped apart by war.

At the same time, Cambodia's Khmer Rouge under Pol Pot were doing almost the same thing as the NVA, rapidly taking over their country. The sweep of fragile governments in South East Asia was happening over a year sooner than Lt. Gray had predicted during the WestPac.

I sat by the swimming pool at the apartment, tanning myself and sipping on a cold beer as the news came on the thirtieth that Saigon had fallen. There was no more "South Vietnam." It had definitely been exhaled into oblivion. I felt useless and impotent. There were plenty of beers left in the fridge to console my remorse.

Zipper Sandin was visibly upset when the news spread throughout the squadron. "Hey Thos, what do you think of all that crap happening over there? It pisses me off, I mean, what the hell was it all for, anyway." He pulled out his Zippo and lit a cigarette. He didn't smoke it; he just stared out the window, letting the rising ribbons of haze ascend to the low ceiling where they slowly dissipated into the ether like so many dead pilots' souls.

The merchant ship *Mayaguez* was seized by Cambodian Khmer Rouge soldiers May 13. The last American troops to die in Indochina gave their lives in the battle for that ship and its crew.

THE FLAMINGO CAFE IN Chula Vista. Just a few blocks from the apartment, it was like an emergency room for the pathetically hung over. That often meant Pete, Malcolm and me. The Formica tabletops and Naugahyde covered booths routinely withstood the assault of our bodies dropping their weight. Coil springs poked through the bench seats, steel fingers searching for a tender spot. The ashtrays never seemed to be completely empty.

"Hi Hon," came the dependable greeting from Betty, who was always on the midmorning shift. I called her "beehive Betty" for her teased, dyed and piled-up hair. She could stick three pencils into it and not lose a single one. Too much lipstick and eye shadow fleshed out her look. She was old enough to be my mother and acted like it.

"You boys look like you've been hootin' with the owls all night. Ya' can't soar with the eagles the next morning if you do that, now can ya'?"

"No, Betty, you're right," we would chime in unison. "Coffee, and lots of it, OK-please?" I begged.

She looked right at me, shook her head and said "My-my, and you should know better, Hon. I'll just leave the pot right here." She would set the hot carafe in the same spot she had for decades, right where it had singed a brown halo into the Formica.

"The usual for you boys this morning? Or is it afternoon ..." Sometimes a chilicheeseburger omelette—our favorite—was just the antidote to too much booze and world politics. The food was modest and plentiful. If the cook had an off-day some hot sauce made up the difference.

Outside, the Flamingo sign pulsed pink neon blood through its veins, flickering on and off to the rhythm of a short in the wiring.

By the time the North Vietnamese Army had taken control of the territory south of Saigon, five of us aircrewmen were at NAS Willow Grove, Pennsylvania, for training on the AQA-7 sonobuoy data-processing device. That little piece of electronics gear would be the shipboard antisubmarine detection equipment gracing the *Ranger*. Learning how to interpret the signals was an art form. The two instructors were seasoned vets of the S-2F "Stoof" world. The *Hawk* had two S-2F Tracker squadrons hunting subs but the *Ranger* would not; it would just be the Black Knights and the AQA-7. We were going to have the leading edge of technological wizardry with the little machine on board, but it was a long way off from being a reality.

Willow Grove was almost like a vacation. The small base had

the best chow hall I had experienced, and after classes we had time to jog around the base and still go into town for a few drinks at the local pub.

One evening as I was riding the bus into town a man who had been at the front gate bus stop with me struck up a conversation. "So, you are at the base, yes?" He had a thick Eastern European accent. "I am too. So, you must be learning many things there, yes?"

"Well, mostly just hanging around," I responded, very cautiously. We had been warned about discussing our trade. There were governments that would have liked to have known what I knew, if only to help plug leaks in their security by eliminating sources of information to the West.

He chuckled. "You don't trust me because I am foreigner, right? Of course, yes, I am spy. Yes, a spy." He laughed some more. "My name is Zorko. Anton Zorko. Trust me or not, I will buy us drinks, and we will dance with American women."

And so we did.

I never did trust him; at the very least he could have been a plant from the DoD, at worst a real spy with the perfect cover of saying he was one. The only secret I revealed to him was that I still loved Marsha.

It was rumored that the base commander, aptly named Bird, got airsick when he flew his required hours. I was reminded of *Catch-22* and the incongruities that saturated the military.

The five of us didn't do any flying, we just studied sonobuoy data, doing our best to grasp the exotic-looking information and "find" the Soviet subs buried within all the other noises carried by the ocean.

Two weeks later we finished the schooling. Once again I was given an official Navy certificate. Cdr. Bird even signed it. I finished fifth out of five. They weren't about to flunk me but I didn't impress them with my absorption of complex information. I always did better once I was in the aircraft, hands on and flying. Time would tell if that would hold true once I was sitting in front of the *Ranger*'s AQA-7.

PETE, MALCOLM AND I kicked back on our apartment's couch, drinking Coors and reflecting on how many days we had left in the Navy.

"I'll grab us a few more beers," Pete volunteered. As he got up slowly we heard a thud. "What the fuck was that?" we uttered in unison. Pete entered the dimly lit kitchen, declaring, "You guys should take a look at this."

We found Malcolm's SH-3D helicopter model lying on the dingy yellow linoleum. He had bought it in the Philippines only a few months before. Made of monkey pod, the wooden model had sat proudly on top of the beer-filled refrigerator. Painted in fleet colors of white over gray, with our distinctive squadron accent of vibrant orange on the sponson points, tail rotor housing and main rotor cover, it was a miniature of the real thing. It was complete with five little rotor blades that turned on a small spindle. But there it was on the floor, a big dent on the forward right side, about where the pilot would sit. We held the same thought, was it an omen? A jinx? We couldn't help but be superstitious.

"Whoa! That's really weird," was my drunken response. "How the hell did it end up on the floor? It looks like the damn thing just flew into it."

"It must have been vibrated off by the refer motor. Or maybe it was an evil spirit," Pete mused, handing us another round of beer. Not wanting to think about the strange event too much, we diverted our short attention spans to something less ominous, like the lack of women in our lives.

A few days after the model helicopter crash in the cramped kitchen, Pete and I were scheduled to go out on a two helo mission. We had volunteered for night ops, so we went in late, often flying into the early-morning hours. Malcolm was supposed to go but got sick so Pete filled in for him.

Looking at the flight schedule, I was puzzled. "Hey, who made out the schedule? I usually fly with Lt. Rolek. Pete, looks like you're going out with him tonight instead." An Annapolis graduate, Lt. Leo Rolek was a fine pilot and all around good guy. Built like a linebacker, his sandy blonde hair framed a square, high cheekboned face quick to wear a smile. I had flown with Leo a lot on the WestPac and was a little let down someone had broken us up as a team.

"That's the breaks of naval air," said Pete, drawing on his repository of Navy lingo.

As Lt. Rolek entered the ready room from the officer's lockers he looked at me and asked, "You flying with me tonight, Manthos?"

"Hell no, I don't want to die." I shot back. Bravado wasn't in the green nylon and canvas flight gear issued to naval aviators, but it was there nonetheless. It was one of the survival items.

"Fuck you very much, Thos!" Leo quipped, smiling his wide grin. The mutual respect Leo and I had allowed for a lot of ribbing, but I would have flown into the swirling teeth of a typhoon with him without hesitation.

The rest of Rolek's crew assembled. Leo's copilot was Lt.j.g. Neville, new to the squadron. Tall and lanky, he walked with the grace of a wide receiver. Brady Turner completed the crew roster.

Rolek, Neville, Pete and Brady strode out to their helo. My crew also assembled at our assigned helicopter, parked next to Pete's. As our two crews readied helos for the flight into a Southern California evening, I waved to Pete as he preflighted aircraft number 740.

That helicopter had a famous past. It made five Apollo pick-ups as side number 66. Many photos and newsreels showed the helo hovering over Apollo capsules floating in the Pacific. It had also flown President Kennedy, and the crew of Lt. Rolek, Commander Pearigan, Chief Hatch and myself had flown the Shah of Iran out to the *Kitty Hawk* in it just months before. 740 was destined for the Smithsonian museum once its flying days were done, a nice piece of aviation history and we all felt privileged to be a part of that.

My helo was having problems making it beyond the start-up of the number one engine. The generators weren't functioning properly so we shut down, canceled the mission, and proceeded to the maintenance shack to write up the "gripe" sheets, the paperwork that would begin the process of correcting the problem.

740 taxied out to the runway and lifted off into the cool coastal

air. My crew went its separate ways after the paperwork and short debrief. I shed my cumbersome flight gear, cramming it in my gray metal locker. Slamming the steel door shut and snapping the combination lock closed, I walked outside and mounted my Super Glide, always parked next to Pete's Sportster.

Back at our little safe house of an apartment, I decided to have a few beers and listen to some Crosby, Stills, Nash and Young. I waited for Pete to get back to talk over his mission, but gave up after several hours and went to bed.

In the morning I went into Pete's room to roust him. I hadn't heard him come in but he had to be back by then.

"Hey Pete, rise and shine, let's get going or we'll be in trouble."

"I clathed lasst night," was his sleepy response.

"Bullshit. Get your lazy ass up, time to be Navy!" I retorted.

"Noh, noh, I really crashed lasst nihh, I ain't goin' anywherr."

"What? Why didn't you get me up when you came in?"

"We crashed late, didn't get picked up for hours. Fuckin' Coast Guard made the rescue. And if that don't beat all, the fucking bastards at squadron want me come to muster. Fuck, Mr. Rolek is still in the hospital."

"Dammit, I can't believe it. Let me look at you." He looked like a well-used speed bag at a Golden Gloves convention. Pete's face was bruised purple and red, his tongue swollen and he was complaining about a throbbing headache. "Where did they take you?"

"It was a gagglefuck from the beginning. Oh, Balboa. They finally got us to Balboa. And the idiots there were just standing around the pad when the Coast Guard helo landed. I had to yell at them that there was a hurt pilot inside. Mr. Rolek was getting pretty weak by the time we got there. I don't know, I just don't know..."

"Look, I'll get to the squadron and cover for you for muster. Chief Rice must be able to get you a few days off, at least off the flight schedule for a while. Take it easy, OK Pete?"

It was hard to take it all in. Just a few hours before, I had waved to Pete as his helo taxied to the runway. And what had gone wrong? And why were the Coasties making the rescue? We were the premier base for helicopter search and rescue; why couldn't a helo from IB make the pickup? It was a very weird thing, and it would get stranger yet. And what about Mr. Rolek and Mr. Neville and Brady? I couldn't get to the squadron fast enough to find out. I folded down the chrome kick-start lever of my Harley, giving it a good punch with all my body weight behind it. The finely tuned V-twin engine coughed up its distinctive throaty song and off I sped to the hangar, a knot slowly growing in my gut.

I rolled up to the gate and the gray-suited guard checked the front fork for the base sticker. I passed the guard shack in a blast of dyno-tuned power and raced to the squadron hangar. There, a cloud of quiet apprehension hung over the Black Knights. We had tallied 40,000 flight hours without an accident—that was a lot of flying.

The usual banter and chatter among crews and personnel was absent; everyone was wondering the same thing: what happened out there? The pieces would slowly be put together. My piece of the puzzle was made of guilt.

I watched from the hangar gallery as fragments from the wreck were brought in by other helos; an orange seat cushion, a canvas jump seat, a strobe light, remnants of the famous 740. It went down in over 2,500 feet of water—not much would ever be recovered. The fuselage would slowly become encrusted with sea life half a mile below the surface of the Pacific. Instead of residing in the Smithsonian, 740 lay in a museum of failed aerodynamics in water too dark to see.

The story slowly took form. Rumor spread that the runway tower spotted double red-star flares the crew had shot, known to every aviator as a distress signal. Somehow the tower thought kids were playing with fireworks on the sandy fringes of the beach. Hours went by. As the West Coast helicopter search and rescue base, NAS IB somehow, painfully, ironically, could not, did not, get a fully functional rescue helicopter to the scene. The fleet training squadron, HS-10, managed to get a Sea King to the site, but it was mechanically incapable of performing a simple rescue, an event we, as a fleet aviation arm, took great pride in executing.

It must have been infuriating, so near everything they needed yet for so long unable to get any help. Eventually a Coast Guard H-3 made it to the scene of the four soaked flyers huddling together in the darkness, their black rubber flotation gear making an eerie "sqweee, sqweee" sound as the inflated bags chafed together. Finally the big Coastie helo set down in the water, lowered the rear ramp and pulled in the crew. Pete was continually yelling at the Coast Guard crew, "Get your asses in gear! We got a hurt pilot here!" For Pete things were moving in the frustrating pace of a bad dream, where no matter how hard you tried you couldn't move quickly in a molasses-filled world.

Once at Balboa Naval Hospital, Pete again encountered sloth-like performance from the receiving personnel. His resentment and anger at the way things had developed would simmer underneath his calm exterior for months.

The hospital released everyone but Lt. Rolek. Lt.j.g. Neville had some facial lacerations and bruises, but seemed in fair shape. Brady looked pretty good. Pete could walk, but had a neck ache that turned out to be a cracked vertebrae. This he would not know for six weeks.

"Those idiots, they gave me the wrong X-rays. My fuckin' neck is broken and I didn't know it all this time! All it would take is to dump my Sportster and I could be paralyzed."

I asked Brady how he got out of the wreckage; I wanted to know what he did to escape, just in case I ever needed to. When the water/air temperature was below a combined 120 degrees, aircrewmen had to wear their rescue swimmer wet suits under all their flight gear. It made things unbearably hot and, with the added buoyancy, I wondered if that made it tough to get out of the sinking helo.

"I don't know, I was just out, just through a big hole and out," was all Brady could say. He seemed distant. All the training for disorientation awareness either worked subconsciously, or things just simply happened. Reliving the long night was taking its toll on him.

The mood at the squadron was tense. Much of the night's events went undisclosed, but I was close to both Pete and Brady, and I repeatedly asked about it. Pete had the most complete story to tell.

"We were in a sonar hover, had about a hundred feet of cable in the water. Everybody was tired. Seems like we started to slip backwards, then things seemed OK, but the tail rotor hit and that was all it took. The noise was deafening: tearing metal, rotor blades thrashing, cold water rushing in everywhere, it was fuckin' crazy."

All the usual after-accident elements occurred: a renewed commitment to safety, a new replacement aircraft for 740, the sense that even after 40,000 hours, routine flights can unravel.

Lt. Rolek never returned to the squadron. He died not long after that night. The whole squadron tried to donate blood, but since most of us had taken the big malaria pills while off the coast of Vietnam, our blood was rejected.

Brady Turner quit flying. He turned in his wings, never to step into a Sikorsky SH-3D Sea King again. Wearing the striking gold wings of a naval aircrewman—looking so classy against the dark Navy dress blue uniform—was a proud thing. Brady decided it wasn't worth the bragging rights; his wife and baby daughter came first. No one begrudged him his decision; it was volunteer duty and for obvious reasons. He left the squadron shortly after the crash, rumored to have been sent to a destroyer sonar shack. He would be missed, after going through so much with him over the years.

Lt.j.g. Neville continued to fly as did Pete. He and I would fly together as well, as friends and squadronmates. He would also continue to fly at night, even as he struggled with nightmares about being trapped in a sinking helicopter.

After a few days I went to take another look at Malcolm's helicopter model. There it sat on top of the refrigerator, a big 740 painted on its side, the same number as the famous helo on the bottom of the ocean. I took it down, glancing at where it hit the floor. There, on the right side where the pilot would be sitting in the cockpit, was a big dent, the gray and white paint chipped off. It was right where Leo had sat in the real 740, where his body absorbed the impact. A chill ran through me. I stood there looking at the damaged model, wishing I could have picked up the real 740 as easily and set it back to where it was safe.

Pete had seen his future, his fate, his destiny, that night we stood gazing at the wrecked model. Did that make it an omen, or just a strange coincidence?

What began as a simple training mission changed me forever. Why was I stupid enough to say something to Leo like, "Hell no, I don't want to die"? What would have happened if I hadn't said it? Of course there could be no logical connection, no jinx, but the questions and guilt began to build. What would have happened if I had flown with Leo? Could I have prevented the crash? Why did our own helo have to fail to fly; if we were airborne we could have been right there when the crash occurred. We could rescue pieces of dead aircraft, but not living crewmen.

Too many questions. It would become the longest night of my life and I didn't even know it at the time. I would relive that night a thousand times, each time playing out the different possibilities of an alternate universe where Leo lived and all was well. After a one-day safety stand-down we got back to the business of aviation. The notion that shore-based flying was routine and just a job had been shaken free of its moorings and set adrift. The loss of one of our own on top of losing the famous helo got everyone's attention.

"I want to see everyone's nose in their NATOPS," ordered Chief Rice. "You turkeys better pass your checkrides on the first try or I'll have your ass. Chief Dominguez won't cut anybody slack with their tests, either. And Manthos, you're the aircrew training petty officer, I want my lectures read to the division on a regular basis."

He was right, we had lost a bit of that edge we had honed while on WestPac, and even if that had nothing to do with the crash, we needed to get it back.

―◗◖―

NEW GUYS SHOWED UP as Brady Turner cleaned out his locker. A reservist named Rich Keene checked in with a single-mindedness I would not understand until a few months later. Tony Dinkle sported a good attitude. John Dungan had settled into the squadron as Jose Guzman and Clyde Dog were getting short.

"I'm so short I can sit on a dime and dangle my legs," teased Clyde Dog. "How long you got left, Thos? Over a year? Well sumbitch."

"Rub it in Clyde Dog, we're going on a plane guard det for two weeks, that will be a nice way to end your naval career!"

"Yeah, but I got news for you. I'm done flying, turned in my wings yesterday. I'll be a brownshirt, I don't care, I'm too damned short to die in a helo crash. I've got football to play and women to chase." He had a point. A handful of aircrewmen had quit flying; Jose was one of the first, several more followed. Clyde Dog didn't mind being a plane captain; he was certainly qualified.

Once aboard the *Ranger* I could see him through my crewman's window as he stood by the starboard landing gear wearing his flight deck helmet and brown flotation vest, waiting to pull chocks and chains. I would manage a resigned smile as he grinned his toothy grin and waved, wishing me a safe flight with no guarantees of one.

The *Ranger* was almost identical to the *Kitty Hawk*: same weight, same flight deck, same cramped quarters. The biggest difference was in the deck load, no S-2 Trackers for ASW. The other aircraft were very familiar: F-4 Phantoms, A-6 Intruders, A-7 Corsair IIs, EA-6B ultra-secret electronic jamming planes. The EA-6s had a gold-lined cockpit to prevent radiation damage to the four-man crew. Nice to know the Navy spared no expense to protect their assets. The E-2 Hawkeye turbo-props, the "hummers," added air protection along with the A-3 Skywarriors, or "whales." The A-3 was a massive twin-engined jet and it was a tight fit on the flight deck when a Skywarrior landed.

My all-time favorite plane remained the RA-5 Vigilante. It looked like it was flying at 1,000 miles per hour standing still, and could top that in the air. The front landing gear was positioned so far behind the cockpit that when they were taxiing on the flight deck the pilot could be over water and not see the ship. It was sleek, fast, and elegant. Everything the Sea King wasn't. But for all its ungainly bulk I still loved the H-3; it was as dependable as a Wyoming saddle horse.

I always took books along when I was shipboard: coveted portals into other worlds, other minds, other realities. At one point I had been drawn into the evangelical fervor that swept in young impressionable minds. The sailors who drew me in promised eternal life and a short stay on earth as the end was near, while at the same time they were investing in real estate. That seemed a contradiction. Within a short time I rejected apocalyptic predictions and teleological arguments; I was much more fascinated by the nature of time as expressed by the Hindu calendar and the nature of reality as envisioned by Buddhism. I read books on both, letting my mind absorb nonwestern concepts. The age of the Hindu creator god Brahma was such a mathematically complex and huge number that I was entranced by the sheer magnitude of the idea. That Buddhism talked of illusion being our normal everyday perception caused me to question my world as I saw it.

And I loved the sight of an F-4 on afterburners as it left the flight deck at night, the harmonic rings of J79 jet engine exhaust pulsating in perfect harmony with nature's laws as the fighter streaked to altitude to assume Combat Air Patrol. That was one hell of an illusion.

⊱ ● ⊰

BACK FROM THE *RANGER*'S short cruise we continued to get new crewmen mission qualified. With another ASW training flight completed, my crew headed back to IB. The West Coast sun was beginning its downward slide into the Pacific Ocean as our tires hit runway 27, skid marks from thousands of landings marking the optimum spot. Amid the angry fanlike noise of five big rotor blades, we taxied in a roll to the flight line.

I was looking forward to firing up my Harley and going for a cold beer to unwind. AWAN Dinkle collected his swim gear as I opened the side hatch to help get the helicopter shut down. Searing-hot turbine exhaust billowed in, followed by Feek.

"Hey Feek, the old gal is still able to fly. Still leaking some hydraulic fluid though, see, by the transmission."

"Thos, that just means you have some fluid left, don't sweat it. I'll check it out when you get back. You ain't done yet, got a message for ya'." He handed me the dispatch, shrugging his shoulders. I relayed the information to the pilots.

"Mr. Gross, Mr. Jankowsky, we've been ordered to Twentynine Palms Marine Base for a medevac. I sure hope it's worth it, I'm dog-tired."

"They call it 'twenty nine stumps' out there, Thos. Look up the base radio frequency and find the maps while I get us some fuel," Gross ordered. "And we only need one crewman, figure out who it's going to be, we'll be going back out ASAP."

Dinkle wore a look on his face like he had a date lined up or wished he had or was going to go try to make one happen so I cut him loose. "Catch ya' later Dinkle; you can still make happy hour at the EM club if you hurry."

I dug out the maps for Mr. Gross as Feek got us topped off with fuel. We adjusted our flight gear, wiped the sweat out from under our flight helmets and taxied back out to the runway, launching into the ever-ripening orange ball of sun. Turning back northeast we put the setting sun behind, climbing to altitude to clear the mountains that stood between San Diego and the high desert.

After a quiet hour of flight we dropped down into the desert and its flat, desolate, sun-baked world. Two Phantoms overtook us at our nine o'clock, the last rays of sunlight glinting off the sleek fighters. Standing at the open top hatch of the crew door I gave a wave, and a quick rock of the wings from the lead F-4 connected me to those aviators as they sliced through hot desert air to their own destiny.

Darkness crept into our helicopter. Fatigue set in as the full day ended, and wearily we adjusted to the night. Jankowsky turned on the instrument panel lights, glowing red and dancing in front of our eyes.

Finally in radio contact with the Twentynine Palms tower, we received instructions to our landing zone. By then it was pitch black and moonless. In the barren Mojave there were few lights to give any sense of civilization, save for the Marine base. We were instructed to land in a sports field, where a corporal would guide us in.

Once we had him sighted the pilots maneuvered onto the scrub-grass of the field while I was hanging out the back, clearing the tail wheel of any obstructions. Scattered debris and dust were kicked up by our rotor blades, and the downward force flattened the scrubby grass far into the night. Our young Marine waved us in, getting us settled down onto the field. I slid the cargo door the rest of the way open as the corporal ran up.

"Glad to see you guys, we have an emergency at the hospital. Don't know any more than that, just need you to stand by."

"Corporal, how long do we have to 'stand by'? We don't have enough fuel to sit here all night."

"I'll radio in and find out what I can. OK, the ambulance is on its way." Soon an old blue Cadillac ambulance pulled up in the darkness, backing in toward the cargo door. A transparent incubator, complete with access holes in the side, was gently carried to the helo by two civilian doctors. This didn't make sense at a Marine base.

In the dim red cabin light I could barely see what was inside. I had to get real close but there, in the center, was a tiny little body, wrinkled pink and barely bigger than my two fists put together. A lump formed in my throat as I gazed at the tiny premature baby, whose first major life experience outside the womb was to be a ride in my helicopter.

"Hey Manthos," Mr. Jankowsky asked, "what shape is our Marine in back there?"

"Sir, it's not—it's not a Marine at all, it's a little baby, can't be more than a few pounds. I've never seen a baby so tiny before." This had caught us all off guard. Expecting a wounded Marine—tough, conditioned and trained for combat—we had a tiny new life instead. Dwarfed by sophisticated war machinery, the helpless child lay oblivious to all around her. Engaged in her own struggle to live, she gave us renewed energy.

"Well then Manthos, let's get this helo in the air and on our way!" came his reply.

It was a quiet flight back to San Diego. Gross had our helicopter at the 144 knot red line while Jankowsky and I watched for air traffic and backed him up on the instruments and radios. Occasionally I would steal a glance at the premature baby, wondering what her life would be like, wondering if she would ever know about her first ride in a helicopter. I couldn't help but smile.

She survived the flight back to San Diego, and by the time we got back to Imperial Beach it was midnight.

We had been in that helo for ten hours but I had forgotten that I was dead-tired, forgotten that I really didn't want to make that extra flight. And I would never forget the sight of that tiny little body wrapped in blue hospital blankets, lying in that small incubator in the back of my big Navy Sea King. She would always be my little Desert Flower.

———— • ————

MY GROOMING FOR SHIPBOARD ASW electronics gear continued. In late June, two weeks after the crash of 740, another pod of HS-4 aircrew was sent to a specialized school, this time at NAS Moffet Field, in the San Francisco Bay area. Doc Bliven was in the group as well as myself and Chuck Fields.

Moffet was a paradise. And it was where all of my A school class went save for Brady and me. Home to the West Coast P-3 Orion squadrons, it was a huge base once housing the dirigible USS *Macon*. An enormous hangar was constructed to house the lighter-than-air craft, so large it created its own weather inside.

Next to the base was the Ames NASA research center. Our barracks room was close by and at night I could hear the huge wind tunnels pummeling whatever the scientists were subjecting to the manmade hurricanes. On more than a few occasions after class I slipped through a chain link fence surrounding Ames and wandered about burial grounds holding metallic skeletal remains, castaways from past experiments. Everything lying about was aerodynamic: fins, flaps, cowlings, tails, wings, capsules and fuselages dotted the grassy field like so many disassembled and discarded raptorial robots. It was like seeing Flash Gordon's scrap heap. My mind wandered to velocities unattained by even the Vigilante. There was no way to tell which pieces had been part of a success and which flew apart under experimental rigors of flight, but they were all successful in at least one way—something was learned from their design.

I was learning a lot about designs too, as sound burned onto paper graphs. Lines depicting noise sources in salt water were deciphered in class. We would be using a smaller version of the AQA-7 taught at Moffet aboard the *Ranger*, but the principles were the same: sound gave away secrets about its source.

There was plenty of time off. One weekend Doc Bliven went to see Frankie Valli and the Four Seasons while Chuck and I went to a massage parlor. A beautiful woman claimed me as "hers" for the next few hours and we ended up just talking. I asked her if she wanted to get together for the 4th of July, maybe get some Sangre De Toro and find a hillside to watch fireworks from.

"Yes, I'd like that, it sounds sweet," she said. "Here's my phone number. Call me, cutie pie."

I felt wonderful; a voluptuous woman was paying attention to me and seemed genuine in wanting to get together. I focused on figuring out where we might go.

After a couple of days I called her number from the barracks hallway telephone. It rang and rang. I tried again every few hours. No answer. I tried again the next day—no luck. I was wearing out my dime for the pay phone.

The Fourth came and went as I sat in the base club drinking bourbon and staring at the bogus phone number she had given me, wondering why she would play with my mind like that. It was making me consider the ascetic life of a mendicant monk; somehow it seemed that would make life so much simpler.

The final weeks of training passed and I managed to get through the academics. It was a satisfactory-unsatisfactory program; I was "sat" and by how much I didn't know. I got still another official Navy certificate dated July 19, 1975. I was now trained to use the little AQA-7 we would be getting for the *Ranger*.

We made our way back to San Diego aboard a Lockheed L-188 Electra, the civilian version of the P-3 Orion. I was looking forward to getting back in my flight suit and doing some real helo flying again.

———◗◖———

IT WAS TIME TO prepare for my next promotion. Petty Officer 2nd Class was the equivalent of sergeant in the Marines and Army. If I made 2nd Class and 1st Crewman I would be in good shape. I had been flying as a 1st Crewman but it couldn't be made official until I had enough hours and checkrides. One of the preparations was flying as the maintenance test crewman, which meant going out on flights after work had been done and checking out a helo to make sure it was air worthy and mission capable. On one such flight we were hovering over a practice pad as hydraulic control began to fail. The test pilot set the helo down and I got out to see if there were any signs of a problem. It looked like the helicopter had been shot in the head—reddish purple hydraulic fluid was running down the airframe from the transmission area in rivulets as the control system was dying. We were damn lucky the system failure hadn't happened 100 miles west of IB or 10,000 feet in the air.

I took the exams for E-5 and did my best not to show how much I wanted out. Vietnam—the war—was over, and a sense of malaise settled over the Navy. We were in need of a sense of direction even as the Soviet Union continued to show the world its bluster. The Cold War was a puppet show of lethal implications, and proxy wars were straining to break out all over the African continent. The Middle East was seemingly on the verge of implosion. At least the Shah was in power in Iran and a US ally in the region.

We had a WestPac coming up in 1976 and were training vigorously for it. I continued to read esoteric books and ride my Harley across Southern California. I also continued to find release in massage parlors, since I had not found a girlfriend in San Diego. I wasn't proud of it; it was just a fact, sort of like the weather—stormy clouds with impending rain.

One night Pete and I hit the strip clubs downtown. We rode our bikes up from IB and went to all the classy joints, places with oak floors and brass bar rails. After we spent most of our E-4 pay on overpriced drinks and tips for the dancers, we headed back south.

"Hey Pete, whadduya wanna do now?" I yelled over the throaty exhaust notes of the two big Harleys as we sped down I-5.

"I'm starving, let's go to the Flamingo and get a chilicheese-burger," Pete suggested. It sounded really good: filling, nurturing. But after watching lithe female bodies gyrating in front of me and drinking watered-down whiskey, I longed for a different fulfillment. My hunger was of a more evolutionary kind.

"I'll catch up with ya' later Pete; I'm heading over to the H&I." The H&I. Massage Parlor. A place where despondent servicemen engaged jaded women in a time-honored exchange of money for, well, it wasn't really sex, it was more a servicing of basic vital systems, like an oil change or a tire balancing. I was feeling way out of balance.

It was another session of suspension of disbelief. After all was done I headed back out into the cold coastal air to climb aboard my green Super Glide and head back to our apartment. Except it wasn't there. My motorcycle. It had disappeared into the early morning like a vaporized cloud. Calling the police made everyone nervous, but it had to be done.

That made two exquisite, powerful motorcycles stolen in less than a year. It seemed as though the universe was going to keep tak-ing motorcycles away from me until I understood I was going to kill myself on one. Riding between lanes of traffic on the Interstate high on speed probably increased my chances of fulfilling that destiny. But my beloved Harley was gone. I had plowed fistfuls of money into her—dyno tuning, a Mikuni high performance carburetor, new electricals—it was a fine, well balanced machine. Now someone else was enjoying her mechanical perfection. It was an embarrassing walk back to the apartment. I would have to tell aircrew that my bike was ripped off. Would I tell them from where?

I bought an old beat-up '63 Chevy Impala to get me around until we went on the next WestPac. I never owned another motorcycle.

———◦———

FAST EDDIE SHOWED UP one day out of nowhere. That's how guys who were traded off or discarded showed up, out of thin air. He was wearing his blue working jacket, and it was a hot Southern California day. I knew he was enlisted by his dungaree uniform, but I couldn't tell his rank; his crow was covered by his jacket sleeve. His name was Edward Douval but I named him "Fast Eddie." I had seen that name etched into the valve covers of a tricked out Sportster and it seemed to fit; Eddie was all revved up. It was like his mind was a roulette wheel and the next scheme was whirling around the race waiting for the world to slow down enough for his idea to drop into a slot, didn't matter red or black, he would make it work, to his advantage, with your help. He had that bony look of someone who didn't eat much, his metabolism running like a hummingbird's. And he arrived in my division. He was an aircrewman but he wouldn't show up on the flight schedule; he was an S-2F Stoof man in a helo world, so why was he there? There was a reason: HS-4 needed someone with hands-on real world experience with the AQA-7 and the Navy detailer had scoured the roster for someone qualified on the gear but who wasn't needed in his squadron, or anywhere else but there.

His face—high cheekbones, thin black mustache, slicked back black hair, Marlboro dangling from his lips—made me think of a blackjack dealer working a table on the graveyard shift. Finally Fast Eddie dropped his jacket; he felt uncomfortable with everyone staring, wondering what he was hiding. It was his crow, his petty officer patch. It was half gone, or half there, depending on whether you were a half empty or half full kind of guy. He had been a First Class, an E-6. Not a bad rank to have, but now he was in limbo. I didn't know what he was, if he outranked me, or if it even mattered. I did see the wince on his face when his jacket hit the deck, there was a moment of embarrassment quickly followed by banter telling how it all happened and how he was in the wrong place at the wrong time and how the Navy was his life. He seemed older than his years.

I felt a certain magnetic pull into Fast Eddie's way that happened in a split second. But I listened to some inner voice that said stay clear, don't tangle yourself in that man's web. Regardless of his intentions, it felt like a pull into a place that would do me no good. Do the professional bit; work together, accomplish the mission, but don't collude or delude or concede or collide with him. Accomplices aplenty would make themselves available; that was assured. He would hold court to willing minds, attentive ears. I preferred to encounter what life had to offer in the far corners of the world in my own way.

———◆———

AUGUST. I WAS AT sea again. It seemed like the squadron was either going on a short cruise or getting back from one. Between special schools and condensed deployments time was passing quickly.

The *Ranger* was a classic supercarrier, the crown jewel of the surface fleet. It was the eighth ship to bear the name, the first being wooden hulled and commanded by John Paul Jones. If he could only see what the modern Navy had. The *Ranger* had been an attack carrier with seven WestPacs to Vietnam. By late June all attack carriers—CVAs—were re-designated CVs. This reflected, in part, the very integration of ASW capability HS-4 was intimately involved in. The upcoming WestPac would test our abilities—including using the little AQA-7 gear—and our successes or failures would factor heavily on whether or not the Navy decided to continue using helo ASW alongside so many fighters and attack jets. By joining *Ranger*'s Air Wing 2, our tail code had also changed, from NH to NE–November Echo.

Many personnel changes had taken place over the previous months. Clyde Dog was headed back to Kentucky. Jose Guzman and Chief Rice and Allen and a handful of experienced aircrew had also moved on. Teddy Bear was still with us and would be for some time; he was a rent-a-crow, six long years of commitment. But we gained new aircrew leadership through Chief Dominguez and our new aircrew chief, R.A. Beaty. John "JD" Dungan, a third generation sailor, was racking up short cruises and shipboard experience. Still, nothing like a full WestPac to cement one's pedigree as a salty dog. He was going to get his chance. Pete and Malcolm had enough time left to do the upcoming cruise. None of us relished the idea. Some of the new guys were curious. While on the August cruise Dinkle was asking a lot of questions.

"What's it like over there in the Philippines, Thos?"

"What's it like in the PI? And call it 'the PI,' it sounds like you know what you're talking about. I can guarantee it's like nothing you've ever seen back in Indiana. Everything will seem cheap, even life itself. The bar girls will want you to marry them and who can blame 'em—anything to get out of that life. You'll see a miniature castle in the bay, World War Two wrecks and artillery pieces all over the place. You'll walk across Shit River and wonder how anybody could get near it and yet see kids swimming and diving in it. You'll smell that ditch before you even get close. You'll see beaches that look like they're right out of Michener's *Tales of the South Pacific*. You'll sweat and stink and probably grow fungus on your feet and some kid in Olongapo will sell your own watch back to you before you know it's gone. You'll see rice paddies and water buffalo and giant jellyfish and sea snakes and dolphins and beggars and lepers and you'll drink San Miguel until you can't stand up. You'll swear you'll never drink another San Magoo but you will, I guarantee it. You'll even drink a Mojo or two. You'll think you fell into some sort of alternate-universe Old West and in many ways you will have done just that. Don't fuck with the national police and be off the streets by midnight. And, be careful of the benny boys, I doubt you want to take that route."

"What's a 'benny boy,' Thos?"

"Dinkle, go ask Chief Beaty."

SEPTEMBER STARTED OFF WITH yet another school. It was one I knew was coming since the WestPac—four days of intensive training in the loading and arming of a nuclear weapon. If I hadn't signed the nuclear weapons reliability form back in February of '74 I wouldn't have been in the ordnance loading school, but then I wouldn't have still been in HS-4 either.

It was a no-nonsense seminar on the very intricate process of getting a nuclear weapon attached to the side of a Sea King and making it "deployable." The bomb looked like a Hollywood version of one, like something out of a '50s science fiction movie. It was so bomb-like it seemed a parody. It reminded me of an exchange I had with a woman I briefly dated when I was home on leave.

"Is this your flight jacket?" she asked, slightly accusing in her tone as she rubbed her hand over the fine leather.

"Yep, see my WestPac patches? This one is for the air wing, this one is for the cruise..."

"Yeah but, do you have a real one?"

"A real one *what*? I was issued this from our paraloft. See my name on it?"

"OK, well, but I know somebody who has a *real* one."

It was as if my flight jacket was so real it looked fake to her. I was feeling kind of the same way towards the bomb.

On September 5 the Nuclear Weapons Training Group Pacific Command endowed me with the knowledge of how to get a multi-megaton weapon of mass destruction attached to the side of my helicopter. The official certificate had a mushroom cloud as a backdrop, looking like a radiation watermark.

I had a year to go on my enlistment. A handful of short cruises and a WestPac and I would be done. I passed my 1st Crewman check-rides in mid-September. If anyone had told me three years before that I would be given a certificate designating me as such I would not have believed them. I wanted to see that old master chief back at Memphis and tell him thanks for pushing me along. I wanted to tell

Chief Lawson thanks for giving me a second chance. And I was in a balancing act: one side of me disliked military life and wanted out in the worst way, the other took pride in making it as far as I could.

September 22 was the date of my official 1st Crewman certificate, signed by the squadron CO. On September 30 Ali KO'd Joe Frazier in Manila. Brady Turner wasn't around to take any bets. In the newly united country of Vietnam reeducation camps were established to "cleanse" the minds of former ARVN. In Cambodia a primitive and deliberate slaughter of the innocent was taking place. I was oblivious to both.

There were just a handful of months to go before we deployed on the WestPac. Pete, Malcolm and I made the most of it. We partied and raised hell in our apartment. And I found out why Rich Keene joined up—he wanted to earn enough money to buy a Hammond B-3 organ. Renowned by jazz and blues players the B-3, coupled with big Leslie speakers, was the ultimate electronic keyboard. Rich bought one. And he lived in the barracks. It would hardly fit in his locker so he asked if he could keep it at our apartment. He could play "Light my Fire" like he wrote the tune. The big spinning horns of the Leslie speakers would send throbbing reverb through walls, across rafters and within the foundation into the neighboring apartments. We were not very popular.

I had been learning to play the flute on my own over the previous year. Without any formal lessons I would hyperventilate for months until I finally learned how to get a decent tone. I figured a flute would be easy to pack in my seabag and maybe provide some sanity once back out in the South China Sea. Rich would kindly accompany me as I struggled with Neil Young tunes.

I also kept at my yoga routine. It was making a big difference in my flexibility and I thought it would be something I could do aboard ship. If I could find a spot with some privacy. On a carrier that might prove to be impossible.

The *Hancock* returned from the debacle in the South China Sea in mid-October. I couldn't help but think had I stayed with my original enlistment I would have been home and out of the Navy. I kept telling myself the last year would go by quickly, that a final voyage to a far-away sea over seven thousand miles away would seem dream-like soon after it was over.

I had plans to go back to college using the GI Bill. It was a great program and I was getting eager to flex my mind. I studied differ-ent schools and was thinking of somewhere in northern California.

And we partied hard those last few months on the beach. Mal-colm's 20th birthday was one to remember. We started with beer that morning just to get in the mood. Around noon a few bottles of wine were opened. That afternoon the Wild Turkey was brought out. Fortunately there was a liquor store nearby; nothing lasted very long. Aircrew showed up throughout the day as our neighbors dis-appeared into the community.

Rich Keene warmed up the Leslie speakers with some jazz while Teddy Bear and Pete jousted in the short narrow hallway. Later on in the evening the pizza delivery guy didn't want to come close to the front door but we assured him it was relatively safe and tipped him heavily after offering and being refused a hit off a joint and a swig of whiskey. Malcolm said he was going out for a "six pack of cigarettes" but we didn't let him go on his own.

We were going back out to sea in a few weeks on yet another short cruise. I would be getting some OJT on the little AQA-7 under Fast Eddie's guidance. He knew his stuff, there was no doubt about that. And he always seemed to be one step ahead of ship's security following the trail of dope smoke.

I always passed on the offers to "take a hit" aboard ship. I had a bad experience while stoned, one I was ashamed of and lucky I didn't get in big trouble for. I was on ready duty at the apartment, the one to be called if the squadron needed a crewman for a rescue. By 11 p.m. I figured nothing was going to happen so I lit a joint and listened to some music. As my body relaxed and settled into the papasan chair the phone rang. Malcolm answered.

"Hey Thos, it's for you."

"Don't bullshit me, Malcolm, just tell whoever it is I'll call 'em back later."

"No shit, it's for you, it's the duty office. You have to go fly."

Goddamn it. I was in a mess. I got in my Impala and drove to the base in the slow motion of stoned motoring. The whole way there I pondered my fate; I would have to tell them I couldn't fly. I would lose my wings. I would be drummed out of the squadron and sent to some other unit, my crow patch half ripped off my sleeve. But I couldn't risk someone else's life; not in the air, not my helo crew, not my friends and squadronmates. I was on my way to a very dishonorable end to all my hard work and struggle to get where I was.

Once parked by the hangar I got up the flight of stairs as best I could, only to run right into Lt. Grupe, the ready duty pilot. He looked at me as if he could read my mind. A brief second passed as he took it all in—I had no idea what he could tell but he didn't seem happy. I was hoping I was just a little late. Just as I was about to confess, the squadron duty PO looked around the corner at me—it was Bob Loving from aircrew. He was already in his flight suit and pulled me aside.

"Where the fuck have you been? Hey, what's that I smell—look Thos, we have a medevac out on San Clemente Island. No big deal, we don't need a second crewman and I'm already set to go."

"I'm a little stoned, didn't mean to, I just didn't think—well, never mind, anyway, I'll suit up just in case but man, you have this baby all the way, OK?"

The mission brief was short. Nobody was in the water, no ships were on fire, no pilots had ejected into the cold dark night, just some sailor who hurt his shoulder wanting to get to Balboa. In the middle of the night. The crew got the helo in the air minus my usual hands-on preflight. Loving handled everything as I stared at panel lights dancing their glowing-red jitterbug.

Once we landed all we had to do was lower the door and get the sailor onboard and strapped into a seat. We dropped him off at the Naval Hospital and by the time we landed back at IB I was clear-headed enough to not feel like I was hanging out in Haight Ashbury. As I headed out the door to make my way back home Lt. Grupe gave me one last glance, laced with disappointment. I never wanted to see that look again. I got lucky that night, but I would never again put myself in jeopardy by running another risk like that.

Lt. Grupe apparently didn't say anything about that night and my E-5 and AW2 test scores were fine. I was designated a 2nd Class Petty Officer selectee on November 1. I would have to wait until February 16 to sew the double chevrons on—there were a lot of AWs ending their tours within a few months and once they were civilians again room would open up in the rate. But it was the last accomplishment I could possibly make in the time I had left. If I could just keep from getting the short-timer's attitude Papa Gire warned me about I might finish out my time with few regrets. With a WestPac looming just a few months away, it would be a challenge.

———◆———

CHANGE WAS CONSTANT, WITH squadron commanding officers rotating through faster than most enlisted. They had a two year assignment—one as the executive officer, the XO—and one as the CO.

Our newest CO was Commander C J Stokes—a lean, tough man and a dead-ringer for Lee Van Cleef. Put Stokes in a cowboy hat and chaps and he could have walked on a spaghetti western movie set and fit right in. His tight, focused gaze and set jaw lent him a hawk-like appearance, and he seemed to absorb every detail within his field of vision. He led by example and didn't stifle his understated sense of humor. But I sure didn't want to be on his bad side. After my stupid comment overheard by Commander Rich at Mombasa and my narrow escape from demotion and de-winging the night I showed up stoned for a flight, I didn't feel like tempting fate with my new CO. He had my fullest confidence. I didn't know if I had his.

New guys filled in the empty spaces left by aircrew returning to civilian life. Bob Hart had left a job making sonobuoys to become the one throwing them out the cargo door. He was a rent-a-crow like Teddy Bear, another six year sailor. Hart and I would be teamed up a lot in the coming months.

One new AW, rumored to be the son of an admiral, was dead

weight from the day he got to the squadron. I dreaded flying with him and was amazed he had passed the rigorous training. He didn't seem to care one way or the other about much of anything, even whether or not his fellow aircrewmen survived a mission. I dubbed him "Fuck-up."

Even with a full WestPac looming ahead I plotted my escape from the Navy to collegiate life. After considering a couple of other schools I set my sights on Humboldt State, a small university nestled in the coastal redwoods of northern California.

Mom wanted me to come home for a holiday, any holiday, before we deployed but I passed on using my leave. I wanted a full thirty days on the books so I could make that my last month in, in effect cutting short that last year. I skipped going home for both Thanksgiving and Christmas, instead taking watches and duty for other guys who wanted to go home.

I wanted out of the Navy so bad I could taste it. But at the same time I was an E-5 selectee, soon to be in a supervisory and leadership role. And possibly a role model as well for the younger guys just getting checked in to aircrew. That was going to be some balancing act.

We had a Christmas tree in the apartment. We weren't particularly pious but it was a reminder of home. We failed to give it any water, instead opting to hang tin foil from it. By New Year's Eve it was time to do something with the tree so we hacked it to pieces with our official Navy survival knives and stuffed it in the otherwise never-used corner fireplace. We lit the dried-out tree, needles and all. It burst into a violent ball of flame, sounding like a freight train conflagration crashing through the apartment. There was no fire grate, no cover, no screen, just rapidly combusting air between us and the tree. It was over in seconds. We ended 1975 by almost burning down the fourplex.

PART FIVE
1976

PART FIVE

14: ONE MORE TIME

"I think the best way to celebrate the new year is with chili-cheeseburger omelettes. I mean, we won't get many more chances to have one of those beauties. Besides, if we survived last night we were meant to live forever." It sounded like a good idea to me anyway.

"Sounds like a plan, Thos, but next time let's either water the goddamn tree or burn it outside," Malcolm suggested.

"Next time I'll be in the Berkshires," Pete said wistfully. "You can come visit for the holidays but you better bring your down parkas, it gets fuckin' cold back there."

"This time next year I'm planning on being snuggled up against a sweet young thing keeping me warm."

"Dream on, Thos. And since you're going to be a Second Class soon, you're buyin' breakfast."

"OK Pete, it's on me, but dibs on the seat without the springs poking through."

The Flamingo Cafe never disappointed. Betty was her usual motherly self, peppering her small talk with homilies aimed at our youthful excesses. "Now you boys should know better. I heard all about the forest fire in your apartment last night; the neighbors could smell it for blocks. What are you going to do out on that big boat of yours, sink it? Well then, what's it going to be, the usual? Ok, three chilicheeseburger omelettes coming up and coffee is on the way. I guess I won't be seeing y'all for a long while, be careful over there." It seemed like she knew everything. Maybe she was married to a master chief.

After the hearty breakfast the three of us retreated back to the smoky apartment and began the process of thinning out our possessions, there wouldn't be much room aboard ship. I needed to make plans for getting rid of my Impala and storing the rest of my stuff, including my prized stereo equipment. I had promised myself if I came back with anything from Subic it would be a Teac reel-to-reel tape machine. I had sold my camera. I just couldn't imagine wanting more pictures of helicopters, ships and water.

The *Ranger* was due to leave North Island on January 30. CV-61 hadn't been past the 180th meridian in over a year, and had been tied up at the pier for a month. Both Air Wing Two and ship's company were stale. Even with all the short cruises the previous year, our skills would need refining on the high seas.

Before we shipped out the squadron had plans for me to attend one last Navy school. Chief Beaty broke the news. "Thos, get yer butt up to North Island, you're going to attend Career Counseling School."

"Chief, what the fuck for? I'm almost under 250 days. Hell, it's 249 and a wake-up, and if I get my school cut it's even less than that. What makes somebody think I'm going to counsel anyone on a Navy career? If I 'counseled' them at all it would be to do everything they could short of punching an officer to get out as soon as possible. That really confuses me, Chief, I just don't get it."

"Didn't anyone ever tell you that if you're not confused, you don't understand the situation?" The chief lit his pipe, rocked back on his heels just a bit and grinned. All I could do was jump in my Chevy and head north on the Strand.

The school was a cluster of petty officers taught by a senior chief. Everyone there had at least one WestPac under their belt. Some guys were enthusiastic. I could barely keep a straight face. It was a short seminar; I understood all the benefits that lay waiting behind the reenlistment ceremony, I understood how young I would be when retiring after twenty years, even if it seemed an impossible distance away. The senior chief told us all the good things to say to young men who were sitting on the fence about re-upping. Would I ever be my own client?

The certificate, signed on January 14, proclaimed that I had satisfactorily completed Career Information and Counseling School. I kept asking the senior chief how I could get a school cut plus use up my saved leave and slice two months off my enlistment. He told me I was in the wrong school. I ended up with a certificate authorizing me to talk young men into reenlisting. Someone had gotten to Feek already. I spotted him at the line shack after a maintenance test flight.

"Hey Feek, I heard you re-upped for six big ones. Hell, by the time that's over you'll be halfway to retirement, then they really have you. What do you have to say for yourself?"

"Unfuckingbelievable." We would be doing another WestPac together.

With two weeks to go things were frenzied. I got my personal items stashed in a warehouse. The hallway double closet full of empty beer bottles got cleared out. I had arranged to donate my car to a group home. Our rent was paid up through the end of the month and soon all that was left was to turn in the keys.

The *Ranger* underwent a P.O.M.—Preparation for Overseas Movement. The task of readying thousands of compartments plus the hangar deck and Steel Beach for a seven month cruise was a daunting task. From the engine rooms to the flag bridge, an almost infinite amount of details had to be taken care of.

HS-4 once again packed up its heavy cruise boxes and we formed working parties to get all of the squadron necessities onboard. Once again we were ensconced on the 0-3 level, right under the flight deck. The ready room was more spartan than the *Kitty Hawk*'s, but the aircrew space was close by and the communications office, where Pete worked, was just a few frames towards the bow.

The aircrew space held an ominous sign—a pipe as big around as a garbage can ran along the overhead of the small compartment parallel to the ship's centerline. It was a steam tube for the port bow catapult, capable of heating the close quarters air to over 110 degrees when the cat was being used. On top of the tropical humidity we were heading towards it could render the space uninhabitable.

Red lighting switches lined the passageway from the ready room to the flight deck; that would help with night vision for the inevitable nocturnal missions. The enlisted berthing compartment was aft of the ready room by a hundred frames. It was a straight shot along the portside, and looking down the passageway I could see the knee knockers set in the frames in ever-decreasing size due to the distance. It almost appeared like I was looking at a mirror reflected into another mirror—the image recessing into infinity.

We had time to ready the working spaces and pick our berthing. Since I was an "old salt" with some rank I was able to lay claim to a top rack, the penthouse of the triple stack. No more getting my face stepped on; I would be the "stepper," not the "steppee."

Our clothing storage was under our racks; the mattress and frame—all two inches thick of it—acted like a horizontal door, hinged and raised up for access to the shallow locker underneath. The rows of racks were open with scant curtains between the joining tiers. Less privacy than the *Hawk*. Less privacy than a prison. It would have to do.

We would be deploying without Doc Bliven. He had turned in his wings and slipped into a shadowy beyond leaving only rumor in his wake. I wasn't sure why he did it; he never told any of us, except for Chief Beaty. I thought it might have had something to do with the death of his daughter a year previous, but he never told me much about his personal life. Someone said he went to submarines, quite a switch from sub hunting helos. His experience would have been invaluable on the cruise.

A handful of replacements filtered in from the training squadron. "Cowboy" Johnny, hailing from Steamboat Springs, Colorado, seemed OK. We even had our own new "Tex," Walter Tarnbeck from Dallas. Our last Texan, Terry Mistrot, fell for the mail buoy ploy under the tutelage of Master Chief Romney. The master chief was still with us and already scoping out his next victim, hopefully from Texas. Our Tex—tall, stout, good natured and gullible—looked ripe for the picking. The dead weight crewman, Fuckup, just took up valuable space.

It was finally time to pack my seabag, stuff my parachute bag with everything but a parachute and ship aboard the USS *Ranger*, CV-61, for my last deployment to the South China Sea. I tried to call Dad to say goodbye but couldn't reach him.

The *Ranger* pulled out of NAS North Island on Friday, January 30. We were headed over 7,000 miles west, following the path of the *Kitty Hawk* and every other carrier that had sailed for the South China Sea. The war was over in Vietnam. We were going back there anyway.

———— • ————

ONLY THREE DAYS OUT—halfway to Pearl Harbor—a feeling of dread settled in my bones. I wasn't sure I could do a seven or eight month WestPac and maintain my sanity—the first casualty of a cruise. The days were already taking on an endless quality and we weren't even past Guam. My short-timer's calendar was slowly being filled in— 227 days and a wake-up. 1976 was a leap year, February holding one more long day for me to spend aboard ship. I would turn twenty-three in five weeks and I was feeling old. It was definitely time to let the younger guys pick up the slack.

The weather off Hawaii was rough, gale-force winds whipping the Pacific into a froth. The *Ranger* rode out the storm at sea but managed to send two Sea Kings in to Barbers Point. I was on a crew and drawing on past experiences had a plan. To do laundry. Even a handful of clean skivvies would make the transit to Subic more civilized.

After landing at Barbers I asked around until I found out where a laundromat was. One wasn't far and as I stood doing wash in my flight suit I drew some glances. One woman looked at me and smiled as if she wondered why I was there and not at the PO club having a steak. There was no way I could have explained it to her. Another flyer was there, also in his green Nomex, doing the same thing. I didn't need to explain anything to him.

Back at my Sea King waiting for the pilots to return I heard a friendly and familiar voice. "Hey, is that you, Manthos?" A slow, deliberate southern drawl rolled the words my way. I turned to see who it was as a chief came up to me.

"Well I'll be damned, Hatfield. And look, you made chief! That's cool, man."

"Nice to see ya'. I remember you from sonar school, hell, there were days you couldn't find a sub in a shitcan. And then, just when I thought you were getting the hang of it, you were tracking crap I didn't even have programmed in! But you did OK, finally." He let slip a wide grin as he razzed me a bit. "What are ya'll doin' here anyway? These your helos?"

"Yep, I'm headin' to the PI once again. But I'm getting short, startin' to count the days. Seems like a long time since you taught sonar school."

"It has been. I've been here a while and don't rightly mind it much. Say, why don't you come work for me? I could find something for you to do around here, it's great duty and I think you'd not regret it."

"Shit Chief, I don't know, I'm really thinking about going back to college. I made a mess of it last time I tried, but I think I'm ready for it now."

"Why hell, work for me, take night classes in college and before you know it you'd be starin' a commission straight in the eye. Think about it, the offer is open any time."

"Thanks Hatfield, I mean, 'Chief' Hatfield, I'll kick it around. And I guess I know how to find you! Take 'er easy."

"Ya'll be careful up on Steel Beach. Fair winds and following seas, shipmate." Hatfield turned and sauntered back to his squadron area as I climbed into my helo and stowed clean skivvies in my parachute bag. Sitting on the red metal ordnance box by the aft station door, I settled in and pondered what Hatfield had said. He had offered me a job. I had never been offered one like that before. I felt like I was at a crossroads, much like when I had a chance to wrestle for the NAS Millington base team. My orders and future would have changed if I wrestled, and it would change again if I accepted Hatfield's proposal. Something inside said keep with the plan, but I would often wonder what might have happened if I took Hatfield up on his offer.

The *Ranger* pulled in to Pearl Harbor after the storm subsided and docked across from the *Arizona* Memorial. Oil bubbled up from the shattered hull of the battleship, coating the water's surface. It was still bleeding.

I had two days of liberty and made the most of it. Cowboy Johnny and I rented a car along with Feek and we proceeded to tour the island. We also downed copious amounts of Michelob and Feek scored some local "Maui Zowie," his all time favorite. I didn't take a toke but couldn't help but get high from being cooped up in the small rental car all afternoon. I wasn't going to be flying for several days but I was already at high altitude. We stopped periodically to take a plunge in the warm Pacific waters. I managed to cut my right foot on razor-sharp coral. It was pretty funny, but then weed made everything pretty funny.

We looked in vain for red coral necklaces, prized for the depth a diver needed to go to collect the ruby-colored prize. Cowboy settled on a shell necklace while Feek took home two of white coral. I passed on the natural jewelry; I was never one to wear any. The newly forming scar on my foot would suffice as a reminder of the beautiful island.

Back by midnight, I had the better part of the next day to recover before Feek and Fast Eddie dragged me along for another shot at Waikiki. We ended up on the beach at midnight. They wanted to go swimming in the nude, creating their own memories of skinny-dipping on Waikiki Beach in the middle of the night. I passed on the swim but took my flute and played melodies from my heart as I sat on the warm sand in the dark.

After everyone had a chance to call home, mail a letter, get drunk, cruise Hotel Street and buy souvenirs, the *Ranger* put to sea with a full hold of boiler oil, aviation fuel, fresh food and water.

I hoped the transit to Subic was uneventful. Everyone who was on the *Hawk* back in '73 couldn't help but think of the fire that ravaged that ship midway between Hawaii and the PI. We would be flying the usual mixed bag of missions during various exercises with the carrier battle group while en route. We wouldn't set foot on dry land for almost three weeks. The steam catapult pipe in the aircrew space made life miserable; it heated the room into a steel-walled sauna. I would easily sweat out the beer I drank in Hawaii.

"Hey Master Chief, when's the next mail call?" I sensed Master Chief Romney was in a good mood and ready to have some fun. I didn't mind playing the straight man to his highjinks. The ready room was full of potential victims.

"Why Manthos, it ought to be any day now. What we need is a mail buoy watch. Let's see the duty roster for tomorrow, hmm, OK, Looks like one of yours, Airman Tarnbeck over there, and one of mine, Airman Przygurski right here, are on the list. They should do just fine. Hey Tarnbeck, you're from Texas, right? Gotta call ya' 'Tex.' We call Przygurski 'Ski' of course, every unit has to have at least one 'Ski' and he's it, right, Ski? Who can pronounce P-r-z-y-g-u-r-s-k-i anyway. So we have 'Tex' and 'Ski' for the mail buoy watch tomorrow. Don't get any better than that." Romney refilled his heavy ceramic mug with freshly brewed coffee and sauntered back into the maintenance shack.

"You're really from Texas, uh, 'Tex?'" I had to know.

"Yep."

"What part?"

"All of me. And hey Thos, what does the master chief mean by 'don't get any better than that'?" he asked, his eyebrows raising up towards his newly-shaven head. "This isn't like some seabat hunt is it?"

"No, no, nothing like that at all. What he means is that tomorrow you will make an invaluable contribution to your new squadron. Mail is vital to our morale as you already know, even just a few weeks into this WestPac. The master chief will explain what you have to do tomorrow and I wouldn't be late for your buoy brief; if you're on time you're already late. Do us aircrew proud, Tex, do us proud. And when you're done with your watch the duty section needs to get a gallon of relative bearing grease for the helos; got to keep those compasses working out here in the open ocean, so grab us some. Vital son, it's all vital."

I had a plane guard flight the next day with JD Dungan as my swimmer. When we got back we saw Tex still standing the mail buoy watch on the port-side catwalk.

"When is somebody going to tell him, he's been there for a long time." JD smiled; his dad had been career Navy so he knew exactly what was going on.

"I'll leave that up to the master chief, JD; he always has impeccable timing." As I turned over the helo to Chief Beaty in a hot refuel and crew switch I glanced over at Tex. He looked at me with a long face and throwing up his hands, shrugged his shoulders. I gave him a big thumb's up. He only had a few more hours to go.

<hr />

I HAD A HARD TIME convincing Tex that there was going to be a real mail call until he had confirmation from the 1MC.

"That don't mean a buoy watch, does it?"

"Of course not Tex; this is the real deal, real mail brought on by the COD, real letters going back home the same route, it's all good stuff."

"The 'cod'? Ain't that some kind of fish? Are you pulling my leg again? And you said the mail buoy watch wasn't like a seabat hunt and it sure was."

"No, no it wasn't, it was more like staring at the horizon for hours and hours looking for nothing; a seabat hunt is very different.

And the COD, or C-O-D, is a plane, the 'carrier onboard delivery' airplane; 'cod' is just easier to say. Now, the smoking lamp is out of lamp oil; go see the master chief for instructions on where to get some more."

"You're not fuckin' with me again, are ya'? If ya' are, I'll, I'll, well, I'll do *something*."

"Now Tex, that's no way to talk to a Second Class Petty Officer is it? Well, in a few days I'll be an E-5 and you just don't mess with E-5s, now do ya'?"

He shrugged his shoulders once again and went to find the master chief. Tex had a long cruise ahead of him.

I had my novels to keep me occupied in my spare time. Pete Cassidy had a wonderful book, a huge publication with color plates of all the National Parks. Grand Canyon, Glacier, Rocky Mountain, Yosemite, Yellowstone and Crater Lake were parks with gorgeous scenery, each picture taking up a whole page. We had only been at sea a few weeks and already Pete and I were getting lost in the beauty of nature captured by the photographers. From where we were, enshrouded in steel, it seemed like we were looking at a book about a different planet.

Before we pulled into port we got word that a Soviet Victor-class sub was patrolling the Philippine Sea, which lay between us and Subic Bay. The Victor was a nuclear powered class of carrier-hunting subs. We were its prime target. We went into full ASW mode flying around-the-clock tracking missions. I put my new-found expertise in loading the nuclear bomb to task as we went through the motions. The bomb still looked like something out of a science fiction movie, except on the flight deck under actual flight operations it took on a more sinister aura.

President Ford had authorized wheat sales to the Soviet Union, at least 6 million tons per year. The sailors on the Soviet submarine searching for us might have been eating bread made from Kansas wheat.

Two weeks after we left San Diego it was made official; I was a second class petty officer. The iron-on patch for the working uniform made the change easy. I took my Tropical Dress White shirt to laundry services and had the double chevron crow sewn on. We would be standing the inevitable inspections and changes of command and I would need an updated dress uniform. And I was elevated to a leadership role, if for nothing other than overseeing E-4s and below pulling a field day. I also collected collateral duties including assignment as the Human Relations Petty Officer. As such I would see Cdr. Stokes in action at a Captain's Mast.

WE PULLED UP TO the Alava Pier on the twenty-ninth of February with as much grace as 80,000 tons can exhibit. Subic looked the same. It smelled the same. The greenish water around the moored ship was clogged with trash and spilled oil and bits of flotsam and jungle debris washed down from the surrounding mountains. Dockworkers and shipfitters and gawkers crowded the pier as boatswain's mates got us moored to the big cleats. Guerrero taxis lined up awaiting the inevitable flooding tide of business. Olongapo would absorb the influx of sailors without batting an eye.

I opted to stay aboard ship most of the time in port, reading Solzhenitsyn and Vonnegut and Conrad under the dim florescent light over my bunk while shipmates poured across Shit River into town. I swore I wasn't going to have sex with bar girls. I had escaped getting any diseases on the last WestPac and it was all seeming like a rerun anyway, the sixteen months we spent in San Diego already fading into a dim memory, as if it had been a long dream. The overpowering sounds and smells and sights of the PI wiped away everything but being in the moment.

Evenings I would walk the flight deck, breathe in the thick humid air, hope for a cool sea breeze to make its way into the bay, lean on the catwalk railing and look into the black night water surrounding us. I tried not counting my days left; I was under 200 but until I was a "two digit midget," ninety-nine or less, it was just too many days to try to think about.

Once Clyde Dog got out Chuck Fields absorbed his moniker and became "Chuck Dog." Chuck Dog went into town and got a custom belt buckle made of Baguio silver inscribed with a short-timer's logo. The shortest guy in aircrew got to wear it, and Chuck Dog was short, almost a two digit midget.

"I'm so short I could take a bath in a bottle cap," Chuck Dog would say. He was eager to get back to Pennsylvania and resume his life, even if he refused to let himself believe he could do that without being a changed man after two WestPacs. I waited impatiently for my turn to wear the quickly coveted short timer's buckle.

We had a modest flight schedule out of Cubi Point while in port. Taking a big gray bus over to Cubi to make a flight took me past some piers and there was the freighter *Mayaguez*, of Cambodian Khmer Rouge fame—it was right there, moored to the dock. It was a remnant of the final firefight, of the final deaths of Americans, in South East Asia the year before. It sat there like a big period in a long sentence of living history.

Flying out of Cubi was a pleasure, even if we ran the slight risk of getting shot at by Huks with rifles or hill tribes with bows and arrows.

Between flights one afternoon I sauntered down to the water's edge where a boat ramp led into the bay. I was drawn in by a black-hulled contraption that looked like a huge, fat torpedo. It looked thirty feet long and sat on a boat trailer frame, as if ready to be launched into the murky green water. A sailor in green jungle fatigues stood near the mysterious machine.

"So, what *is* this thing, anyway?" I had to ask.

"It's classified," came his reply. I could now see the SEAL emblem on his shirt, along with 1st Class Petty Officer insignia.

"Looks like a mini-sub, kinda," I reflected. He said nothing. "So, how fast will it go, this sub-like thing?"

"That's classified."

"Oh. OK. Gee, how deep, I mean, can this thing go very deep? And how many guys can ride on it?"

"That, Sir, is classified. There is really nothing to discuss here, Sir. Matter of fact, Sir, would you please step back?"

I conceded him his space, slowly turned and drifted back up the ramp towards the flight operations Quonset, looking back every now and then, hoping to catch the little sub disappearing into the dark water. It just sat there. Seeing the small but lethal looking weapons platform did nothing to make me sleep better on a big hulking carrier.

On my way back I passed the area where the F-5s had been parked in 1974, awaiting flight to South Vietnam's Air Force. Nothing had replaced them. I recalled back in '75 seeing on the news an F-5 being used by a defector to the Communists during the fall of Saigon. He was a pilot who, perhaps all along, sympathized with the North and when his moment came, took to the air to support the North's takeover of Saigon. I couldn't help but wonder if his fighter was one from the group at Cubi two years before.

⬤

WITHIN A FEW DAYS it was time again to enjoy the hospitality of Sarge and Company at JEST training. Chief Partz had retired and Senior Chief Reginald Davies stood in his place. Sarge was still there. He looked younger than he did over two years before; all that fresh bat meat must have been his fountain of youth. He took us through the ritual of making fire and utensils from bamboo. Sarge did his standard "big nosed Westerner" bamboo cup, endlessly amusing himself. We couldn't find him in his jungle.

A new phase was added to the day—vectoring in a rescue helo by hand-held emergency radio. It proved to be a fun afternoon. Watching a big Sea King ease in over a bamboo stand at forty feet as I fed the pilots detailed information as to where to "find" me was exhilarating. I was able to step outside my aircrewman mindset and appreciate what a helicopter rescue was like from the survivor's point of view. The SH-3D looked magnificent.

After my turn at the radio I relaxed and unzipped my zoombag to my navel to let a scant bit of air in. I had my HS-4 hat cocked at a jaunty angle like I had seen Dad do in his WWII photos, his complete with the "fifty mission crush." Mine just smelled like jet fuel.

My attention turned to the bamboo and I grabbed a brown, dried-out cane and took a closer look. Marveling at the sectional beauty of the big grass, I brought the dead cane, which was several inches in diameter, close to my face and commenced to split the top section in two with my fingers to further see nature's wonder. It split easily, distinctly down the middle. This action also exposed the biggest, meanest looking spider I had ever seen. He was all stretched out inside the section of bamboo, minding his own business, maybe sleeping, when his world was split open. He was pissed. He was also gigantic. My two eyes got huge, my heart jumped, sweat broke out; his eight eyes got huge and he rocketed out of the bamboo at the speed of light. I knew he went down my flight suit, he just had to, it was hanging wide open, the perfect place for a gigantic spider to hide in. I was hopping like a barefoot lunatic on hot pavement, trying to get out of that suit as fast as I could. I grabbed my hat and swatted at every part of my body I could reach. Swearing, cussing, waiting for the fatal bite that would kill me on the spot, I finally managed to get the larger part of my body out of that spider-filled flight suit. My skin was all tingly and crawly feeling, I knew he had to be somewhere close, real close. I looked and looked, and looked some more, and looked everywhere, but no spider. It had simply disappeared.

Sarge watched the whole thing and was laughing his ass off. He probably would have eaten the spider as a snack.

My final Navy training certificate went into my service jacket, dated March 3, 1976. I would turn twenty-three three days later. I could still feel the elusive spider crawling on my skin as I downed a birthday Mojo at the Airwaves Club.

Aircrew had laid claim to the Airwaves. It was close—just past the bowling alley on the first road to the right after crossing into town—and as every chief had suggested, we hung around one bar, got to know the owners and staff, respected them, and they treated us well. I got my ass kicked playing chess with the waiters, but the San Miguel was close to cold and we would bring in Wild Turkey and they would sell us safe ice to chill it. After a while the bar girls knew who wanted to go short time and who just wanted to hang out, so they wouldn't pester me, instead going after Tex and Cowboy Johnny and Fuckup and the newest of the new guys, Chuck Carrier.

"Is that really your name, 'Carrier'? So you're Carrier on a carrier?"

"Yes Thos, it's my name and it's ironic but what the fuck, what if my name was 'Saylor'?"

He had a point. It reminded me of a guy I worked with back when I was dating Marsha, before I got myself enlisted. His name *was* Saylor and I was sure he would end up in the Navy but he talked more about the Army, if for no other reason than the obvious.

The neon sign out in front of the bar only lit up the first five letters of the name, so at night it read "Airwa…" I started calling the place "The Airwuh."

Malcolm took a liking to the mamasan of the joint and a romance blossomed. I was holding fast to my self-imposed celibacy, or at least resisting going short time, or long time, or any time with a bar girl. But it was still early on the WestPac; I wasn't sure how long I could hold fast to my resolution.

I STILL HAD A duty section and as a 2nd Class my watch stature was elevated to a slightly higher degree. No more fire and integrity watches, I was standing a longer section watch but with more flexibility. If we were in port I could leave the ship for a short time while on duty, just not leave the base. That meant I could have a meal at the Spanish Gate Cafeteria, skipping the ship's galley.

"Who wants to go grab a bite at the Spanish Gate?" I polled the ready room to see if there were any takers. A few hands went up and since I had the duty I did a quick check of the deserted aircrew office spaces to see how things were before we disembarked. With no one around and no paperwork to be done it was quiet in the two adjacent spaces. Something struck me as odd—I thought I smelled a sharp, edgy odor, like someone was welding nearby. Someone *was* likely welding; the ship was under almost constant maintenance while tied up at the pier. I sniffed around but didn't see any smoke or reason to think there was a problem. I went to have a burger and fries, downing it with a shake made from powdered milk.

Within twenty minutes we heard general quarters sounded on the *Ranger*. Pete, Cowboy Johnny and I looked at each other; GQ was not a good sign in port. I had never heard of it happening before. We went outside and gawked at what we saw—black smoke pouring out of the *Ranger*'s portside, up by the flight deck. We rushed to get back aboard but the afterbrow was closed off; no one was getting aboard or leaving. Reclined on the grass across from the Spanish Gate we watched in amazement as the battle waged against the fire.

"Could be anything: some plane on fire, some welder setting something ablaze, who knows." Speculation was all I could come up with.

"I dunno, maybe somebody threw a lit cigarette butt into a shit-can full of scrap paper," Pete added.

"The whole thing is gonna blow if it hits the bomb deck," Cowboy tossed in.

We waited for a timeless hour to pass before we were allowed to board the carrier. We made our way up to the 0-3 level. As we got closer to the ready room the thick acrid smoke hanging in the still air became thicker. Fire hoses ran along the water-drenched port passageway, leading us to the fire's core. The hoses ran right up to the aircrew space. The entire area was blackened and burnt like the inside of a pot-bellied stove. The smoke was solid and unyielding. Young sailors from the firefighting duty section were putting the finishing touches on ensuring the fire was dead. They looked young to me, much too young to be carrying that much responsibility, that much risk. And they contained the fire and killed it. That part of the 0-3 deck looked like it had been attacked by napalm. Water sloshed between the frames, knee knockers keeping it contained between them.

The duty section mustered in the ready room and our work began. "Who has a secret clearance?" asked Lt. Casey, our new division officer, as he scanned the gaggle of Black Knights. "Manthos, aircrew has the clearance; we need you to go in and secure the secret files before anyone can get in to start the cleanup." The smoke in the ready room made everyone's eyes water. We were a good ten frames in front of the fire's core.

"Roger that, Sir."

"OK, get topside and the fire crew will get you set up to enter the space. It's a mess in there, be careful."

I went up to the flight deck where the firefighting crew was regrouping. And coiling hoses. That didn't make sense; the fire was below. A young fireman approached me and asked why I was there, in their way.

"I'm from HS-4, I need to get in the space and take care of some things."

"OK, you're the man, we've been waiting for you."

"I gotta ask, why are hoses topside? The fire was below, wasn't it? It sure looked like it was."

"It was, in *your* space. It was so hot we dogged-down the hatch and cut a hole through the side of the ship and poured water in that way. It's one hot sumbitch in there, I tell ya'. Now here, put this on."

He handed me an OBA, an Oxygen Breathing Apparatus. They were re-breathers with a canister of chemicals converting carbon dioxide and moisture into oxygen. I had seen them but never needed to use one before, and in spite of their life-saving value they could be dangerous themselves.

"You've never used one and you're a Second Class? Geez. Anyway dude, here, I'll get you going. Now, don't touch the canister, it gets fuckin' hot, and it's making oxygen. A fire likes oxygen so keep that in mind. And watch the timer, you have maybe thirty minutes of air. If the mask gets foggy, get out fast and back up here."

He helped me get the contraption on, the facemask held painfully tight by head straps, the bulk of the device like a front pack. I felt like I was SCUBA diving in air.

"Any questions?"

I didn't know what to ask so I gave the guy a thumb's up and made my way down into the burned space, looking like some alien insect sailor. It was almost impossible to see. The bulkheads were hot near the space, and it was as dark as the inside of a buried coffin. I could still sense the smoke as I felt myself breathing the chemical air. The only illumination was a powerful emergency lamp, its cone of light piercing the dark. It revealed total devastation. The space was destroyed. I saw daylight through the hole they had cut in the port bulkhead. It looked beautiful, a perfect circle of blue penetrating the small cubicle of hell.

Our flight gear had been stowed along one side on hooks welded to the steel bulkhead. Each survival vest held several types of flares. One flare was discharged by a .38 caliber cartridge. Each vest held a dozen cartridge-flare combinations, plus the larger smoke/flare pack attached to the lower part of the vest. Their combined potency gave the flames a massive boost once the gear caught fire.

Clumps of smelly rubber were all that was left of everyone's custom wet suits. The interior bulkhead was warped several inches. The temperatures must have been staggering to cook and bend steel several inches thick. The row of flight log books was charred, looking like a burnt roast. I was fascinated by the devastation, pissed off that it happened to us, and wondering why it happened at all. Then I remembered to check the OBA timer. I had used up half my air just taking it all in. I tried to slow my breathing to save oxygen as I got to work securing the secret files.

We were granted access to a sponson gun mount, allotted to us to use as secure storage for whatever we could salvage. I started piling classified documents outside the space and other aircrewmen shuttled them down to the sponson where we could start to recover what was left of sensitive secrets. I was getting soaked in the smelly water contained by the space. The residual heat made me feel like I was in a blacked-out sauna. I watched for flare-ups just in case, although I was convinced there was nothing left to burn. The firefighting crews brought in pumps to suck out the water. Once the secret files were secured I got out of their way. It was time for me to go anyway; the mask was fogging up. I was out of chemically produced air.

Surfacing from our little piece of perdition, I stood on the flight deck and peeled off the OBA, returning it to the young firefighter. The pungent air of Subic never smelled so good.

"Fun, ain't it?" the kid said. He fought fires for a living. Brave sons-of-bitches I thought to myself. He disposed of the hot converter canister and secured a fresh one—the OBA was good to go for the next user. Hopefully that would not be for a long time. The tight fitting mask left deep red marks in my face for hours.

I spent the rest of the day and most of the night either on the sponson or in the space, shepherding critical information to safety or overlooking what was left of aircrew's reason for being.

It would take days to even begin to straighten out the mess. Zipper offered a bottle of Scotch to anyone willing to go in there and recover his log book. Aircrew had no usable flight gear. It made the entire squadron impotent.

Wheels turned fast. Paraloft issued new gear. We also got new log books, the burned ones unusable. I was not granted a new wet suit. "You're too damn short, Thos," Chief Beaty declared. Fair enough.

An accident investigating officer was assigned, a commander from one of the fighter squadrons. Conclusion: clothing stuffed between the steam catapult tube and the overhead combusted when the tube got hot from in-port testing. It was Fuckup's clothing. He had nothing to say, not even an "I'm sorry."

We were just a few weeks into the cruise. Most of the new guys were still working off their first San Miguel hangover. Things had a way of happening before you were scheduled for things to even start to happen.

I hated myself for not sticking around another ten or fifteen minutes when I had smelled something. I would never know if I could have stopped the fire before it became an inferno.

I would fight that fire at its pyrotechnic inception in my mind for the rest of my life.

15: ON PATROL

After the in-port period the *Ranger* headed out into the South China Sea. The day before we pulled out the squadron had an all-hands picnic at Cubi Point. Roast pig, lumpia, fried rice and gallons of San Miguel made for a pleasant day. The ops space fire had punched a hole in the squadron and the relaxed atmosphere of the gathering helped morale, especially the day before deploying on line. A lot of beer was consumed. A lot. Both pilots and aircrew settled into the warm sand and watched the sun set over the bay. Some looked intently for the "green flash," when the sun illuminated only water before it vanished into the sea.

Bright and early the *Ranger*'s anchor chains did their noisy dance into the chain lockers. Fortunately my berthing space was way aft of the chains. That also meant my top rack was directly under the number three arresting wire. I felt every landing. I quickly learned that I could judge landings by the sound; there was a weighty thunk to a good one, bad ones had more disturbing resonances. Bolters, a missed trap of the wire, had an elongated roar as the jet engines kept the aircraft at full power so they could go around and try again. At least that morning, flight ops weren't scheduled until we were well out to sea. By then I would be over my San Miguel blues.

The pace picked up as we hit blue water. The ever-critical launch and recovery qualifications resumed for the air wing as ship's company held their own drills. HS-4's "planeguardinstarboarddelta" helo made its lazy orbit. Soon it settled into a perfect, computer-aided hover at forty feet over the sea. The winds were calm and the water's surface like glass. The *Ranger* continued on its way. Soon there was an increasing distance between the ship and helicopter, the wide expanse of sea ahead of the *Ranger*, the interval between it and the helo increasing.

"Black Knight helo seven-two-four, this is *Ranger*, over." All quiet on the radio.

"Black Knight helo seven-two-four, this is *Ranger*, uh, coming with us today?" Silence.

"Black Knight in starboard delta, are you declaring an emergency?"

At last, faint gasps broke the static. "Uh, right, this is, let's see, this is Black Knight seven-two uh, four, we'll be along ASAP, we were experiencing, uh . . ."

"Black Knight seven-two-four, current *Ranger* heading is two-one-zero degrees, speed thirty knots. Resume starboard delta, which is up here now, when you get around to it. Don't make me call the air boss."

The entire helo crew had fallen asleep. The power of San Miguel was not to be underestimated.

Within a couple of days we had our edge back. We were close enough to Subic to get mail via the C-2 Greyhound COD transports. They had the same engine setup as the E-2 Hawkeye, their fuselages larger to hold cargo. Even after a short time it was great to get mail.

Cdr. Stokes received a large package a few days out. The ready room was crowded and curious heads leaned in close to see what he had received.

"Now give me some breathing room here, shipmates. Hmm, what's this? Look, it says 'opening this will bring you closer to God.' Master Chief Romney, what do you make of that? I don't like it, I mean, I'm not ready to meet my maker just yet."

"'Closer to God,' Skipper? I don't like it much either, let's call EOD, I know the chief down there. Let's let him deal with it, just in case."

The box was heavy, it had a solid, metallic clank to it. Stokes's eyes narrowed, his mind thumbing back through the pages of his command, checking to see if anyone might have held a grudge. That someone would send him a package bomb seemed unlikely, but being at sea could do strange things to men's minds.

The box was from Bill Clemens, the ordnanceman I had helped rescue after he was thrown overboard by jet exhaust back on the *Kitty Hawk* WestPac. As an ordnanceman he would know explosives, and quite well. He had returned to civilian life and then—according to rumor—joined the French Foreign Legion. Did he harbor some malice towards Cdr. Stokes? I couldn't imagine why; Stokes was a fine skipper and excellent pilot.

Still, the skipper wasn't taking any chances. "OK, clear the ready room, everybody out, now. Master Chief, get your EOD buddy up here pronto. Everybody else stay clear until EOD has figured out what the hell is going on with this box. It's way too heavy to be cookies. Hell, it's too heavy to be fruit cake." He smiled his tight smile and ushered us all out.

Explosive Ordnance Disposal. They undid what frogmen tried to do, which was blow things up. Much of their training was the same, their goals polar opposites. The EOD chief showed up, respectfully told Stokes to wait somewhere else, and did his job. It was over in a few minutes. And it remained very quiet.

"Sir, if you care to step back in please, I'll show you what I found."

We crowded in behind the skipper, peering around and over his shoulders. The box sat opened on the duty desk. Inside was a squadron-issued .45 Colt semi-automatic pistol and 200 rounds of ammunition, plus some tools. It could have been rigged to explode but was instead a confessional. Clemens had apparently "appropriated" the items and was overtaken by guilt. Bill assuaged his god and cleared his conscience. He also scared the hell out of the skipper, although Stokes showed no outward signs of it.

"You just never know, do you," was all Stokes said as the items were returned to the squadron ordnance locker.

"If I get my hands on Clemens I'll keelhaul his ass," said the master chief, sipping on his coffee.

The ready room resumed its normal pace—flight crews briefing and debriefing, the odd adrift Black Knight seeking a place just to sit, the big coffee pot gurgling its uneven ballad of caffeine.

THE *RANGER* PATROLLED THE South China Sea. The little Soviet AGI "fishing boats" dogged us as before. They seemed even rustier than the last time I saw them. I wondered how long they deployed for, if their crews longed for letters from home, if they got "Dear Ivan" notes severing a relationship. HS-4 continued to hone its sub hunting skills in the new attack/ASW carrier combination. We were having to prove our worthiness and the only way to do that was to find subs.

Fast Eddie was in charge of the new mini AQA-7, which received signals from the sonobuoys we tossed from the Sea Kings. Both the P-3 and the S-2 had launching systems for the buoys; we just slid back the wide cargo door and after selecting the channel, threw them out. Not very sophisticated but it got the job done. The best part of a sonobuoy mission was that we had to fly quite high to act as a relay station for the signal, from the buoy up to us and then back down to the *Ranger*'s tiny space where the AQA-7 was. The higher we flew the cooler it was. The tropical air at 10,000 feet was wonderful-cool, fresh, clear, clean. If I could have packaged it I would have made a fortune selling it to the ship's crew.

Flight operations would often go around the clock. This wore everyone out; the high-tension atmosphere permeated the entire ship. Trying to sleep was an attempt to push past the constant pounding just a few feet above my head, to block out the metallic screeching of the arresting cables as they ran below the flight deck and close by the berthing compartment. There was no escape on the 0-3 level—you were either below the catapults as we were in the ready room, or below the arresting cables where aircrew slept. It was akin to getting used to a building next door being eternally demolished while you went about your routine.

I managed a shallow, restless sleep, enough sleep to be able to get up—often rousted out by a sailor with a wake-up sheet—and fly and function, but never enough to be fully rested. I made up for it in port but during the long days and nights of flight ops I slowly became a semi-zombie. I would try to read myself to sleep under my dim sixty-cycle lamp.

On the night of March 20 I was in my top rack winding my way up a murky, slow-moving African river in *Heart of Darkness* as jets pounded down on the flight deck. Every sentence was punctuated by a concussion as a jet slammed into the deck. One after another, as the far-flung planes came home to be refueled, checked over, rearmed and reassigned—I read of a quieter time.

Ten, maybe fifteen landings were textbook perfect—some part of my brain was registering it all even as I read Conrad's words. Then WHAM, it felt like a whole airframe slammed into the deck belly-down, sounding like giant steel claws being raked across the flight deck above my head. That snapped me back to total presence. "Uh-oh," I said aloud. No one was asleep at that point. Within seconds the call was sounded. "General quarters, general quarters, all hands man your battle stations."

The ship became a beehive of activity as sailors in all stages of dress rushed to their assigned GQ stations. Everyone had to be located; the XO of the ship made sure of it. Aircrew mustered in the ready room. Pete Cassidy was absent.

The closed circuit TV was replaying what had—just moments before—happened. An F-4 came in too low and hit the rounddown, the trailing edge of the flight deck. It immediately burst into flame as the wreckage slid at 150 miles per hour across the flight deck and into the ocean. That's what I had felt, just a few feet over my head, over 40,000 pounds of jet slamming into the ship and bolting across steel decking in a ball of fire.

The two-man crew ejected. The RIO backseater landed on the flight deck. The pilot hit the water just aft of the ship. Pete was the rescue swimmer who plucked him from the ocean. Pete, who had himself crashed at night some nine months before, was back in the water, that time as the rescuer. It took a lot of nerve to fly again after what he experienced in his own crash. To fly nights and enter the water in a rescue capacity, taking more risk, was exemplary.

No one was killed. It amazed me after watching film of the wreckage slide across a heavily populated flight deck at night that no one was incinerated or obliterated by the plane. It spoke to hundreds of tired young men working unforgiving hours under stress and pressure and constant threat of harm using their training, and perhaps instincts, to survive. It was also a stark reminder that the flight deck was dangerous and no place to be hanging around if I didn't need to be up there. Steel Beach wasn't very friendly most of the time.

The helo crew brought the pilot back aboard and within an incredibly short period of time the flight deck was fully functional. There were still planes airborne with nowhere else to go.

———◆———

AVIATION ANTISUBMARINE WARFARE OPERATOR—AW. My official title. Aside from all the missions—from medevacs to delivering mail—that I flew, hunting submarines was my primary assignment. By adding the AQA-7 aboard the *Ranger* and sonobuoy relay equipment on the Sea Kings, our capabilities were heightened a considerable degree.

The Soviets had 400 submarines for anti-shipping, anti-carrier, and nuclear ballistic attack. The AW rate was intended to act as a barrier to that threat. Our new little gadget was going to help us out. If we could get it to work.

Fast Eddie had hands-on experience but even he wasn't sure what made the odd looking thing tick. In addition to the paper graph the new mini-7 had a heads-up electronic display. It looked like a tiny square sonar scope with signals shown in a cross section. A series of evenly spaced spikes might reveal something, a single one perhaps; a salt and pepper background showed the usual sea noise.

Many hours were spent staring at the scope as helo crews flew high in the cool tropical air relaying signals to the ship. It was stifling hot in the AQA-7 space, a tiny unventilated area not much bigger than a walk-in closet. A single oscillating fan churned out a modest breeze—if I stood right next to it. But it wasn't for us—the electrical equipment needed to be kept cool; we could endure but it was fragile and susceptible to the heat.

One afternoon a Lt. Cdr. from the ship's company came in sporting a hand-held calculator the size of a pocket dictionary, eager to try out his own schooling and utilize his fancy new device. "So, shipmates, how many sonobuoys do we have out there?"

"Two dozen Sir, but nothing is coming in." I hadn't been able to get a signal to show up from any of the channels. Fast Eddie was leaning against the bulkhead smoking a cigarette, watching.

"Mind if I try?" He was polite but chomping at the bit to show his know-how.

"No Sir, go right ahead. But, I'm really not getting anything from a buoy; what's on here just looks like some odd electrical noise. It doesn't look right somehow, I'm not quite sure, but..."

"Now Petty Officer, pardon me, but I *do* think I can figure this all out. Now let's see..." He compulsively entered complicated data into his calculator. "That is, by my calculation, the second harmonic of the port side rudder, given its mass and surface area, plus factor in our speed of twenty-eight knots, well, yes, OK. Now, this other signal is most likely, uh-huh, a freighter's warped drive shaft turning at such and such an RPM and hmm, yes, the freighter is going sixteen knots." He continued to find sources for the myriad of lines showing up all over the screen. But I wasn't convinced; there was no salt and pepper, no background—ambient it was labelled—noise, and water is saturated with noise if from nothing else than its own motion. The heartbeat of the ocean could always be heard, even if there were no whales or porpoise or Soviet submarines lurking nearby.

Fast Eddie looked at me, looked around the room, took a long drag off his cigarette and sauntered over to the steel rack holding a host of assorted electrical equipment. Including the fan. He shut it off. The screen and graph went blank. So did the Lt. Cdr.'s face. Every line showing up was generated by the fan. Somehow the mini-7 was picking up and displaying, for all to see, the intimate electrical secrets of the fan.

Fast Eddie rolled his eyes, miming that he was going to go smoke something a little different, while the officer quietly slid his fancy calculator into its belt holster and wandered off.

The fan was the only thing we caught that day.

———◆———

I CONTINUED MY SEARCH for quiet and solitude. We were surrounded by water, 5,500 of us crammed into steel tunnels and steel caves with nowhere to go. Flying was an escape, there were times I looked forward to a mission even if it meant courting chance and death; at least I would die in the solitary world of ten tons of aircraft falling quietly towards the sea. But aboard ship there was nothing but noise and chaos everywhere I went.

I searched and I explored until that wonderful day I took a chance and opened the always-closed hatch. It had no markings other than the X-ray setting, meaning it was closed and should be. I opened it anyway. Anything could have been on the other side: propellers, sick bay, bombs, paint, food, M-16s, five inch shells, nuclear weapons, toilet paper. Anything. But I never expected to find nothing. And yet there it was, a dark cavernous void, a structural support for the angle deck above, a nautical engineer's solution for supporting the armor-plated steel flight deck as it jutted out over the portside hull, strong enough to withstand thousands of shattering concussions from planes slamming down at 150 knots. And I had found it. It was filled with nothing. Of course during flight ops it would resonate with the pounding from above, but when there were no flights it was almost soundless. A few meager bulbs struggled to illuminate the darkness.

The space was wedge-shaped, starting four stories tall at midships and tapering out to about three feet at the edge. I had to crouch to sit at the outer limits. It ran fifty feet deep. There were a few other hatches from other decks scattered about, and as I sat in the humid stale air and thought nothing, light would periodically wink from afar as someone else probed the little known space.

I staked my claim on a small corner of the void. I exerted as much self-will as possible, leaving my sanity behind as a holding force when I left.

I would visit my sanity from time to time. I found it lonely but holding up OK. It told me to play my flute more and pretend I would be the next Herbie Mann. It told me to forget that I was an aircrew petty officer team member for loading the B-57 nuclear device. My sanity mentioned I should read another book by Kurt Vonnegut, that I could use a dose of his humor.

I didn't tell very many people about my discovery; I wanted to keep it low key, quiet, a sanctuary of tranquility. Monotony punctuated by chaos and occasionally fear made for a very unstable environment. Along with doing yoga, the void kept me on a more even keel.

I had developed a fondness for the yogic headstand; it left me feeling like my senses had been fine-tuned. Finding a place to do it onboard was always challenging. Pete had the keys to the secret communications space since he worked there, so occasionally at night off-peak times we would don cutoffs, turn the lights to the red setting, put some jazz on his turntable and do headstands. That could be tricky if the *Ranger* was riding a high sea state, but more often than not we could get into a good headstand, with our bodies rocking slightly to the ship's swaying.

One night, as the ship slipped silently through the South China Sea, Pete and I decided to go for a heavy duty headstand, one that would tune our senses like never before. We were ready; after a couple of weeks at sea we needed something to get us centered. Flight ops weren't scheduled that night so it would be relatively quiet above. Pete put on Chick Corea's latest album, we placed folded towels on the hard linoleum covered steel deck for our heads, and set the lights to red. Onto our headstands we went. It was perfect.

I had no idea how long I had been on my head when the burst of light blasted through the door. My eyes had adjusted to the red light of the space so when the door opened letting in standard white light from the passageway it momentarily blinded me. I twisted my head just enough to see what was going on. There, in the doorway, was Lt.j.g. Neville, the communications officer. All he saw was dirty feet bathed in red light swaying to the ship's motion as jazz filled the room—his office. I thought I saw him shake his head in disbelief as he quietly shut the door.

———•———

Time stretched at sea, seeming like an eon surrounded by an infinite expanse of water. I wanted to get away from the ship, to take some leave in Australia, but it was prohibitively expensive to travel to. I had thirty days saved up and thought about using it overseas but couldn't afford to go anywhere exotic besides where I already was, and that was for free. I would sneak off to the void when I had a chance and mull over the future and its possibilities. Sometimes I would just sit in the dark and breathe in stale air, clearing my mind of all thoughts.

I had another technique for claiming a tiny piece of privacy. It was risky but at times the consequences seemed worth it. Part of the class structure aboard ship was evident in the heads. The enlisted heads were rows of tightly compacted stalls with barely enough room to sit and do what had to be done, infrequent as it might be aboard ship. I was lucky on occasion to find a stall with a clear plastic curtain; usually it was face to face. The officer's heads were cavernous by comparison; real stalls and just a few to a space with nice big partitions, a real door on real hinges, plenty of room to take some time and relax. I would glance in as I walked the 0-3 portside passageway—they looked luxurious.

The 0-3 level was populated by aviators: pilots, navigator-bombardiers, RIOs and . . . aircrewmen. I had been mistaken for a pilot while in my flight gear; why not take the chance and be mistaken for a pilot while on a toilet? RHIP—rank has its privileges—but I wasn't going to let that stop me. If I was going to try it I would need to steer clear of HS-4 pilots' territory; that meant I'd have to risk it in fighter country.

I wasn't a fighter pilot like Dad but I was sure as hell going to try to crap like one. It wouldn't be as if I was stealing anything, just taking up some unused space that wasn't allocated to one of my position and not for long, just a small slice of the time/space continuum experienced in secret. I didn't know if I could go through with it but I was longing for some privacy and needing to clear my system.

The cooks did their best, but recombining dehydrated cottage cheese with leftover dehydrated vegetables chased with bug juice taxed my system to its limit. The speed line burgers were as tough as roofing shingles, the beans and franks outdated me, and the occasional box lunch for long flights often tasted like jet fuel. The small cans of warm pineapple juice in the boxed meal would barely chase away the fuel aftertaste. I would never drink pineapple juice again.

One day I decided to go for it. I knew enough of aviation to hold down a casual, bathroom-type chat. After all, officers weren't all that different from us enlisted, especially in that place. I rehearsed:

"The fuckin' air boss thinks he's God, doesn't he?"

"If I get any more night time I'm gonna run out of red ink."

"They didn't tell ya' about this at Pensacola, did they?"

At last I gained enough confidence, and urgency, to test my plan. Hide in plain sight. Waltz right in and sit down like I had the right. I would be a Phantom of a wholly different type. The plan was simple: stash my name tag embossed with enlisted wings and just walk in.

I did. It was fairly quiet, just a pair of well-shined brown flight boots showing underneath the farthest stall door and no one at the sinks.

The empty stall door swung in gracefully on well oiled hinges. And there it was, a shrine to decency, a porcelain receptacle of glorious proportion. The black plastic seat was clean and there was plenty of toilet paper. The elbow room was almost sinful. I was giddy with anticipation—a quiet, big space all to myself and a mission to complete. As I eased out of my flight suit and down onto the cool plastic seat, I closed my eyes in reflection of a special moment. I wanted to savor it, to dwell in the uniqueness of it all. I could sense that the occupant of the other stall was aware of me, waiting for my commitment to the event.

I ran my mental checklist: toilet paper, check; door latch closed, check; flight suit and T-shirt clear, check. I was ready, I was oh so ready, when the impossible happened.

"General quarters, general quarters, all hands man your battle stations!"

It couldn't be, it just couldn't. But I had to obey, it was the 1MC bellowing a direct order to do as it instructed. I squeezed my cheeks, zipped up my flight suit, and bolted from the stall.

I nearly ran over the young officer exiting the other stall. As our eyes met I couldn't help but say, "They didn't tell ya' about this at Pensacola, did they?"

I made it to the ready room in time to find out it was just a drill. It was also the leading edge of a major exercise, including a complicated ASW scenario that was to run for twenty-four hours. Missions would be back to back, the flight deck crowded and hectic, the pace rapid and crews stressed.

The sunset was beautiful but few noticed. Bob Hart and I had been teamed up and flew a lot of nights, which meant we would be launching after dark. The ready room was alive with crews coming and going, the flight deck buzzing with hot refuels and crew changes. Sonobuoys were loaded, rescue hoists checked and last minute once-overs of the helos done all while the rest of the air wing pursued their own assignments topside.

I was getting too short to take any chances; fortunately Hart was sharp and eager to learn. We stood on the starboard side waiting for our helo to be brought up on the aircraft elevator. The night sky had turned purple-black, millions of stars glowing in the clean ocean air.

Bob looked up, then looked puzzled. "Hey Thos, those stars, they're jumping up and down! They're moving!"

"What the hell are you taking about, Bob, what moving stars?" I couldn't get what he was talking about. I had seen some pretty strange things at sea but never jumping stars.

"No, really, if you look at the stars next to the island they're moving up and down, almost in tempo to something."

"Uh, Bob, *we're* moving, it's the ship. I mean, sure, the stars *are* moving—in space—really fast too, but not like that, I mean, the ship is just rocking side to side. We're on a boat, remember?"

Bob found out just how easy it was to get confused on the flight deck. It was too easy; that was in part what made it so dangerous. I figured I knew my way around pretty well. Bob would too, all in good time.

We had a tiring four hour mission including cargo and personnel hoists as well as sonobuoy deployment. We made it back for a hot refuel and crew switch. The helo was going back out on another mission and needed to be loaded with a fresh batch of buoys, and Bob and I helped get the clumsy units aboard.

There were two Sea Kings on landing spots three and four. Some deep, ingrained instinct told me there was never enough clearance between the helos as they sat on their designated zones. I stayed close to the front helo as I shuttled the buoys into the cargo area from the buoy locker. I was carrying two at a time—one on each shoulder, just like the old Springfields back in bootcamp: right shoulder arms, left shoulder arms.

As I approached the helo with the last load I thought I heard a whooshing sound emanating from the dark. I looked back and up and realized I had just walked under the spinning tail rotor. In all my flight gear there was at best three inches of clearance; with sonobuoys poking up above my head my mind flashed on the possibilities. The adrenaline rush had already coursed through my body and dissipated by the time I had a chance to take in what had just happened. I would never know how close I came to contacting the speeding tail rotor, but I would hear that menacing buzz created by the five blades in my mind for the rest of my life; all I had to do was close my eyes and listen.

I was done for the night and probably good that I was. I didn't have a flight until the next afternoon so I hit the speed line for some wrinkly, rubbery hot dogs the color of brick and a glass of green bug juice, then hit my rack. The 1MC rang eight bells—0400 hrs.—as I tried to forget my earlier blunder. I thought I was infallible up on Steel Beach. Even the time when an A-3's exhaust almost blew me off the flight deck before the blast shield blocked the force, I was aware and took measures to keep from going overboard. But walking under a tail rotor, even on the big Sea King, was a lapse in judgment regardless of how tired I had been or how dark it was. Being a short-timer could get me hurt or killed if I let that cloud my thinking.

◆

IT WAS NIGHT ON the flight deck. By instinct I approached the helo in a crouched position, even though the big H-3's rotors were high off the ground. But I had to crouch lower; the blurry path of the five blades seemed close to the ground and getting closer. I crouched even lower, but the whirling blades, five blunt scythes in a strobe-like effect, cut ever closer to the deck. I didn't remember having to crouch that low, but I finally got on my hands and knees and shuffled forward. I had to get on board; it was my responsibility to take the next mission, but damn if I could get through those rotor blades. I could feel the wind churned up by the blades against my face, even with my clear helmet visor down. I wasn't going to make it that way, the slicing motion of the dull black rotors inching ever so slowly toward the deck and my body. Finally I got on my belly, dragging my gear behind me, trying not to look up. I pressed my face against the hard, rough surface of the flight deck, scratching my cheek on the nonskid. I flattened myself out, I couldn't go back, I had to get inside that helo, but those blades were as menacing as sabers twenty feet long whirled by a demon, and they were aimed right at me. Closing my eyes to somehow feed the illusion that if I couldn't see the deadly blades they wouldn't be so menacing, I began to feel them buffeting against my flight suit, slapping at my body ever so slightly. An inch lower and I would surely be shredded and become "one with the flight deck." The brown shirts would have to hose my body off the nonskid. I wanted to cry out but I couldn't; I just had to make myself as much a part of the steel deck as I could, and slither under the giant fan above me. I knew what was coming next—I had watched the progression already; the rotors would continue to dip down until I was caught up in whirling high-technology metals and taken for a spinning dance of death.

The nightmares had started.

THE NEXT DAY I went to the sponson where we had stored the damaged secret materials from the fire to shake off the bad dream. It was low on the port side and had a simple railing circling it. Facing the bow, I reclined against a gun mount and put my legs up on the rail, catching the breeze and breathing in some fresh air. It was a stunningly beautiful day. I was endlessly fascinated by the intensity of colors at sea: blues that defined "blue," billowing white clouds that seemed so close I felt I could reach in and take a handful, letting it squeeze out between my fingers.

The immense gray ship slicing through the sea looked unstoppable. As my eyes took in the graceful curve of the hull sweeping down from Steel Beach to the sea sixty feet below, I noticed a pipe opening twenty feet from the waterline. I then heard a gurgling sound carried back by the wind. Suddenly a torrent of brown slurry gushed forth from the outlet, like the ship had diarrhea. Colors remained vibrant, especially the brown.

I knew folks back home had a tendency to think of a WestPac as a romantic tropical voyage, so I wasn't sure if anybody would believe me if I told them about the pipe.

I had 172 days to go to find out.

On course for Manila and a few day's liberty, Cdr. Stokes held a Captain's Mast. A holdover from the days of sailing ships when it took place at the foot of the mainmast, it was a court-like disciplinary session where the CO was empowered to assign punishment for certain offenses. Being placed on report by a petty officer or commissioned officer was necessary to be "called before the mast." Bread and water for three days still stood as possible punishment. At least flogging had become unfashionable.

Since I had been appointed the Human Relations Petty Officer it was my duty to attend the Mast as an observer. I had no idea what was going to happen; somehow I had managed to avoid experiencing one first-hand. A maintenance senior chief named McGalliard had placed one of his men on report, and now it was his chance to explain to the CO why.

"OK, Senior Chief, why is this man on report?"

"Well Sir, he's been negligent in his duties."

"Oh? Then why are his quarterly marks so high?"

"Sir, just lately he's been tardy and disrespectful."

"So where was your leadership during all that; didn't you counsel him to be more punctual? Didn't you take him aside and remind him of his responsibilities towards officers and petty officers? No? You mean you just one day decided to put him on report without any prior advisory action on your own behalf? Do you know what the UCMJ says about putting a man on report? It is to be used as a last resort, not a first action. And by all accounts the quarterly marks you assigned him lead me to believe he is a decent and hard working sailor, and now you're telling me he isn't?"

"Well, yes, Skipper, I guess I am."

"Senior Chief, you can't have it both ways, and I see no reason to pursue any disciplinary action at this time. Your actions were unwarranted. The report is dismissed."

I was stunned. I had just seen my CO confront and upbraid a senior chief. I was no fan of McGalliard myself—he had put me on report for being tardy when we flew into Cubi the first time and I had bunked in the transit barracks. There was no watch wake-up list and I had overslept, getting to his muster late. Not a good thing to do but hardly an offense worthy of being put on report. He wasn't even in my own division; he knew nothing about me other than I was aircrew and that was all he needed to cause me trouble. Chief Dominguez tore up the report and told me don't give the guy another reason to mess with me. And I had just seen the skipper dismiss McGallaird's animosity towards selected individuals with laser-like precision. Justice had been served.

After Mast was over I looked at Stokes, raising my eyebrows with an expression of amazement. He looked right at me with his intense gaze but I thought I detected a slight grin—not much, hardly a real grin at all—but still, something was there along with an almost imperceptible glint of amusement in his eye. I felt the squadron was in good hands.

We entered Manila Harbor on April 1 for three days of liberty. I had decided not to go into town; I was going to stay aboard, save my money, get caught up on sleep, read, and dream about going home.

The ship was a quiet place in the harbor; with thousands of sailors on liberty and no flight ops it seemed deserted. On the second day I headed down to the void to reflect on nothing in particular. The hatch was padlocked. I was denied my sanctuary. There was always the secret comm office for a yogic headstand, if nothing secret was going on.

After the brief visit we slowly made our way back to Subic, qualifying new pilots for launches and traps on the way after Steel Beach surrendered to the carrier's reason for being.

Squadron area inspections continued in fine naval tradition and we had the first one in the aircrew ops space since it had been an inferno. The warped steel bulkhead was gleaming with its new coat of paint. Nothing was stored between the steam tube and the overhead.

As a newly minted E-5 I had the additional assignment of accompanying the XO, Cdr. Redman, on the inspection. I had a clipboard with a blank piece of paper on it, a sure sign I didn't know what I was supposed to be doing.

When we got to the aircrew space the XO gave it a close look, running his finger over the door jamb and under desks. Clean, I made sure the guys caught everything. Having done countless field days myself I knew what to have them take care of. Then the XO's gaze locked on something that had caught his eye. Uh-oh, had I missed something? He was looking intently at our modest book collection.

"Mind if I borrow a few of these?" he asked no one in particular as his fingers caressed a row of Louis L'Amour paperbacks. The XO, in the blink of an eye, had become just a guy who wanted to read some westerns. With the owner's permission Redman picked *Sackett*, *High Lonesome* and *Silver Canyon*. "This should keep me out of trouble," he said as he marked off the space as outstanding on his own clipboard.

I had given the XO the nickname of "Fast and Low" which was the way he flew. It made for exciting flights. Cdr. Redman was due to take over the squadron in June as the new commanding officer. CJ Stokes had his style of leadership; Redman his own. We would still be in good hands.

———•———

THE *RANGER* WAS OUR home away from home. The Airwaves Club was our home away from our home away from home. San Miguels chased by swigs of sweet Wild Turkey lubricated evenings at "The Airwuh." San Miguel was basically formaldehyde with some fermented mystery grain served in dark brown bottles to hide what some may have called impurities. Others would claim that was what made San Magoo so unforgettable. It usually took until noon the next day for me to forget my share. The Wild Turkey on the other hand was straight from the base liquor store, and brought into town to augment the local brew. At three dollars a fifth, how could we go wrong?

As usual, Malcolm, Pete and I sat around one of the dark tables which leaned a bit to port from a loosely-anchored top and uneven floor. Chief Beaty sat off to the side, smoking his pipe and reading a well-worn paperback. A small bottle of brandy sat by his tobacco. Watching the bartender clean shot glasses with a rag that looked like it had just swabbed the flight deck, we opted to take swigs of whiskey straight from the bottle.

That night was to be the crowning moment in Malcolm's ever-evolving plan to fuck the Navy. Over the past three months Malcolm had taken up with Suzy, the mamasan of the bar. I could see that Malcolm was "going native." Gazing out from under heavy eyelids, he lit yet another Marlboro with his Zippo and proceeded to fill me in.

"Thos, I got a plan, and it's foolproof."

"Oh jeezus, I don't believe what I'm hearing. Malcolm, a walk in the park ain't foolproof, shit happens and you know it. Just what the fuck is it now; you gonna cook up some scheme so you can go home on emergency leave?"

"Just listen to this idea, I got it all worked out. Suzy, you know her, well, I love her, I really do, and I got a way to get out of the rest of the cruise so I can be with her."

"Sure, have it your way, but do you really want to spend the rest of your life in the PI? Don't you think you'll get homesick? I can't wait to hear this one, so let me have it..."

"OK, it's simple. I know this ex-Marine dude who owns a bar not far from here. He says if I go into legal hold, I have to spend sixty days in limbo until my case could be heard. By then the *Ranger* will be long gone, and I'll be out."

"What do you mean 'I'll be out.' Out of what? And what's going to get you into legal hold?"

"It will work like this. I'll start a fight in this guy's bar but it won't be a real fight, it will be a fake fight, a staged brawl, just enough to get the shore patrol there and get arrested. Then, I have this card, see, this guy is related to Suzy and he's the assistant chief of police, so when I get arrested I give them this card and get taken directly to him, and he plays along. Hell, I've been made mayor of Pago Pago! Thos, I know it will work."

I couldn't believe what I was hearing. Ordering another round of San Magoo and taking a swig of Wild Turkey, I just shook my head in disbelief. I thought I caught Beaty's ears tuning into our roundtable discussion. He puffed on his burl pipe in almost a meditative state.

Pete, ever reserved, kicked in his assessment of Malcolm's scheme. "You're fuckin' nuts. Have you seen the Shore Patrol here? They're armed to the teeth and for christsakes there's martial law! And they like hurting sailors. Marcos says it's OK to shoot your ass for no reason at all!"

"No, no, it's OK, I've got it all covered. Jake, the bar owner, will get the police to arrest me, and he'll file a holding order until the quote 'damages' are paid, but there won't be any damages, just a little cash to keep him in the plan, a visit to Suzy's relative in the police and by then that fuckin' aircraft carrier will be long gone."

It was my turn. "And what, once you're in the brig and we sail out into the South China Sea, he'll drop the charges and you'll be set free to live your Papa Hemingway life on the veranda of mamasan's hootch?"

"Exactly! I'll be out of the brig, a short-timer, and living the good life with Suzy. I can sit out the rest of my time in the Nav right here in Olongapo!"

The chief's head was buried in his hands, his pipe now smoldering on the table.

"Of all the lame-brained fucked-up stupid ideas I've ever heard, this takes the cake." Pete was on a streak of eloquent reflection. "This has to be the most crazy scheme you've ever hatched! By comparison it makes those six foot square, 100 pound speakers you wanted to drag onboard look uninspired."

"C'mon, Pete, I hate that fucking ship, I never want to fly again and I really care for Suzy."

Holding the fifth of whiskey by the neck, the bottle tilted at a dangerous angle on the table, I chimed in. "Malcolm, Suzy seems nice enough, but aren't you just a dependable meal ticket for her? In the meantime she'll want an air-conditioned Honda to drive around this shithole. Do you want to do this for the rest of your life? And remember, brig time is dead time, it doesn't count toward your enlistment."

"I won't be in the brig that long, just long enough to miss ship's movement. Anyway, I'm tired of this Navy crap. Hey Thos, got any butts? I'm out."

"Here, you can have the whole pack, they're PI knockoffs. I forgot to say 'American' when I bought them from the kid at the corner. God knows what they use for tobacco to make those things. But ya' gotta hand it to 'em, they're damn good counterfeiters."

Malcolm looked resplendent in a silk shirt, the colors resembling an oil slick captured in fabric. "I suppose she bought that fashion statement for you, too?" Pete chimed in.

"Yeah, so don't give me any shit about it, ok? She wants me to look nice when we go out."

I gave it one final try. "Malcolm, this is the last thing I'm going to say on the matter. If for a moment I thought you were really cut out for this I'd be the first one to shake your hand, but I know you, and this ain't it. Remember how we talked about missing Colorado, the high plains in summer full of wildflowers, magpies singing, and watching those huge thunderstorms build up in the hot afternoons? The sky turning purple under the advancing column of a 60,000 foot-high storm, the wind picking up, the air shot through with wild ozone and horses sprinting back and forth in the charged atmosphere of impending chaos?

"Think of that girl you were telling me about, the one who told you to look her up when you got back. Think, Malcolm, think. Think about straddling a big Harley hog and cruising the open roads of eastern Colorado, the wind and asphalt your only company in the solitude as you speed by in the warm summer sun."

"Stop, dammit, stop, Thos, will ya stop?"

The ceiling fans continued their slow rotation, barely circulating the thick pungent portside air heavy with cigarette smoke and talk. The bar girls stood aside, trying to catch someone's eye for a proposition to go long time. Off in the corner Tex was arguing with Carrier, and Chief Beaty stepped in to calm the guys down. Soon it would be midnight; we either had to find a hootch in town to stay in, or get back to the ship.

"Last call," came halfheartedly from the bartender, replaying a scene done thousands of times before, the only difference was which ship the batch of sailors were from.

The humid tropical night clung to our bodies like a sticky second skin. After we passed around the Wild Turkey until everyone had a chance for one last pull of the sweet bourbon, we collected our strays and headed out the door. I put my arm around Malcolm to steady both of us, and looked over at the big gray hulk of the carrier standing proud above the wharf, the American flag waving beckoningly from the highest point of the ship. "Malcolm, let's go home."

The *Ranger* set sail on April 22 for another tour of duty in the South China Sea.

———◆———

THE FLIGHT DECK WAS a compact, tightly woven fabric of steel, fuel, bombs, rockets, missiles and young men. The crash crew always stood on high alert in their firefighting gear. A full-sized fire truck sat just behind the island. Another stood by the ready. Tow vehicles scooted around dragging aircraft, staging and storing them in the choreographed dance of the airwing. There was a rhythm to flight operations and as always a Black Knight helo was either off the deck first or already airborne.

Watching a Sea King lift off up close was never a reassuring sight—the skeletal frame would twist and torque out of alignment, ripples running through the helo's thin skin at an oblique angle. The whole airframe seemed to contort out of shape as ten tons of helicopter sagged under rotor blades clawing the air. It always looked as if the helo needed a second to decide if it was going to defeat gravity once again before the pilot would dip the nose down and transition into forward flight.

I didn't think about that when I was in the left crew seat; I was concerned with watching the landing gear indicators, the engine fire-warning lights, the double row of gauges that told an analog tale of vital systems' overall health. In the double row there was pressure: hydraulic and oil; temperature: engine oil, power turbine, main gearbox oil. There were two gas generator tachometers. I didn't need to know what the specific readings were; a genius at Sikorsky positioned the double row of gauges so that when in the proper range the needles all pointed up. A quick glance told the whole story.

The two crewmen had plenty to keep them busy on a sub hunting mission. The sonar gear was massive, with a face full of dials, switches, range and bearing indicators, dome depth gauge and CRT scope. To its side was the MAD indicator and multipurpose recorder. The MAD detector itself resembled a blunt missile slung beneath the starboard landing gear sponson. It deployed behind the helo on a cable to get it out of the magnetic influence of its host and into its own space, where it could pick out a mass of steel hiding beneath the waves.

The sonobuoys, their selected signals destined for Fast Eddie's scrutiny, were piled in the back of the helo like so much firewood, to be thrown out of the cargo door by hominoid devices. Sending signals back to the ship by way of electronic relay gear was technological progress. The deployment of the buoys was still a bit primitive.

We were continuing to validate the contribution our H-3s were making to the overall mission of the modern supercarrier. We were finding subs. Torpedoes and nuclear weapons were loaded, the continuing rehearsal for a Cold War blowout perfected and perfected again.

One cool early morning, after our helo twisted and contorted itself into the air, we headed out to an ASW search area across a glass-smooth sea. It was one of those mornings that seemed to embody a tranquility that was both rare and beautiful.

Airborne just before sunrise, our Sea King skimmed along the smooth surface of the South China Sea with power and grace. The tropic air was still, creating an almost divine moment to experience the enormity of water in a state of peace. As the day lightened, the haze-gray sky blended with the water's horizon, as if a canvas stained the color of putty was awaiting the hues from the rising sun to paint the panorama of the sea.

Then I saw a strange apparition on the calm flat surface; it didn't make sense, it was nothing I had ever seen before. Leaning out of the cargo door I peered through my clear helmet visor, trying to make out the odd vision. Humps. A dozen graceful humps protruded from the surface like a collection of watery hillocks. Gray like everything else, the humps made no sense. Sailors of old would likely have had tall tales to weave about such a vision seen from afar, but we instead headed straight for them at 140 knots, our curiosity needing satisfaction.

Near the apparitions in minutes, it was still difficult to see beneath the water due to the reflection of the scant rays of light. Once directly above them, the mystery, the curiosity, the wonderment was fulfilled. Whales. Big, gray, and sleeping whales. They rested quietly, their monstrous forms gently breaking the surface in graceful arcs of thick, smooth whale flesh.

We had disturbed their slumber, their own enjoyment of a calm sea and quiet morning. On our second pass one of the huge animals rolled on its side and looked directly at me, eye to eye, and a jolt of awareness shot through me like a high voltage shock. The whale's eye—huge, round, brown and intense—held an intelligence that struck me as something I had never seen or experienced before or since. That eye spoke volumes; it assessed, it judged, it expressed, in the scant few seconds it stared at me from its watery realm. Then, as if thoroughly annoyed by our noisy disturbance, the whale slipped below the surface and disappeared. Soon the rest of the pod did the same, and our apparitions vanished into the deep recesses of the sea.

Wonders never ceased. When I got back from the whale flight

Dinkle revealed a new discovery. "Thos, gotta try this out, it's amazing. Here, go ahead, use some!" He held out a small aerosol can about a quarter the size of a shaving cream canister. He caught me at a good time; it had been a long sweltering flight once the sun began to bake us in the helicopter and I was hot and sticky in the humid air. "Go ahead, pull your boots off, you're going to love this," he assured me.

I got naked from the ankles down and gave his new find a try. Aerosol foot powder. It was heaven. It felt like I had plunged my feet into a cold Colorado mountain stream.

"Ain't America great?" he boasted. I had to agree, whoever invented that stuff was my hero.

———◆———

WE PULLED INTO HONG KONG May 3 on a film of saffron-colored jellyfish layering the channel. They covered the water's surface like a pulsating, breathing blanket. Red sailed Junks glided across the water as countless steamers chugged their way in, making elbow room for themselves among the armada of commercial ships. Hong Kong would be reverting back to the communist Chinese before the century was out; until then it was still a British Crown Colony doing big business.

The at-sea period had been relatively accident free. JD Dungan and I had flown together a few times and he seemed at ease in the helo. I felt like aircrew would be in good hands, in spite of Fuckup's presence. If Dinkle and Hart and JD and Cowboy Johnny and Teddy Bear could keep things under control with Chief Dominguez' help then just maybe Fuckup wouldn't get anybody killed. I hadn't flown with Fuckup yet but I knew at some point I would have to, it was the law of averages.

Hong Kong's mail call was heavy with news from home. I had been accepted for fall quarter at Humboldt State. The news gave me the means to ask for a school early-out, possibly cutting two or three weeks off active duty. I was getting excited about going back to college. I wondered if all my class skipping when I was with Marsha would come back to haunt me. Marsha—I hadn't thought of her in a long time. I had no idea where she was but I was pretty sure I wasn't going to check all the bars back home to see if she was still mixing drinks.

My brother had written me about his visit to Texas. Apparently Dad was drinking without limits and not getting any suggestions from his old friends to do otherwise. Sometimes he would start drinking at lunch and not stop until he passed out on his couch that evening. I didn't know how a man who had flown high-powered fighters for twenty years with a cadre of exceptional men could end up like that. Sometimes I would be on my sixth or seventh Wild Turkey wondering such things.

At his best Dad could survive victorious from a dog fight with an Me-109, fly at Mach 1, build anything, make everyone laugh and shoot a goose on the fly through the neck with a rifle with eagle-like vision and rock-steady hands. At his worst he could drink all day, blame the world's problems on those unlike himself, alienate his family and berate his children. When he was drunk he would play German martial music, thumping his fist against his chair. When he was sober he would claim music soothed the savage beast.

Swarms of sailors converged on Hong Kong and the carrier became a ghost town. I read, wrote letters, poured over Humboldt's brochures, perused the PX catalogue and revisited Pete's wonderful book on national parks. I stood extra watches aboard and took naps between gaggles of squadronmates storming the berthing compartment with excited tales of Kowloon, Wanchai and "Suzie Wong."

Tex had a fine time. "This lady at the bar kept getting me to buy her drinks and Thos, I swear it was just tea! I mean, I was paying real money for little glasses of 'tea' while she talked me into dancing, and I had to pay for that too! Dammit, I'm just about out of E-3 pay. Good thing we're going back to sea tomorrow, I don't think I can afford much more liberty. I'm so broke I can't even pay attention." He was swaying slightly large amounts of overpriced watered down booze.

"Welcome to Hong Kong, or any other portside joint you'll find yourself in, Tex. Did you really think you were going to get *her* drunk and get in her pants? My boy, you're not the first sailor to learn that lesson, I can guarantee it. Kinda makes that mail buoy watch seem like kid's stuff, eh?"

He just looked at me, rolled his eyes and tossed his thin wallet under his rack where it would be safe, or until we hit Singapore.

We pulled out on the eighth of May for a line period in which we kept Sea Kings airborne almost constantly. Intense antisubmarine missions along with the usual plane guard flights filled the schedule. The future of helo ASW on carriers hung in the balance. My life hung in the balance too. I was finally scheduled to fly with Fuckup. At night. He flunked his preflight brief by refusing to wear his survival gear properly. The junior crewman was critiqued on every flight. I had already started marking down failures for him and we weren't even off the flight deck.

We made it through the night mission. He stared out the small crewman's window most of the flight as I maintained a heightened vigilance over the helo and pilots. I never knew if they were aware I was doing my best to back them on instruments, gauges and engine fire warning lights and it didn't matter; what mattered was getting back in one piece. Fuckup didn't even seem to care about that.

I piled up hours of deciphering sonobuoy signals. The Lt. Cdr. who "tracked" the fan had honed his skills and made far fewer wild calls. "This is the future of shipboard ASW, I can guarantee you that, shipmate," he said. "Some day they'll have a room full of computers doing the data analysis and AWs will be working with screens much bigger than this little thing. Paper graphs will be a thing of the past; it will all be done with computers, I guarantee it."

I still couldn't type worth a damn much less operate a "computer." The AQA-7 was pretty simple; it wrote a story and I had learned how to read it. I couldn't imagine needing more than what it already did.

Fast Eddie had the shack set up the way he liked. Nude foldouts were taped to the wall next to the government-issue three month calendar. Ashtrays were scattered about, never beyond an arm's reach from anywhere in the tiny room.

"Hey Thos, gettin' short are ya'?" he asked as we sailed between China and the PI. "Me too, on this floating piece of shit anyway. Maybe we'll head back to Travis together."

"Could be, Eddie. I can have my seabag packed in about two seconds. I'm almost a two digit midget, if I get a school cut I'm already there. Damn, I never thought I'd get to say that."

"You want another crack at the gear? Chances are they won't have these babies at, where is it you're planning on going, Thunderbolt?"

"Humboldt, northern California, up in Redwood country. I've never been there so why not? And sure, I'll take it for a while, you look like you're ready for, well, a break."

"Roger that," Eddie confirmed as he made a rolling-a-joint gesture with his fingers. I was amazed he never got caught, or maybe he had, maybe that was where his 1st Class Crow went, up in smoke with a busted joint. But he worked hard and knew his stuff. He never volunteered to join us and fly in a Sea King. He had his limits.

After an intense week of flight ops we pulled back into Subic. Flight operations were hard on a carrier and the *Ranger* needed constant repair and upkeep. The cheap labor found in the PI helped some accountant at the Pentagon balance his books. The cheap labor found in the PI helped keep thousands of locals slightly above abject poverty.

Subic meant the Airwuh Club. Aircrew had made it our unofficial gathering place and we were welcomed back in earnest by the owners. Malcolm was reunited with Suzy. I was reunited with Wild Turkey.

Chuck Dog was getting real short, under thirty days. "Hey Thos, I got a deal for ya'. I'm about done with this man's Navy. You'll be wearing the short-timer's belt buckle next. How 'bout if I treat us to a night at the Lotus Blossom Massage Parlor? I'll pick up the tab for everything except your 'tip.' What you want is up to you, Thos, but it's my last night in Olongapo and I'm going to make it one I won't forget."

"I don't know Chuck Dog, I haven't even gone short time on this WestPac; I was hoping to go the whole cruise without, well, without going short time. I don't want to take any diseases home with me and this town is one giant fuckin' petri dish."

"Oh c'mon Thos, here, finish your drink and let's do it, it's just a few doors down."

It was late. I had six or ten whiskeys in me. I hadn't felt a woman's touch in over six months. "Oh what the hell. But I'm not staying past twelve; I'll be damned if I'm going to get stuck in a massage parlor overnight. And you're buying, right? OK Chuck Dog, we're outta here."

It was a short stumble down the sidewalk to the parlor. They often had the best looking woman at the front counter, raising hopes that all the working gals were as attractive. Chuck paid and up we went on rickety stairs to the main floor, where the grand ballroom of sexual waltzing was humming with activity.

Curtained off cubicles—one after another in rows alongside a walkway—housed the business end of things. Sailors and Marines were in various stages of intoxication, anticipation and relaxation. Chuck and I were herded into individual cubicles and set upon "massage" tables. We awaited our personal hosts. Soon my "masseuse" pulled back the curtain and introduced herself. "Hello sailuhboy, my name Tina, you know, like Tina Turner! You want massage?"

"Sure, I could use one, I mean, a real one, why not." Stripped naked, I lay on the table as she proceeded to knead my muscles with the delicate touch of a jackhammer operator and the sincerity of a telephone solicitor. It lasted but a minute or so. I ended up on my back. Her touch was anything but sensual but my self-imposed restraint was growing weak.

"You want sensation?" she asked, looking hopeful for a nice tip. I figured what the hell, a hand lotion lubed handjob wouldn't put me in jeopardy as far as infections went. I wasn't sure what my mind might conjure up as I closed my eyes. It didn't matter, the lotion and motion worked.

It was getting late. Chuck was still in his cubicle. Tina sprung her best sales pitch. "You want to go long time? I make you happiest sailuhboy in PI." She smiled what seemed to be a genuine smile. My body had recovered quickly and was ready for more biological imperative to be fulfilled.

"OK." I was stuck for the night on a shaky table in a tiny wooden cubicle behind a frail curtain with a woman I didn't know in a town I didn't understand in a country under martial law.

I ran into Chuck the next morning in the showers. I tried not to think that the water might be pumped in from Shit River. "So how'd it go, Thos?"

"How'd it go? It was like bread and water to a starving man. It was like the worst date you ever had but it was still better than staying home listening to your parents argue. I hope I don't live to regret it, that's all."

"How could you regret screwing?"

"Because, Chuck Dog, I got this funny feeling I'm going to pay a price, and I don't mean Pisos. There could be an infection in the next county and I'd get it."

"Don't worry, remember what Chief Hatch used to say, 'Don't sweat the petty stuff and don't pet the sweaty stuff.' Besides, there's plenty of penicillin in sickbay." Right. Penicillin. I was allergic to it. It was more dangerous to me than the clap.

Three days later I was at sick call. Goddammit. The only time I had sex in over six months and I got infected. Fortunately the dispensary had an alternate drug to the potentially lethal penicillin. At least the corpsman was understanding. Maybe because he hadn't seen me in the clap line yet. Some guys wore it as a badge of some sort—five, six, ten times wasn't uncommon for some sailors. Carpe Diem.

I felt like an idiot. It was back to my books and yogic headstands and counting days to go on my short-timer's calendar.

16: Typhoons and Sub Hunts

M id-May. We were still in Subic readying for another patrol. I was on the flight deck getting some fresh air and waiting for word on whether or not helo 743 was going to be air worthy before I headed over to Cubi. If the helo was "downed" there was no sense heading over to the hangar. Malcolm came up to Steel Beach with a big grin on his face and his arm wrapped in bandages.

"What the hell? It looks like a wombat got a hold of you."

"Almost, a fucking monkey bit me."

"What? What the fuck were you trying to do, anyway?"

"Nothing! I was just standing on Magsaysay talking to Suzy's cousin when I got this funny feeling, like a rat was chewing on my arm, but instead it was this organ grinder's dancing monkey, the little fucker. The corpsman down in sick bay pumped me full of nuclear strength antibiotics. I'll be lucky if my goddamn arm doesn't rot off."

"So what happened to the monkey?"

"I can sum it up in one word—'barbeque!'"

"You going to avoid that part of town for a while, just in case the monkey's owner is looking for some sort of reimbursement for his business loss?"

"Fuck no, I'm still the 'Mayor of Pago Pago!' But Chief Beaty talked me out of the idea of trying to stay in the PI; he heard everything we talked about at the Airwuh awhile back. But I'm still tight with some locals so I'll be OK.

"Anyway, have you heard? Some bigshot Hollywood type is filming a movie up north somewhere. Maybe we should take some leave and go check it out." Malcolm was excited about the idea and it wasn't a bad one. He said the movie had to do with Vietnam and there were helicopters in it; maybe we could get parts as helicopter crewmen extras in the flick.

"Maybe we should. I have a lot of leave saved up but damn, I sure would like to use it to get out early. But maybe now's not the time to head up north anyway; it's looking like a storm is coming, feel that wind? It's got some punch behind it."

The sky had turned slate gray, with heavy, fast moving clouds. The moist air felt extra saturated, with more than the usual tropical mugginess. Within minutes word got out: helo flight crews get a week's worth of personal items plus all flight gear, and get off the ship. "Now," was all Chief Beaty said as he packed his parachute bag.

Flight crews streamed off the officer's brow; the enlisted afterbrow had already been pulled away. As I stepped on the accommodation ladder to go ashore I felt it shudder and jerk. Looking up and aft I saw a huge crane. The brow was attached to the crane by cables and the operator was trying to remove it from the ship. I held on and waved at the operator, hoping he would see me before he hoisted up the ladder. The shuddering stopped and I made a hasty departure. As soon as I hit the pier the ladder was hoisted away. I was the last aviator off the *Ranger* before Typhoon Olga stormed ashore.

As I left I saw two giant ocean going tugs, bulldogs of the harbor, pulling the *Ranger* away from the pier, keeping 80,000 tons of steel from smashing into the dock. To the west it looked like a rampage of wind and rain was relentlessly hurling towards us.

We were hurriedly bussed to some old Quonset huts next to the jungle. Then it began to rain in earnest; it was so thickly heavy I felt like I was trying to breathe underwater. The sky pressed down with cyclone force, land was obscured and the sea and air were beaten into a frothy mix. Rain fell steadily—almost ten inches a day—for a week, pounding the ground into a soggy, fragile slurry. Winds reached 100 miles per hour north of Subic, near Iba. Subic was protected from the highest winds, but the *Ranger* was trying to break loose of her tugboats and crash into the Alava Pier under the force of the tropical cyclone.

There wasn't much to do during the storm, so I read books with damp, moldy pages and waited until the cyclone passed—we knew we would be called upon to medevac victims and deliver food to the stranded as soon as flying was possible. The storm finally abated after a week of hurricane-force winds and five feet of rain.

I finally got airborne on the twenty-ninth, with Carrier as my second crewman. The day started early in Manila, loading up big sacks of "superbread" to be dropped off at clusters of the isolated and starving. We stopped off at a Filipino air base to pick up our local guide to take us into the mountains. Strewn across the tarmac was a row of F-86 Sabre fighter jets—the same jet Dad flew in the Korean War some twenty-three years earlier. I had heard Lt. Gray talk about how Marcos wanted to be a third world super power. I couldn't imagine how he was going to do it with those relics, even the communist Vietnamese had some newer fighters, including some nice F-5s.

Once we had our Filipino Air Force officer on board we headed into the rugged Luzon mountains. It was a full sky as helos from various units scoured rice paddies and canyons for survivors. Olga had flattened the countryside with unrestrained brute force. Flooding and winds wiped out roads and bridges, making overland travel all but impossible. We were in our element.

Our first stop was into hill country and a primitive village that had been decimated by the storm. As we approached I leaned out the cargo door and was taken aback by a strange sight. A tall man swathed in an electric yellow rain slicker—like the kind I wore in first grade, complete with a wide brimmed hat—was waving like a lunatic. He was the only one wearing that getup; the others were in their native attire—loin cloths. The yellow man waved us into the small plateau. Once we were on the ground he came running up.

"Oh man, I am so glad to see you guys! And not just because of the storm; I've been here for two years, you're the first Americans I've seen in twenty-four months! I haven't spoken English since I've been here. Man, I can't believe it, real Americans. Got any gum?"

He had to yell to be heard over the din of the engines and rotor blades. And he had to yell while grinning the biggest grin I had ever seen. He looked like an overgrown school kid about to jump into a curbside puddle on his way home from school.

"Sure, I got gum, here, and we have some food for you too." I pulled a pack of gum out of my flight suit sleeve pocket and gave him several sticks. He stared at the silver foil wrappers like he had just been given thousand dollar bills. We got a dozen big bags of the superbread unloaded and after a vise-like handshake from the Peace Corps yellow man, took to the gray skies over Luzon.

We made our way up a steep canyon to a crowd of wet and hungry survivors. Once on the ground Carrier and I shuttled bags of bread over to the starving villagers. On our first run back down the mountain we evacuated three young women. I had them strapped into the jump seats facing to starboard, looking directly out the gaping hole in the side left by the open cargo door. The pilot lifted the helo off the ground several feet before pushing the nose over and aiming 20,000 pounds of helicopter straight down the canyon. The schoolgirls looked like they thought they were going to die. I think we scared them more than the typhoon did.

The second trip up the canyon had a whole different feel. The tension was tangible as we landed. The day had grown long and the people restless. There was a Filipino soldier off to the side, a pump-action shotgun slung over his shoulder. He looked nervous, agitated, angry. As I took a bag of bread over to the pile he approached me looking hostile and demanding. I couldn't hear anything he said over the helo's turbine engines, I couldn't even tell if he was speaking English or Tagalog. All I saw was the barrel of his shotgun suddenly pointing right at my head. It looked like I was staring down a dark well, the gaping aperture of the barrel a black abyss into which my mind spiraled.

In a split second I snapped out of it, looking at the soldier with contempt. That made two angry people staring at each other, one with a lethal firearm. I had no time to try out my diplomatic skills and he couldn't hear me anyway, even if he understood my language. He wanted on *my* helicopter and that was how I looked at it, that Sea King was my helo and I said who went or not. He wasn't going. I hoped he was lucid enough to know that if he blew my head off he wasn't going anywhere.

I tried a universal language. I brushed him aside with my arm and with a flick of my wrist dismissed him into the crowd. He was pissing me off and getting in my way. I turned my back to him and went about my work getting food to the starving people.

As we were preparing to make our final run back down the mountain panic set in. It was as if the crowd knew we weren't coming back. People swarmed the helo. I had Carrier secure the front passenger door and then come back to help me with crowd control. The cabin was full of civilians, the floor was packed and people still tried to climb aboard. I ended up kicking people away as Carrier slowly slid the cargo door closed against bodies being pushed and shoved and hands and fingers grasping.

We were being overrun by desperate, starving villagers. There was no way to explain to the crowd that we had weight limitations, that we couldn't take everyone, that we had to stop before we were overloaded and came crashing back to earth, killing the very people we were trying to save. We just had to close the door. Finally in the air I sat a young boy on my knee and gave him my last stick of gum. I held him all the way back to dry ground.

Aircrew gathered at the Cubi hangar after the long day to swap stories and debrief. Cowboy Johnny had been squeezing his cheeks for most of his second flight and made a dash for the commodes. Not thirty seconds later we heard a loud crash as Johnny ran from the heads, scrambling as fast as he could with his zoombag wrapped around his ankles. A blood-curdling scream trailed in his wake as he sprinted down the flight line. We rushed to see what had happened. The stall door hung precariously from one hinge, having been punched out from the inside by Cowboy. As we peered in, a very wet and agitated cobra began slithering out of the bowl Johnny had just moments before occupied. After feeling the probing forked tongue of a deadly jungle snake on his most sensitive and vulnerable parts, Johnny never crapped on base or in town again. Even if that meant taking a taxi back to the *Ranger*.

HS-4 evacuated 300 people and delivered 65,000 pounds of food and medicine over a four day period. Aircrews received the Sikorsky Winged S award for rescue work. Hundreds of Filipinos didn't survive the onslaught of wind, rain, flooding and devastation.

The Navy would eventually decide that during periods of strong southwesterly winds the Alava Pier, where the *Ranger* tied up, was one of the worst possible moorings in Subic Bay. The tugboats held the *Ranger* away from the pier and prevented any major damage. The tugboat crews weathered the typhoon on the water for a week straight as they pulled on the big ship. Those crews deserved a medal for their devotion to their duty, even as I guessed they would have said, "Just doin' my job."

The Iba, Luzon, movie set for *Apocalypse Now* was leveled, setting Francis Ford Coppola back in production by months.

I COULD TELL AIR ops were gearing up; the steam catapult tube running through the aircrew space was getting hot. One hundred degrees was about average in the enclosed steel box of an office once the cats got going. At times like that I longed for a sonobuoy signal relay mission at 10,000 feet, where we punched into a cool air layer two miles above the South China Sea.

The *Ranger* pulled out of Subic on June 4, heading back into old Tonkin Gulf Yacht Club turf. Soviet subs still lurked beneath the surface and we all were predator or prey, depending on the circumstances.

Helicopter carrier ASW's future hung in the balance. The Pentagon was determining if the CV concept—meaning in part the integration of helo ASW with the attack carrier configuration—was worth keeping. It had been an uneasy alliance between the fixed winged squadrons and our helos; primary missions clashed in airspace, tempo, deck load, flight deck configuration and a myriad of smaller details that annoyed sailors all the way down the chain of command. It never failed to amaze me how many men and how much time, energy and equipment it took to launch aircraft. Trying to overlap divergent missions on top of that was an air boss's nightmare. We had to prove our worth.

I had been flying a lot with Cdr. Stokes and he seemed to take delight in ribbing me, maybe because in spite of my bluster and sea experience I was still just a shy kid.

"Thos, you're my crewman today. We're taking up some big-shot to show him how helo ASW is done. Let's not let him down. And when was the last time you got a haircut? You look like a damn hippy. Oh, that's right, you're going back to college, I saw your school-cut chit. Going to grow your hair long and smoke weed and chase college girls? And I'm not sure I'll sign that early-out chit, I mean, you signed up for four, didn't you? That means four years, not three years, eleven months."

He had that laser-sharp look, that piercing gaze framed by faint laugh lines and a betraying glint in his eye. He was giving me a ration of shit and loving it. All I could do was grin sheepishly and remind myself he was shipping out himself in a few weeks, so he wouldn't be signing my chit anyway. But I had a feeling he was ribbing me because he cared, in some way, about how I was doing and it was his way of showing it. I had lots of practice with distant men who spoke in deflective phrases when expressing feelings.

"Skipper, I, uh, well, I *am* going back to college and who knows, maybe I'll come back in the Navy and be a friggin' admiral someday. I don't think I will have gotten enough of the fine shipboard food and comfortable accommodations after this stint."

"Not enough? Well Thos, I can arrange for you to have lots of time to enjoy *Ranger* hospitality! Hell, the brig ain't half full." He almost managed a laugh but caught himself and just smiled. He knew he had a mark and was playing me like a pro. I was outmatched and outwitted. I conceded.

"Uh, Skipper, maybe I'll just fly this mission and take it a day at a time."

"Wise choice Thos. Now, go brief the battle group admiral on the emergency ditch procedures and then get back here in time to launch with me."

I would miss CJ Stokes and wasn't sure exactly why. COs came and went with amazing frequency; he was my third CO and soon to be replaced with the current XO, Cdr. Redman, AKA "Fast n' Low."

I made it back from my brief with the admiral and launched with Stokes on the crucial sub hunt. Bob Hart was my 2nd crewman for what would be our last flight together. It was a hard-charging mission; we dipped the sonar on the elusive sub over and over, slamming powerful pulses of sound against its hull. Working in consort with other Black Knight helos, we boxed in the submarine time and again. The evaluator riding in the copilot's seat was beginning to get the idea that we really could hunt a sub.

Once other Sea Kings had the sub trapped in a giant square of open ocean we reeled in the sonar and deployed the MAD gear—capable of pinpointing the sub with deadly accuracy. Bob and I watched the needle on the graph—it was like an airborne lie detector; it could detect the truth—where the sub was—regardless of the lies the sub might be trying to tell.

Cdr. Stokes was giving the evaluator an overview of how it all worked as we crisscrossed the area, searching below for our invisible foe. Minutes went by. Bob and I were riveted to the detector display. The needle held steady in the center of the graph paper. That wasn't going to impress anybody, and the future of carrier helo ASW—the short range vanguard against numerically overwhelming Soviet subs—hung in the balance.

Then it happened, a tiny lightning strike raced across the graph.

"Madman, madman, smoke away!" I called into the ICS. It was a perfect reading, we had just pinpointed our prey. I punched out a smoke marker from the port sponson as Bob noted the time, heading, aircraft number and who the crew was. I had to interrupt Stokes as he was explaining tactics to the evaluator.

"Sorry to interrupt Skipper, but that was a textbook perfect reading. We got him, Sir."

Stokes turned to his guest in the cockpit. "And that, Captain, is how it's done. We just nailed the target sub. If it were a Foxtrot-class Russian boat heading for the *Ranger*, a torpedo would already be in the water."

And that was that. It was a long flight back to the ship and Bob started to get a flushed look on his face. Soon he began to empty his helmet bag—flashlight, checklist, kneeboard, a can of warm pineapple juice, it all was ending up on the helo deck.

"What the fuck are you doing, Bob?"

"Thos, I can't hold it any longer. I'm in agony, I mean, it's been a week!" He was starting to sweat more than usual in the 100 degree-plus heat of the helo cabin.

"Do what you gotta do," was all I could say. He unstrapped from his seat in a flash and disappeared into the aft cabin area. With his empty helmet bag. I dared not look back as I felt hot tropical air flow into the helo from the open cargo door.

He reappeared ten minutes later looking less stressed out. Without his helmet bag. I just hoped it hadn't been caught in the horizontal stabilizer as he tossed his weighty cargo out the door. Feek would not have been happy.

The squadron received a citation from Vice Admiral Baldwin stating, in part, that: "...their exceedingly successful participation in these operations provided a significant and vital contribution to the art of anti-submarine warfare and attributed to the favorable decision to continue the employment of Helicopter Antisubmarine Squadrons aboard aircraft carriers." We did it. And it was a nice way for Cdr. Stokes to wrap up his tour as our CO.

Bob swore he'd eat more fiber.

We pulled back in to Subic in time for Cdr. Stokes to have his change of command on the twenty-second of June. I got caught up on letter writing and made my last pilgrimage to the PX to buy my Teac reel-to-reel and Technics turntable before we headed back out to sea. And, I got some great news from Lt. Sandin. He got me a two week school cut approved by Redman, the new CO. My strategy in San Diego—saving up leave and not going home—was finally paying off. I was a two digit midget no matter how time was sliced. Short of a major world situation, I was going home on July twenty-fourth. Thirty days leave, the two week school cut Zipper Sandin got me, it was all falling together as I had hoped. Enlisting in September turned out to be beneficial; most colleges started classes that month and the Navy, in its infinite wisdom, felt cutting people loose early to make classes made sense. I tried for a thirty day school cut on top of my leave, but Redman had his limits too.

The *Ranger* pulled out on June twenty-third for what would be my last at-sea period. Borneo lay to port and Vietnam to starboard as we transited to the tip of the Maylay Peninsula and Singapore. Being at sea did strange things to men's minds. George Wine reenlisted for six years. He had a special twist to his plan.

"You're going to do what?" I couldn't believe what I was hearing.

"I'm going to cross-deck to my brother's carrier; it's on its way over on a WestPac and I'm going to ship over to that helo squadron." He blinked from behind his large wire-rimmed frames, smiling enigmatically.

"You mean you're going to do back-to-back WestPacs? You'll be away from the good old US of A for another eight months. Are you crazy?"

"Well, not as crazy as Nietzsche; he kissed a horse and called it his brother."

"I don't know who this guy is, who liked horses, but you're both crazy."

"Nietzsche wrote some interesting books and well, it's what I want to do. Besides, I got a pretty good bonus."

"I don't know George, doing back-to-back deployments just doesn't seem fair."

"Thos, if life were fair cats would be allergic to people." He blinked some more, let his grin widen and went to brief for a four hour plane guard mission.

I was amazed. He had "cross-decked." I had heard about it but never seen it happen. He didn't even particularly like the Navy and yet was committed to six more years and another WestPac starting within weeks.

Malcolm had conjured up a scheme to fuck the Navy and stay in the PI. George, who got to HS-4 at the same time, had just taken a giant step towards being a "lifer." I never could tell what crazy thing someone was going to do.

———•———

WE MADE SINGAPORE IN time for the bicentennial Fourth of July. I was sticking with my plan to stay aboard while we were at anchor, all I wanted to do was survive my last weeks on the ship before I headed back home in twenty days.

Chief Beaty was letting me slide on the flight schedule, and my gear was all but turned in to paraloft. There was plenty of office work to do which I was happy to tackle; it kept my mind busy during the endless hours that could make up a day on the carrier. And we had movies in the ready room. That would transform the frenetic epicenter of flight activity into a smoke filled, darkened space where men could let go of the stresses that defined life at sea and allow their imaginations to plunge into the small screen weaving its Technicolor tale.

And once again in port the ship was manned by a shadow crew as we swayed with the tide in the world's busiest harbor. Sailors by the thousands flocked ashore in liberty boats. I would park myself on the flight deck and dream of a Colorado snow storm.

On the Fourth we had a real Steel Beach celebration complete with barbecue, cake and ice cream. A band made up of Ranger-men belted out close approximations of Jimi Hendrix, The Rolling Stones and ZZ Top.

I settled into the cabin of a Sea King, absorbing its spirit and form into my bones and mind. It was quiet inside even with the band pounding out rock and roll from the fantail. The cabin felt safe, like a small sanctuary. The helicopter was feeling so familiar, so intertwined with who I had become, that it truly felt like an extension of myself. The wiring, the sonar, the fuel, the hydraulic fluid, the canvas troop seat, it all mingled into a pungent balm for my senses.

It had been a long road from bootcamp, from that afternoon I saw a hovering Sea King; a long road from bluffing my way through my first swim test only to be thrust back into the pool with even greater demands to be met.

Looking back I couldn't help but think of what might have been: had I never been pulled from flight deck school and offered aircrew training, had I been found out as an impostor in the pool, had I wrestled for Navy Memphis and had orders changed. And just months before, Chief Hatfield had offered me yet another avenue to take, another junction in my life's journey that might have been profound in its consequences. The new XO wanted to talk to me about reenlisting. I was pretty sure I had my answer.

A new beginning was calling. It was as powerful a force as my feeling in 1972 of needing to enlist, even if it was going to carry a price. Back then I had my youth to spend and in Singapore years later I was feeling like I had made a huge down payment.

I was going to miss the Sea King helicopter. But I wasn't going to miss wondering if I was going to die in one.

———◆———

My brother had sent me a letter in which he had several women scribe pithy comments while they were sitting in a bar getting drunk and not worrying about being killed on a flight deck or in a helicopter crash or falling overboard or even just facing another gut-plugging tasteless meal on a smelly, humid and crowded mess deck after a sleepless night lying a few feet underneath a steel runway. The letter was a taste of normalcy that felt like total impossibility.

We weighed anchor after a few days and headed east into the Singapore Straight, past Bintan and hundreds of tiny islands dotting the sea. A ten day line period stood between me and a flight out of Clark AFB. Soon I would be expertly packing my seabag one last time. It still smelled like new canvas from the bins back at bootcamp. I had penned in red Magic Marker "Thos" across the bottom so I could find it in a pile of identical olive drab bags. That was Dad's idea; he must have dug for his own duffle bag in a heap and found out the hard way that some distinctive mark would help.

I could do it I told myself, I could stave off the short-timer's disease that Papa Gire had warned me about, that potentially fatal lapse of concentration, of attitude, or "Don't give a fuck" as Feek put it, that could get me hurt. But I didn't want to turn in my wings, I was going to go the distance. I had worked too damn hard earning them to give them up, even if every flight felt like the Grim Reaper was aboard.

We sailed southeast and down past Lingga Island towards the equator. At just over one degree north latitude, Singapore visits made equator crossings almost mandatory. We would be initiating a whole new gaggle of lowly pollywogs into Shellbacks.

Crossing the equator on July 7 at a point between Sumatra and Borneo just a few degrees south of the Malay Peninsula, the ancient ceremony played out on Steel Beach. I passed on being a Shellback swashbuckler, opting instead to prepare for my escape from Uncle Sam's grasp. I didn't care to initiate anyone, but the squadron was full of foul pollywogs. Tex, JD, Cowboy Johnny and a handful of other nuggets were ripe for the occasion. Feek had his own crew of new guys and was decked out in a pirate getup that looked like he had picked through thrift store leftovers. "Bitchin'" he proclaimed with a sardonic smile as he herded a small pod of nervous brown shirts down to the hangar deck.

The Royal Baby smeared gobs of heavy grease into initiates' faces, Shellbacks flogged and tormented, pollywogs slithered and crawled along the hot flight deck as the ancient game played out under the unrelenting equatorial sun.

As the flight deck hosted the time-honored event I was content to stretch out on my thin mattress on the top tier of racks and count days. I had decided to have a back-up plan to my Humboldt application and started the paperwork on applying to the University of Northern Colorado. It was situated in Greeley, east of Fort Collins out on the high plains but close enough to home to make visits easy, even if gas was closing in on 60¢ a gallon.

The day closed with the gentle rocking of a carrier riding swells at sea. I went up to Steel Beach to catch the green flash. I thought of Lt. Jankowsky's tapes of Richard Alpert—Baba Ram Dass—and his aphorism to "be here now." I wanted to be 8,000 miles away so badly I could hardly stand it, but I took just a moment to let my mind set with the sun as, for a split second, it illuminated the depths of the sea from 93 million miles in space.

The *Ranger* plowed aside jade-colored waters at thirty knots, running directly towards the last air-ops period I would ever experience. Then something very ominous manifested itself in a swift and sudden action. Unannounced, the *Ranger* pulled the hardest turn I had ever experienced on a carrier. Aircraft strained against anchoring chains as the flight deck tilted at a precarious angle, with 80,000 tons of steel doing an about-face and heading back into the Straights. We were suddenly going the opposite direction.

Something was very, very wrong.

17: Aircraft Carrier Diplomacy

The *Ranger* steamed west through the Malacca Straights and towards the Indian Ocean at flank speed. All my plans had evaporated into dense tropical air along with any hope of going home soon. We were all wondering what had happened. News was sparse. The CO had us mustered in the ready room.

"Shipmates, Lt. Gray will explain the situation as best he can, but before he does I want to say that as the helicopter squadron aboard this carrier we will do whatever is asked of us. We are versatile, multi-mission capable and we will do as the captain and battle group admiral ask. We won't be flying much over the next few days as we make way to the coast of Africa, but there is much work to be done. Aircrews, I want you ready for anything, and I mean anything. More as I have it, until then, Lt. Gray." I noticed a copy of L'Amour's *Lando* stuffed in the skipper's back pocket. He didn't look like a man who had much time to read.

Lt. Gray took the podium and filled us in as best he could. He didn't waste any time getting to the point. "On June 27 an Air France jet was hijacked by both Palestinian and German terrorists and flown to Entebbe, Uganda. The Israeli passengers were detained and threatened with death if Israel didn't release some prisoners it was holding. Negotiations were yielding few results. On July fourth

Israeli commandos and aircrews executed what history may some-day call one of the most daring and precise hostage rescues in history. But I digress. The Israelis got their people out of the Entebbe airport terminal and loaded into C-130s, bound for Israel. With a stopover in Nairobi, Kenya. That's where things start to get crazier than they already were. Apparently Idi Amin has taken offense at his neighbors helping with the rescue and has threatened reprisals. That's all I know. The *Ranger* is headed for the coast of Kenya and I wouldn't bank on liberty in Mombasa. This is a rapidly developing situation and all I can say at this point is—hurry up and wait."

Groans bubbled up to the surface as aircrews digested what they heard. Nobody was going anywhere. Except East Africa. Fast Eddie was pissed.

"Goddammit, I'm due home before you, Thos. This sucks. I'll never know why I'm making the Navy a career with shit like this happening."

"Beats the hell outta me, Eddie, but we're in for a ride this time." I was despondent. I watched visions of college classes populated with lovely young women held in the shade of giant redwood trees evaporate before my eyes.

Chief Beaty took me aside. "Thos, I'll have to put you back on the flight schedule; we're going to be short-handed and I'll need every aircrewman I have. Even Chief Dominguez is likely going to fly his ass off."

"That's OK, Chief, I'm going stir crazy; flying will keep my mind off what almost was."

The *Ranger* made a beeline for East Africa. Aircraft were secured for foul weather and fast transit, plans were being made behind closed doors, and we were waiting. Waiting for everything—fresh food, fuel, news, rumors, plans, everything seemed to require a long agonizing wait.

We punched into the Indian Ocean on the twelfth, and the XO called me in for the required reenlistment pep talk. I had just come back from a six hour flight and was hot and tired, but I needed to meet with him; he knew that, I knew that. Commander Hulson was new to the squadron as the XO just the month before. He had just gotten to HS-4 and within weeks was being sent the opposite direction from where he thought we would be going and had to talk me into reenlisting.

"You know Manthos, with six more years you'll be halfway to retirement and hell, the Navy will pay you twelve thousand dollars as a bonus." Behind him was a poster taped to the bulkhead that said, "Sailors have more fun." If I was having fun I couldn't stand any more of it.

"Sir, I don't think it's in the cards for me; I'm planning on going back to college. I mean, you signed my chit, right, Sir?"

"Yes, I sure did, but you'd be heading for shore duty if you re-upped, four years stateside as an instructor. That's not bad duty."

"No Sir it wouldn't be, but if I did that, then I might as well stay for twenty and then I'm a lifer, er, a career man, and I just don't think I want that."

"Lots of options are available, Petty Officer Manthos. There's NESEP, the Navy Enlisted Scientific Education Program, that would land you a degree and a commission. And then there are the reserves; a weekend a month, two weeks in the summer, you keep your rank and accrue time in rate. The Navy needs men like you Manthos, just think it over." He sounded like the career counseling instructor back in January.

"I pretty much have, XO, I need to get home and back to school."

"What do you think you want to study?"

"Well, I've been studying the flute and I like music, so maybe I'll do that. I've applied to UNC back in Colorado as well as Humboldt State, so I'm not sure, but then I'm not sure when I'll get off this boat, either."

"UNC? Music? I almost became a trumpet major and I got my masters at UNC. Small world. I wonder if they still call Greeley 'greality.' It was dry once, all the bars are south of town. Paul's Place is a great spot to grab a pint." It sounded like he wanted a cold beer as badly as I did. He gave it one last try. "OK Manthos, sign up for six, get the bonus, work towards first class, which isn't that far away for you, next step is chief and you'll have it made in the shade."

None of the chiefs I saw looked too happy to me. I declined, he said he understood, and I went back to the furnace of the aircrew space to baste in the 100 degree radiating heat of the catapult steam tube.

Rumors spread at an amazing rate. One rapidly circulating was that Idi Amin had ordered his tanks to invade Kenya only to run out of gas since he bought his oil from the country he wanted to invade, which had cut off supplies. True or not it made for a great story.

I had been sent down earlier to the combat intelligence center with some important bathythermograph readings I recorded on that day's flight. It was a busy place and as I "milled about smartly" my eyes wandered the room. I managed to see what looked to be very high altitude photos of a city layout in the grasp of a distinguished looking officer. Certain buildings were prominently marked. I had no idea what city, what buildings or what was being discussed but I was detected by the commander holding them. He gave me a "You have no reason to be seeing these, young man, go away" scowl, which I did.

I imagined the Vigilantes of RVAH-5's Savage Sons were busy making high altitude overflights of Uganda and Kenya. Rumors abounded about the ability of their cameras to take pictures of a golf ball from 60,000 feet, while the strobe lights would burn the flesh off your body if you got close when they were set off.

It felt odd to be steaming as fast as possible in a straight line; we were so often sailing in a huge racetrack pattern for air ops in a rough stationary geographic fix. And then we slowed down. After days of a headlong rush towards the Horn and passing the 60th meridian, we settled into a state of uncertainty. The chiefs usually knew what was happening.

"Chief Beaty, what's going on?"

"Nothing Thos, that's what. Whatever *was* planned that got us involved, it's pretty much over. I have no idea if the thought of an American carrier headed his way got Amin to change his mind, or what. Here's the skinny—keep your flight gear handy but be ready to get shipped out. We're going to be sending people out through the Seychelles but you're way down the list. There are people who need to go on emergency leave or are already past their rotation date, so hang tight. And I'd get a haircut, you're not out yet." The chief puffed on his pipe and smiled.

The Seychelles. Fuck. If I went out that way I might be heading home by way of the east coast of the States. The next fly-out was to be from Diego Garcia. My chances of getting out from either one were slim to none.

Zipper got his hands on the lyrics to "Suicide is Painless," and a handful of pilots and aircrew gathered in the comm space, singing the praises of killing oneself in rough tones as I accompanied them with my flute. We let off some steam by singing the banned song, joking with each other and for a moment, forgetting just where we were.

The Indian Ocean is over 28 million square miles of open water. Since the war-that-never-was had ended, the *Ranger* now did another 180 degree turn and headed back the way we had just come. My fly-out date of July 24 was rapidly approaching and we were still thousands of miles from the Philippines. I was riding the *Ranger* all the way back to the PI. I was out of books. I was slowly going mad.

There were days at sea in the IO that labored over every tick of the clock, as if each second had to be carefully sliced from time and inspected to see if it really was time at all—and not some imposter—before it was methodically discarded over the side and consigned to a watery vault. More seconds sliced off, more hours consumed by the rotation of the earth, more miles of brilliant blue water put behind only to be replaced with millions of square miles of more brilliant blue water ahead seemingly pressing the horizon farther away with every turn of the four giant screws below the fantail.

I didn't want to eat, I didn't want to think, I didn't want to exist. I wanted to crawl into my void and close the hatch behind me—don't come for me until I can leave, be gone from that ship, find my future at the end of a transoceanic flight heading east. But the void was locked. I had to eat something, even if it was leathery hamburgers and stale chips chased with near-toxic bug juice the color of radiator fluid. I had to do something to keep busy even if it was taking 120 grit sandpaper to the ready room knee knockers, polishing the step to a mirror shine.

"You're not supposed to be doing that. It's a task for E-3s and below, you know that, Manthos. What are you trying to do, upset the chain of command?" Lt. Cdr. Gray remarked, half seriously. He was right, I had reversed the shit detail up the chain of command but I didn't care. It kept me from launching myself off an aircraft elevator and into the warm, cleansing waters of the eternal sea and swimming home.

Gray had just made 0-4 and was due to leave the Black Knights as I was. He was headed to graduate school and likely a sparkling career. I was headed towards a lot of uncertainty but I knew for sure that at some point I would be standing in the shadow of the Front Range of Colorado, drinking real milk and unpacking my seabag for the last time.

As July drew to a close and my ship-out date came and went Chief Beaty needed me on the flight schedule and I happily went. After being on water-hours and taking Navy showers and sweating in my rack in stifling heat and humidity the escape from the ship was welcomed.

July 30 was my final flight in a Sikorsky SH-3D Sea King helicopter. Pete Cassidy was the other crewman. It seemed a fitting way to end my time in the air.

18: Goin' Home

With the glacial-like movement of inevitable change, we once again transited the Malacca Straights, passed Singapore and entered the South China Sea. I was moving up the list of sailors scheduled to be flown off as the C-2 Greyhound CODs were busy once we got within their range of Subic. I packed my seabag, giving away handfuls of stuff I couldn't take and deep-sixing what no one would have. There was no room for my flight helmet even though the guys at paraloft said I could keep it.

I got my squadron check-out sheet completed and found myself truly in limbo. I was no longer a Black Knight. I was in their berthing, I was in their ready room, I was drinking their coffee, I was still wearing the squadron identification patch on my dress uniform. But I was no longer one of them. I could already feel some squadron-mates start to pull away, create distance, as if I were morphing into a creature unlike themselves. Such was Navy life. As much as I wanted to go home, I was becoming torn between the intense life I was living and the one I was about to enter.

Early August. I sat in the ready room for days in my Dress Whites, waiting for my name to be called over the 1MC for departure by the COD. Finally I got word that I was on the next day's roster for a C-2 flight to Clark Air Force Base, the Philippines. It was my turn to start making the disconnect—saying my goodbyes, wondering if they would miss me, wondering who would take my place. The Navy did need me, the XO was right about that. But I also knew I couldn't stay.

That evening, in a pitch-black moonless night, the *Ranger* went DIW. Dead In the Water. We were adrift in the South China Sea. I recalled the *Kitty Hawk* fire and waited for bad news to blast through the ship like a tornado, but it didn't happen. We just sat there. A supercarrier feels like a ship when it's moving; when it's standing still in the middle of nowhere it feels like an iron island without a reason for being.

My heart sank, no way was I getting off the ship the next day under those conditions. I crawled into my rack and tried to clear my mind of all the possibilities. By morning the *Ranger* was underway. That was a good sign; at least if I didn't get off other guys would, and that would bring me closer to the top of the list. I sat in the ready room trying to stay calm but my anxiety showed. Tex came up and had a solution. "Hey Thos, you look like you could use a cigarette, here, want these? I'm trying to quit."

I hadn't smoked a cigarette in months. Suddenly the nicotine jolt sounded like the best idea all day. At 15¢ a pack I gave him 50¢ to cover three packs and tore one open. I still had my trusty Zippo so I dug it out of my seabag and lit up. I saw Lt. Cdr. Gray with his bags packed and offered him one. He took me up on it.

"Think we'll head home today?" I figured if anybody knew, it would be the squadron intelligence officer.

"Fuck if I know, Thos, nobody tells me anything these days. Let's just hope so." He had been severed from the squadron as well.

After chain-smoking half a pack the next roster call came over the 1MC. "HS-4 personnel Lt. Cdr. Gray, Petty Officer Second Class Manthos, report." I was stunned. It had finally happened. We were close to Subic and at that point were getting people and aircraft off the ship. I made my final handshakes and looked for Pete, but he was already topside for a mission. So were Zipper and Chief Beaty.

I made my way up and walked right into the world of flight ops.

As a spectator. It seemed a beehive of activity as flight deck hands clothed in identifying colors swarmed over airplanes and equipment. The noise was deafening. Two big helicopters sat on the port side, their rotor blades turning in a consort of pulsing sound. Deckhands kept looking at me as if I were a liability, as if some guy in his Dress Whites had no reason to be up there and in their way.

The big C-2 cargo plane was already powered up, the ramp lowered and its twin turbine engines humming a deep drone. Then the engines stopped. The propellers slowly came to a halt. The word came down—the COD was having mechanical problems. The flight was canceled. I felt like the *Ranger* was not going to let me go home, it was going to keep me, maybe coax me into that void and lock the hatch, preserving me as a curiosity.

Someone tried to figure out what to do with us. Lt. Cdr. Gray walked to the starboard side and stared into the deep. I looked over at one of the helos and saw Pete Cassidy in the right seat. He was going out on a plane guard mission. If I made it into the air in the next four hours, he would be flying rescue for me.

Chief Beaty was standing to starboard of the Sea Kings in his flight gear, overseeing the two-helo flight as it prepared to launch. Feek was riding herd on the younger brown shirts as they readied the helicopters. Zipper saw me from the cockpit of the lead helo and gave me a thumb's up.

The flight deck officer returned and notified us that the admiral had acquiesced to our using the C-2 held in reserve for him. The two helos were gone by the time the released COD was ready to take us aboard.

We were shuffled into the cavernous hold of the big cargo plane by the C-2 aircrewman. I picked a spot right under an escape hatch and by a porthole window. If all my training meant anything, it was to survive that flight. We were facing backwards, and as Lt. Cdr. Gray and the gaggle of disenfranchised sailors all got safety helmets and flotation vests on and strapped in, the ramp closed. I watched Steel Beach slowly disappear as if a stage curtain was being lowered after the final act.

We taxied to the catapult and as I looked out the small port-hole window I saw the cat crew holding up the board that read the aircraft's weight. It looked like it read "56,000,000 lbs." I knew that couldn't be but it didn't help my confidence in the big lumbering plane getting airborne. At last the C-2's aircrewman signaled our cat shot and within two seconds I was going 150 miles per hour back-wards towards my new future.

As the COD made a slow left turn I caught a brief glimpse of the *Ranger* fading into the haze of the South China Sea.

Feek was right; it had all been, truly, unfuckingbelievable.

Epilogue

I made it to Clark Field and departed on a commercial DC-8 the next day. The DC-8 experienced engine trouble on take-off and I thought—one more time—that I was not going to escape the pull of the South China Sea. But I made it to Travis AFB, California, by way of Guam and Hawaii. On Guam the B-52s used in Operation Linebacker II stood ready to be sent again, against the next targets wherever they may be.

At the San Francisco airport I came eye to eye with a DC-10 as I stood by the boarding gate. It was the most beautiful aircraft I had ever seen, and it was taking me home.

Later that August I enrolled in the University of Northern Colorado at Greeley. In a week I had gone from Steel Beach to a college campus. Thanks for getting me that school cut, Zipper.

Apologies may be in order for any liberties I took with the Flamingo Café's menu but Betty, or someone very much like her, is still serving up heaping plates of hot, filling food to young sailors somewhere in San Diego.

I learned many years later that members of the draft "class of '72" did not get inducted, even as the last man drafted entered the Army on June 30, 1973. Only 646 men were drafted in 1973, down from 49,514 in 1972.

For several long years I would look for Marsha in Fort Collins, hoping to catch a glimpse of her, hoping she would see me, come to me, warm me. Or perhaps I was just dreaming it. Wherever she is, I wish her well.

AUTHOR'S NOTES

I couldn't mention everyone I remember, and I can't remember everyone I served with. I have done my best to portray people as I knew them. In some instances I changed names and in two cases—Lt. Gray and Roger Feek—combined several squadronmates into individuals in order to streamline my story and include as many unique individual characteristics as possible.

The dialogue is primarily reconstructed, with the intent of capturing the truth of the times and circumstances. In some instances the words written were actually spoken.

The bulk of *Steel Beach* was written from memory. In addition I have a good number of memorabilia such as my quarterly marks, squadron and carrier newsletters, portions of my service records and all of the certificates issued to me, as well as my letters home, as reference material. The letters written to my family formed the soul of my story-writing process, serving as a window back in time to my state of mind and where I may have been at sea or in port. Between the letters and military records I was able to reconstruct a fairly accurate time-line, not without some speculation where I was unable to confirm exact dates.

The following books were invaluable in filling in historical details:

Davidson, Phillip B. *Vietnam at War, the history 1946-1975* New York, Oxford, Oxford University Press 1991

Karnow, Stanley. *Vietnam, A History* Viking Press 1983

Trager, James. *The People's Chronology* New York, Henry Holt and Company 1992

Francillon, Rene´. *Tonkin Gulf Yacht Club-U.S. carrier operations off Vietnam* Annapolis. MD. Naval Institute Press 1988

Adcock, Al. *H-3 Sea King in action* Squadron Signal Publications, Aircraft Number 150, 1995

Also indispensable, as well as nostalgic, was a copy of *The Blue-jackets' Manual*, eighteenth edition, 1969, by the U.S. Naval Institute. This would have been the edition I used in bootcamp. I augmented my fond memories of the Sea King with a reprint of a NATOPS flight manual, NAVAIR 01-230HLH-1, for the SH-3D/H model helicopter.

GLOSSARY

A school: Schooling to attain a rate, most rates having their own A school. There were also P schools—short preparatory courses—and advanced B and C schools.

ASW: Anti-submarine warfare.

Boot: Short for bootcamp. Can refer to the basic training phase or an individual in it or recently from it.

Bug juice: A beverage served aboard ships similar to Kool-Aid. It is rumored to be more than adequate to remove paint and rust.

Chief: Chief Petty Officer (E-7). Also, Senior Chief (E-8) and Master Chief (E-9).

Civvies: Civilian clothes.

CO: Commanding Officer.

Crow: See PO.

Det: A detachment from a squadron or other unit operating autonomously as a smaller contingent. A typical HS-4 plane guard det was two helicopters with commensurate aircrews and support personnel.

Field Day: A thorough cleaning of a space.

Head: A shipboard bathroom, also used loosely to refer to any bathroom.

Helantisubron: Helicopter anti-submarine squadron, abbreviated HS.

MAD: Magnetic Anomaly Detection device, deployed by ASW aircraft and helicopters to locate submarines.

Non-skid: Rough coating applied to the flight deck and hangar deck, containing grit which allowed for traction of aircraft and mobile equipment.

PO: Petty Officer. The three enlisted Petty Officer ranks are: Petty Officer Third (E-4), Second (E-5) and First (E-6), in ascension of rank. The Petty Officer insignia has an eagle as part of the patch, which is referred to as the "crow." Petty Officers and the Chief Petty Officer ranks are considered noncommissioned officers.

Rack: A shipboard bed, also used loosely to refer to any bed.

Rank: The Navy is divided into three basic divisions: Enlisted, Warrant Officer and Officer. Enlisted ranks are E-1 through E-9 (See PO and Chief). Enlisted ranks are also talked about as pay grades. Warrant Officer rank is Warrant Officer, W-1, or Chief Warrant Officer, and W-2 through W-4. Officer ranks are: Ensign (O-1), Lieutenant junior grade, Lt.j.g. (O-2), Lieutenant, Lt. (O-3), Lieutenant Commander, Lt Cmdr. (O-4), Commander, Cmdr. (O-5), Captain, Capt.(O-6), Rear Admiral, Rear Adm. (O-7), Vice Admiral, Vice Adm. (O-8), Admiral, Adm. (O-9).

Rate: The Navy assigns a job title for sailors with specific training, such as Boatswain's Mate or Signalman. Not to be confused with rank. Each rating, assigned a four number code, has a specialty mark integrated into the Petty Officer patch worn on the dress uniform. Enlisted sailors E-1 through E-3 are not rated, but called a "striker" if in training for a specific rating.

SAR: Search and rescue.

Skipper: The informal name for a commanding officer of a unit, squadron, vessel, etc. The formal title is Commanding Officer, abbreviated as CO.

TAD: Temporary Additional Duty.

The island: The superstructure of a carrier that stands above the flight deck on the starboard side.

XO: The Executive Officer of a unit, ship or squadron. The executive officer is informally addressed as the "XO."

Zoombag: A flight suit, made from fire-retardant Nomex.

1MC: A ship's general announcing system.

The Ball Studio, Corvallis, Oregon

ABOUT THE AUTHOR

J eff Manthos has been writing since his collegiate days. His love of writing has been manifest in his numerous poems and short stories. In 1997 he visited Vietnam with a veterans group, producing his journal *Crossing the South China Sea*.

Jeff was born the son a combat fighter pilot in the Langely Air Force Base, Virginia, hospital in 1953. As his family was stationed overseas and around the US, he spent much of his youth travelling. A decade after his father's retirement to their Wyoming ranch and after a move to Colorado, Jeff enlisted in the Navy. His deployments completed his travels around the globe.

After his service he gained a B.A. in Philosophy and then pursued the art of violin making, attending the Violin Making School of America. He has been a professional violin maker for over 20 years.

Jeff's service memoir, *Steel Beach*, is his most recent literary endeavor. He is currently working on two manuscripts, one on his life as a boy on a Wyoming ranch and one about his fight against non-Hodgkin's lymphoma.

Jeff resides in the heart of Oregon's Willamette Valley where he enjoys cycling, gardening and the outdoors.